PRAISE FOR

"I met Sister Annabel Laity wh̶ ̶ ̶ ̶ ̶ ̶ ̶ ̶ ̶ ̶ ̶ ̶ ̶̶ organize Thich
Nhat Hanh's first teaching tour to the United Kingdom more
than thirty years ago now. Since then we have practiced alongside each other and I have seen her transform from a shy young
woman into a formidable teacher of the Dharma. Reading *True
Virtue* has taught me so much about Sister Annabel and her
qualities of faith, determination, and tenderness."

—SISTER CHAN KHONG, cofounder of Plum Village
Community of Engaged Buddhism, France; director of
the humanitarian projects of the International Plum Village
Sangha since the 1960s; and author of *Learning True Love*

"More than just a personal biography, this is a first-hand account
of the early years of Plum Village and the unfolding of Thich
Nhat Hanh's vision and the activities of the Order of Interbeing.
Venerable Annabel recounts her early years as a monastic and
her subsequent life helping Thay to realise his aspirations in
spreading the cultivation of mindfulness and compassion in all
directions throughout the world."

—JETSUNMA TENZIN PALMO, founder of Dongyu Gatsal Ling
nunnery and author of *Reflections on a Mountain Lake:
Teachings on Practical Buddhism*

"Sister True Virtue was among the first three monastic disciples of
Thich Nhat Hanh ordained more than thirty years ago. This honest and delightful book tells of her journey as a spiritual seeker,
brave activist, and a lifetime practitioner. As the first Westerner
to be ordained, her trailblazing spirit has allowed many monastic and lay practitioners alike to follow in her footsteps."

—SISTER CHAN DIEU NGHIEM, senior Dharma teacher
in the lineage of Thich Nhat Hanh, former abbess
of Plum Village Lower Hamlet

"Sister Annabel's poignant memoir is a powerful and much needed reminder of the strength to be found in cultivating stillness and mindful attention to the present moment. It is a moving testament to the courage and deep compassion of those who follow Zen Master Thich Nhat Hanh's path of Engaged Buddhism in the world."

—CHRISTINE TOOMEY, Amnesty International award-winning journalist and author of *In Search of Buddha's Daughters*

"Sister True Virtue's memoir is a simple telling of a spiritual journey with many twists and turns. Beginning with her childhood in the English countryside, winding through the Indian Himalayas and many cultures, Sister True Virtue arrives home at Plum Village and her path to awakening slowly accelerates. Her candid remembrances of interbeing with Thich Nhat Hanh and his community are heartwarming, innocent, and evocative."

—KARMA LEKSHE TSOMO, PhD, cofounder of Sakyadhita International Association of Buddhist Women and editor of *Buddhism through American Women's Eyes*

"I have always thought of Sr. Annabel as my elder sister in the Dharma and Sangha . . . . Her presence and her erudite talks are an inspiration to everyone in the audience and if there are any doubts on understanding the sutras, Sr. Annabel is the person to seek out for clarity. She also has an 'Ananda'-like memory and remembers what Thay taught and in what setting and reference . . . . She cultivates the path of 'peace in oneself and peace in the world.'"

—SHANTUM SETH, DHARMACHARYA, Ahimsatrust.org, and pilgrimage teacher and guide, Buddhapath.com

WITHDRAWN

TRUE VIRTUE

THE JOURNEY OF AN ENGLISH BUDDHIST NUN

SISTER ANNABEL LAITY

The First Western Monastic Disciple of Zen Master

THICH NHAT HANH

PARALLAX PRESS

BERKELEY, CALIFORNIA

Parallax Press
P.O. Box 7355
Berkeley, California 94707
parallax.org

Parallax Press is the publishing division of
Plum Village Community of Engaged Buddhism, Inc.
Copyright © 2019 by Sister Annabel Laity
All rights reserved
Printed in The United States of America

Cover design by Jess Morphew
Text design by Gopa & Ted2, Inc
Maps © John Barnett
Author photograph with permission of
Plum Village Community of Engaged Buddhism

Printed on 30 percent post-consumer waste recycled paper

ISBN 978-1-946764-27-0
Ebook ISBN 978-1-946764-28-7

Library of Congress Cataloging-in-Publication Data
Names: Laity, Annabel, author.
Title: True virtue : the journey of of an
English Buddhist nun / Sister Annabel Laity.
Description: Berkeley : Parallax Press, [2019]
Identifiers: LCCN 2019007112| ISBN 9781946764270 (pbk.) |
ISBN 9781946764287 (ebk.)
Subjects: LCSH: Laity, Annabel. | Buddhist nuns—Biography.
Classification: LCC BQ970.A5475 A3 2019 | DDC 294.3/927092 [B]—dc23
LC record available at https://lccn.loc.gov/2019007112

1 2 3 4 5 / 23 22 21 20 19

The first virtue is the virtue of putting an end to the afflictions: letting go of anger, craving, fear, and delusion. The second virtue is the virtue of loving: having the capacity to accept, forgive, and embrace the other person with compassion. The third virtue is the virtue of insight: the ability to look deeply and gain insight so you can resolve your difficulties and help other people.

—THICH NHAT HANH

Contents

Preface

NOT LONG after I had been ordained as a nun, my teacher Thich Nhat Hanh would ask me to write about my life. He saw that I did not respond. I did try several times in notebooks to write about myself, but I never felt it was good enough. A friend offered to transcribe one of these notebooks and, in the end, these writings became the basis for what is in this book.

Thay ("teacher," as we affectionately call Thich Nhat Hanh) always tells us that writing about our life is a meditation, a practice of looking deeply to know and understand ourself better. The various events of our life that we hold on to as memories can all be lessons helping us to develop the three virtues that exist as seeds in our consciousness: putting an end to the afflictions, loving, and insight.

Our self is always changing from moment to moment. It is not something we can grasp but is more like a river, which we can learn to understand in its different manifestations every day.

Looking back at yourself as a child, you might be tempted to ask: "What does that child have to do with me?" You could also ask the same question of yourself as you were one week ago. When you were a child you did not stop to try to understand yourself. You grew up without noticing that you were growing up until one day it was time to leave home.

When I was a child I used to look up at the stars outside my bedroom window and tell myself that I would never leave my home in the Cornish countryside. I could not imagine living anywhere else. But the day came when I was put on the train to go to London University and the farmhouse in Cornwall ceased to be home.

Still, that child in the photograph does have something to do with the seventy-year-old now. The joy, the sadness, and the roots of virtue have grown and changed, but if my childhood had not been like that, the present experience would not be like this. Writing a memoir is seeing connections between what is remembered as then and what is experienced as now.

Thay gave me the name True Virtue when I was ordained as a lay member of the Order of Interbeing and I kept the same name when I was ordained as a nun. Virtue is the translation of the Chinese 德 and the Sanskrit *guṇa*, the inner quality of virtue. On my ordination certificate my name was written in French "*Vraie Vertu*." I was not impressed by the name and I tried to forget about it, but one day, while lying in his hammock in the Upper Hamlet, Thay told me that True Virtue was a good name. From that time I began to think about how I and the name could become one. I felt happy when I heard about the virtue of cutting off afflictions (斷德). I felt that this was something I could do bit by bit.

Your teacher uses his or her intuitive insight to give you a name. It is for you to meditate on and use as a guide on your path of practice. In this book I can look into how true or how imperfect my practice of virtue has been.

Sister Annabel Laity
New Hamlet, Plum Village, France
July 2018

✳ PART ONE ✳

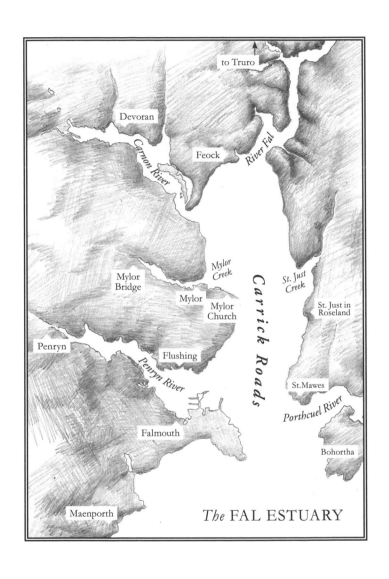

The FAL ESTUARY

※ CHAPTER ONE ※

Childhood in Cornwall

I GREW UP in a part of England on the southwest coast that enjoyed the effects of the Gulf Stream. Although temperatures did fall below freezing sometimes and even snow fell, it was not cold for very long. The nearest village was called Flushing. It was on the Fal estuary opposite the town of Falmouth in Cornwall. Because of the mild climate, daffodils can grow in Cornwall in the early months of the year and palm trees can be seen in many of its seaside towns.

It was a lovely place to grow up. Our house was on a hill above the sea. To the north you could see Austrian pines towering over the roof of the house. Crows nested there and the wind soughed in the pine branches. The fragrance of pine wafted through the windows facing north. You could play in the pine needles under the spreading branches in a dark and mysterious place where fallen trunks two feet in diameter were boats to sail across foreign seas. To the south of the house was the flower garden, the orchard planted by my great-grandfather, and then the vegetable garden. On coming home from school in the autumn, my younger sister, Sarah, and I would climb the apple trees to each pick the apple we wanted to eat and together we would sit right there to enjoy eating them in the tree. There were many ancient varieties of apple—Orange Pippins, Julipers, Beauty of Bath, American Mother, Bramleys—each with its own particular flavour, and our family would pick them to eat immediately between July and October, or to store in crates until the following March in the coolest part of the house. Sarah was two and a half years my junior. Our younger brothers, Stephen and Thomas, played other games.

The orchard was the place for orphan lambs in spring. Sheep often have difficulty in giving birth, so sometimes the ewe dies. The orchard was walled and the lambs were very tame and never wandered far from the house. As children we enjoyed helping our mother take care of the lambs, feeding them from bottles of cow's milk.

The house was 500 years old in parts, and was haunted by a decapitated ghost who carried his head around on a tray. Sometimes people would hear footsteps on the landing, but no one was to be seen. When my mother put me to bed I would ask her to look under the bed to see if a ghost was hiding there. She left a night-light flickering on the bedside table.

When I was born, the house had no electricity, and in winter when temperatures would fall, the only warm place was the kitchen, where my mother kept the stove alight twenty-four hours a day. We snuggled up in bed under layers of several blankets.

The sitting room had a fireplace, and in the winter a log fire was lit late in the afternoon. The warmest place was in front of the fire, so we took it in turns to sit in that spot. No other room had heating, although the kitchen stove provided hot water for all our needs. As soon as outside temperatures began to fall in the late afternoon, all doors and windows were closed, and when night fell, we would draw all the curtains. Father was strict about this and supervised

About three years old.

it. When I was a teenager and needed to study in my bedroom, Father bought me a greenhouse heater, which was
designed to keep the heat above freezing in a greenhouse.
Still my fingers grew numb from cold as I was writing.

Father was a farmer. As a small child there was nothing
I enjoyed more than following him around feeding the animals, the cows, the pigs, the sheep; watching him repair
farm machinery; riding on the tractor; looking to see how
the crops of barley, oats, kale, potatoes, and mangolds were
growing. My mother looked after the vegetable garden, the
hens, and the orphaned lambs; she made butter and sometimes helped working in the fields at harvest or planting
time. Mother had four children to take care of. Often she
forgot to drink anything while she was caring so much for
her children and husband, and at the end of the day she
would say, "My goodness! I have not drunk anything,"
and pour herself a glass of spring water from the glass jug.
She devoted herself to caring for husband and children
from early morning to late at night, cooking, cleaning,

comforting and consoling us when we were sad. We did not have a washing machine or refrigerator and neither did my grandmother. When I was very small I used to like watching Mother and Grandmother washing clothes. There was a piece of equipment called a mangle, which we used to wring the water out of the newly-washed clothes. It was made of two rollers connected to a handle. The wet clothes were passed between the rollers, wringing the water out of them. It was hard work for a small child to turn the handle and usually my mother or grandmother had to do the work.

My mother took care of the animals too. The little lambs whose mother ewes had died or who were born prematurely had to be wrapped up and put in the bottom oven to keep them warm and then fed cows' milk in a bottle. Many cats lived on the farm, some of whom were very tame and some were half-wild. As children we liked the little kittens. The pregnant mother cat would seek a warm place in the hay or straw of the barn to give birth to her kittens and when we went into the barn we could hear the gentle mewing of newly-born kittens. We knew that Father wanted to keep the cat population down and would sometimes drown the kittens while they were still blind. Father would never drown a kitten once it could see, so we tried to hide the kittens until their eyes were open.

Around the house and garden was a cobbled yard; cows walked there when they were brought in from the fields, and the cats would run about their feet. Leading from the cobbled yard there was a lane, which led to a pond and then down to the sea, simply called Pond Lane. When you had walked down the lane a quarter of a mile, you would see the wide-open sea.

In autumn the blackberry bushes that lined the lane and the hedges in the fields were ripe for picking. Each child had a colander or basket to fill. We made blackberry pies or stewed blackberries or blackberry jelly. The best thing about blackberries is their fragrance! Arriving home our hands were purple and our clothes a little stained too. If there was time, we would take a picnic lunch or tea with us when we went blackberrying. We children helped Mother to prepare picnics. There would be sandwiches, a large thermos of tea, and a small bottle of milk. Sitting on hills 200 feet above sea level, we could enjoy the beautiful views of the sea and the creeks winding between forested banks. It was a true childhood paradise.

When Father was busy, he could not come home from the fields for lunch or tea. One child, myself or my sister, would be appointed to take his lunch to him. She could sit with father as he ate or leave the basket by the gate for him to pick up later.

I was born not long after the Second World War. Food was strictly rationed during the war and for some time afterward until 1954. Mother, my teachers, and the parents of my friends did not want to waste any food. We ate everything on our plates. Much of what we ate was produced locally: potatoes, runner beans, and brussels sprouts came from our own fields and garden. Tangerines were a once-a-year treat at Christmastime. Picking food in the wild was such fun, mushroom picking especially. In August, if the weather conditions were right, mushrooms would spring up everywhere in the fields.

A mushroom is a miracle. Their spores, which are always in the air, can land in the grass blades and spring up as mushrooms in the course of the night. They only take one night to grow and the next day they can be eaten. The secret is to wake up early before the other villagers, and go out picking when the grass is wet with dew. The mushrooms are closed tight, perfectly round like little buttons. It is a game of hide-and-seek finding them in the grass. You may feel a little greedy taking them all, so you leave some behind for those who did not rise so early. When you come home you would eat them for breakfast fried in a little butter or baked on toast in the oven.

Water came from a spring at least half a mile from the house. It was pumped by an engine driven by a windmill, and in dry weather there was not always enough. We were taught to use water sparingly. When we were small, two children would share the same bath. When I was three years old, my father had enough money to bring electricity into the house. My father said it was a real blessing not to have to heat the iron in the oven or clean the paraffin-filled Tilley lamps and the black marks they left on the ceiling— just a flick of a switch and we would get a bright light. Father had his own chair in the sitting room and at table. Mother had her own chair too, which was quite small, by the piano. Father came in late and would eat on his own. He also ate breakfast earlier than the rest of us. Sometimes we would sit near to Father as he was eating, and he would give us a tiny piece of meat or potato or a bean off his plate.

My mother was very tolerant and accepting. She was the peacemaker in the family and could accept people as they were and make friends with anyone. She had been a nurse when she was very young, and I suppose she chose that vocation when war broke out because of her compassionate nature. She worked during the blitz in London. She had been trained in a large teaching hospital in London in the 1930s. It was a very strict training, and she was especially afraid of the matrons. The first principle all nurses had to learn was that the comfort and well-being of the patient matters above all else.

My mother's mother, whom we called Granny Smith to distinguish her from my father's mother, Granny Laity, was proud of the compassion my mother showed to the patients. Her father, my grandfather, had been a drunkard and beaten my grandmother, but when my grandmother ran away to Cornwall he followed her, and she agreed to live with him if he mended his ways, which he did. My mother must have suffered a great deal as a child although she never talked about it very much. She had a sister who was two years older than her and they loved and supported each other. The worst thing for my mother growing up was when her sister contracted tuberculosis and was sent to live in Switzerland for two years. The best thing was the holiday times that she spent with her maternal grandmother in Yorkshire. When her sister, Pam, was not in Switzerland, my grandmother, mother, and aunt would be together. They would spend time on Filey Beach, riding the donkeys, or singing and dancing as my great-grandmother played tunes from *The Scottish Students' Song Book* on the piano. As a result of all my mother had been through, she was both compassionate and stoical.

My maternal grandparents lived in a large house by the Mylor dockyard, situated on Mylor Creek, a tributary of the Fal River estuary called Carrick Roads. It was only a kilometre across the fields from where we lived, but we did not see much of them. As a child I felt that my father did not approve of my grandmother too much, although he never said so, and we spent far more time with our paternal grandparents. My maternal grandfather was a mechanical engineer who mended ships' engines, and my father was also an engineer, so my father and maternal grandfather conversed together with a certain camaraderie. My maternal grandmother and my father had nothing in commmon to talk about and her ways were very different from the ways of my paternal grandmother. Maternal grandmother's house was never very clean and tidy. Later my mother told me that the fact we spent less time with maternal grandmother than we did with paternal grandmother was painful for her. Although my maternal grandmother had no dislike of my father, she too must have felt his disapproval. Once she had seen my father and us children in the dockyard near her house, but we had not gone up to visit her. She told my mother about it and my mother instructed us that whenever we were visiting the dockyard we should call in on my grandmother.

My maternal grandmother used to catch shrimps in a net and cook them in boiling water. She liked painting and writing fiction about events that had happened in history. She would pick up shells on the beach and glue them together to make shell flowers, which she then painted. She gave us a chance to learn this art, but her shell flowers were always the most beautiful and remarkably delicate. She loved her little rose garden, which went down to the edge of Mylor Creek, and she transmitted her green fingers to my mother.

As children, we benefited from Mother's training as a nurse. Whenever we were sick, we had her undivided attention. She kept us warm and brought us what food or drink was needed. Whenever she had a moment and we were recovering, she would read to us. Mother read aloud very well; her expressive voice engaged us in the story she was reading. My mother has always been the model of loving kindness for me, the virtue of loving.

We had a motor car but we did not use it much. We walked to the village, Flushing, or took the ferryboat across the estuary to the nearest town, Falmouth. The way we lived was quite simple; we didn't consume much, and we produced very little refuse. There was the compost pile, an occasional bonfire, and for metal that the scrap iron man did not take, there was an old quarry.

Just after my fifth birthday I had to go to school. Later on, I learned that it was quite a sacrifice economically for my parents to send me to school. I could have gone to the local state school, but my father believed that a private education would train our character best, so he paid for all his four children—myself, Sarah, Stephen, and, later, Thomas, to go to private schools. My school was called Truro High School for Girls. It was an Anglican foundation school, founded by a Bishop Benson. This meant that we began our day with Anglican prayers and hymns, and we had an annnual service in the cathedral for the whole school and parents. We had to study the Bible twice a week in a class called Divinity.

The students entered the kindergarten by the conservatory. It was warm in mid-September in the autumn sunlight. On those first days of school, even though I was there only for the morning, I missed my mother so much I cried my

Six years old. Sailing with father in Little Falmouth (Flushing).

eyes out. I was five years old and it was the first time I had been separated from my mother. She had always been there somewhere in the house, or grandmother had been there to replace her for a few hours. I missed my father too. He had started to teach me to read when I followed him around the farm before school began. He taught me the names of the stars and the wildflowers which grew in the meadows.

In the conservatory there were pegs for us to hang our coats and hats, and lockers for our shoes—we wore laced shoes outside and buckled shoes inside. After a week or so at school I managed to find peace with the new situation. I even managed to stay on happily for two hours longer on Tuesdays to attend the ballet class. Everyone had a tiny cardboard case, and inside were a pair of ballet shoes and a ballet tunic of pale blue, green, or turquoise. We walked for a mile or so in a crocodile to the senior school for the ballet class holding our little cardboard case. We learnt all five positions of the feet, plié, and arabesque-en-posé to the sound of the piano. My best friend and I enjoyed the class so much that we would play games that included ballet dancing. I used to enjoy dancing for my mother and my grandmother. Many years later when my mother, then in her nineties, was very weak and had dementia, I would ask her: "Mummy, can I dance for you?" She always said yes, and watching me dance helped her forget her sadness and anxiety.

Just before my sixth birthday, the youngest child of my parents was born. We were now four. Tom, my youngest brother, sometimes had great difficulty breathing when he was a baby. He would be gasping for breath. When that happened, we needed the doctor to come quickly. One time the doctor was a bit reluctant to come out so my grandmother took my little brother to where the telephone was in our home and placed the mouthpiece so that the doctor could hear him gasping for breath. The doctor came immediately.

When I went to school, my sister, then three years old, took my place as my father's favourite. She became the one to follow my father around the farm. In my mind I felt that my father loved my sister and did not love me anymore. This was not true. It was just that I was difficult by nature and my sister was easy-going. She had a sweeter nature than I did. Strangers liked her, and I withdrew like a tortoise into its shell. My perception caused me to suffer from jealousy of my sister.

Father would take us to the nearby Anglican church on Sundays. Mother did not like religion very much, but she would come to early morning Communion with me after

I was confirmed, formally entering the Church of England at the age of eleven. I am always grateful for this. I know she would not have gone if it had not been for me, and she wanted to support my spiritual life because she knew it was important to me. She had to work very hard in the house and on the farm during the week and could have stayed in bed a little bit longer on Sundays, but she sacrificed that.

We lived on the Flushing-Mylor peninsula. Near the north shore, in a valley just where the Mylor Creek begins, is the Mylor Church. The architecture of the present-day church is Norman and a thousand years old, but it had been part of an even older monastery dating from the fourth century. The founding monk had come by sea from Wales and was martyred by a pagan king. The whole area around the church, including the seashore, always has a spiritual significance for me because it has been a place of Christian practice for so long. It figures in my happiest dreams as a seat of awakening, as a place where the fruits of spiritual practice can be fully realised. After I became a nun, even if I visited my parents for only a very short time, I would go there to savour again the spiritual dimension of my dreams. Sometimes I have seen that place in other parts of the world—like Wisconsin, where the lake replaces the sea—because there does not need to be a one-thousand-year-old church to make a seat of awakening.

When I was nine or ten years old, if my father was busy and unable to go with me to church, I was allowed to go alone. I would walk down the narrow Cornish roads banked by high stone walls, hundreds of years old, which are now covered in vegetation. These hedges have become habitats for all kinds of plant and animal life. In springtime they are fragrant with the delicate scent of primroses and violets, and birds twitter in the oak trees that have sprung up on them.

To go to church meant to wear your best clothes. My Sunday best was bought in Plymouth, a town sixty miles northeast of where we lived. We would go there once or twice a year as an outing, sometimes by train, sometimes by car, a two-and-a-half-hour drive. The roads were narrow and people drove slowly. A twenty-mile drive would take one hour.

One Sunday when I was ten years old, I noticed now my father did not hold my hand anymore. He only held my sister's hand. This just added to my perception that my father loved Sarah and not me. When we arrived home, I went to our bedroom and cried. Of course, it was only natural that Father should hold the younger child's hand. Father did not like children crying, but mother tried to console us. "Come," she said. "Put back on your Sunday best and we'll take a photograph of you. Wash your face." At this point I felt I could smile for the camera.

We had a vast 300 acres to play in. We explored every nook and cranny, every stream, every little path, the woodlands, pastures, mossy banks. I had a secret hiding place, a tree that was easy to climb. It was a refuge when I felt there was an unpleasant atmosphere in the house. It was near the house but in a place behind the barn where grain was stored, and people never went there. I would stay there a long time until I felt ready to face other people again.

Another refuge was my paternal grandmother's house in Falmouth. It was separated from our house by a quarter-mile stretch of seawater. I have very fond memories of my paternal grandmother. She took care of me when I was ill. She lived on the other side of the estuary and could easily be reached by ferryboat. There was a ferryman who rowed people across and landed just below where my grandmother lived, but he grew old and we had to use the motor ferry. A ferry ride at that time cost only one penny. Then I would walk up a very steep hill to Grandmother's house. The atmosphere in her house was different from that of my own. Grandmother did not seem to have that much to do and she could devote her time to her grandchild, walking into the town, taking the bus to the beach, playing on the beach. On the way home I would run ahead of Grandmother and sit on the steps of her house waiting for her to arrive; I would pretend that I was an orphan and Grandmother would take me in. Since I usually stayed on my own with my grandmother, I devised all kinds of games I could play on my own and with her.

Grandmother spoilt us, but she also instructed us. Whenever we cried, she recited: "Laugh and the world laughs with you. Cry and you cry alone. This poor old world has troubles enough of its own." There is some wisdom in this attitude to life. It helps us to be aware of what is going well rather than always thinking about what is going wrong.

My father, her son, had learnt this lesson well. He never complained or cried. I have seen tears only once in my father's eyes. It was in his eighty-third year when I bid him farewell to return to the United States. I suppose he was unsure when and if we would meet again.

When I stayed with my grandparents, Grandfather was

the first to rise in the morning. He would go downstairs in his pyjamas and dressing gown to make a pot of tea. At the same time he would carefully quarter and peel two or three apples and pears (sometimes he would have me go out and pick them) and prepare a small glass of orange juice for each of us. As soon as I heard Grandfather stirring I would get up and follow him downstairs to help him prepare this little meal. He would sing as he worked, sometimes a song from *The Scottish Students' Song Book* or an extract from Handel's *Messiah*. He could not sing in tune but still I learnt many songs from him. Grandmother would be sitting up in bed waiting for her cup of tea. English people of that time liked to drink a cup of tea in bed before rising. Maybe it helped them get out of bed "on the right side," feeling more awake and ready for the day.

Grandmother and Grandfather lived independently of each other in many ways. Grandmother had her own sphere of action that little interfered with Grandfather's. Grandmother never set foot in Grandfather's sailing boat. Grandfather had a circle of male friends and was a mason. The masons were a secret society, so of course Grandmother knew nothing about them. Grandfather once showed me his masonic robe of blue and gold, and that was all I ever heard about the masons. Grandmother, on the other hand, stayed at home and kept the house in perfect order. She had learned to be independent from early in her marriage. Grandfather was a mining engineer, and when tin was running out in Cornwall, he made his living in India and South Africa. Grandmother preferred to stay at home and bring up her children in England. It was not always easy for him to send money home, and Grandmother and her children had to live very simply. They did not have money to buy luxuries like sugar, so it was something they did without. She made her own bread and pastry, which were very light. The bread she kneaded with just two fingers making holes in the dough, and the pastry she mixed by making cuts with a knife, so she never had to touch the dough.

Grandmother came from a devout Methodist family. Her grandfather had been a stalwart of the local chapel and was known for his concentration in prayer and good works. Her mother was also devout. Grandmother had converted to Anglicanism from Methodism on marrying Grandfather, but she confessed she did not feel at home in the Anglican church. Before she was married she had been a schoolteacher, teaching in a school where the children were very poor. Many of the children came to school unwashed and the first thing the teachers did was to help the children wash their hands and faces. Grandmother was strict but also kind. She would correct wrong behaviour but never with anger. Her way of life was like her house: orderly and neat. It was a joy to be with her because of this.

Next to Grandmother and Grandfather's bedroom was a little room that my grandmother called "the pigsty." It was the only place in the house where order did not reign. It was Grandfather's own terrain. Grandmother never went in or disturbed anything in there. It was full of papers, photographs, and postcards. There was the skin from a python Grandfather had shot in India and other mementos. While Grandmother and Grandfather were drinking their tea, I would go in there and pick up one of the many photo albums bursting with old brown photographs. I would bring it in and place it on the bed in front of Grandfather. To encourage Grandfather, I would open the cover and point to a photograph: "What is that? Where is that? Who is that?" and Grandfather would tell a wonderful tale of his life in India or South Africa.

Grandfather believed in God, but he told me that as far as he was concerned when you died you became nothing. I could not agree with grandfather about this. At the very least, I thought, you would become a tree that grew out of the place where you were buried.

The spirituality of my early years consisted in going to church and Sunday school on Sundays, the daily assem bly at school, and Divinity lessons. From the time I was seven years old I enjoyed studying Divinity very much. I had ancestors on my paternal grandmother's side who had been praised for their practice of Christianity, and maybe my interest in Divinity was inherited from them. I used to receive the Divinity Prize at the end of the school year, and I never knew why this was so. I did not feel I put any special effort into studying this subject. On Sunday morning I would go to church and on Sunday afternoon to Sunday School. One day the vicar asked: "Why did Jesus come into the world?" I raised my hand to answer: "So that we can be like Jesus."

That was not the right answer. I should have said that Jesus came into the world to save us from our sins. So even as a young child I was somewhat at variance with the teachings of the Anglican Church. I felt very close to Jesus as an example of a wonderful human being, but "God the Father" was something or someone my child's mind could not grasp. Nevertheless, I would kneel at my bedside every night and ask God to bless my mother and father and grandmothers and grandfathers. Today I am sure that my Vietnamese monastic brothers and sisters brought up in Buddhist families felt close to Shakyamuni Buddha as children in the way I felt close to Jesus.

My school environment also played a part in forming my character. After a year in the kindergarten I went to the Truro High main school. There were four hundred pupils from the age of six to eighteen. The school was ten miles from our home and we had to go by car or by bus. At school we ate a cooked lunch in a very orderly fashion, everyone beginning and finishing together. The head of the table served us. The head mistress or one of the most senior mistresses sat at the head table—each table of ten children took it in turn to sit at that table with them. A teacher or senior prefect sat at the head of all the other tables. The children took it in turns to go and fetch the food from the kitchen, and the teacher or senior prefect would serve food for the children. You had to eat what you were given and stay at the table until you had eaten it. Since milk upset my stomach I was loathe to eat anything containing dairy, but I did not have the skill to express this to my teachers. The concept of allergies or food intolerances, much less freedom for children to choose what to eat, was then unknown.

During playtime before lunch, I would stand by the wire fence around the play yard and look down into the kitchen windows to see what was being prepared. If I could identify tinned fruit salad for dessert, it was a tremendous relief. If it was a milk pudding, I knew I would sit for hours trying to force it down. I remember once sitting at the table until three o'clock in the afternoon with some milk pudding I could not eat.

I suffered a great deal because of this, so my parents decided to send me to a school of Catholic nuns who were less strict. This school was more like a family. If you could not eat something, you did not have to have that dish. It was a tremendous relief to go to school and not to have to worry all morning what was going to happen at lunchtime.

So in my eighth year, I began to be taught by a French order of nuns—though they were mostly Irish—called Les Soeurs de la Croix. These sisters were for the most part gentle and understanding. They conducted their careers as religious and not primarily as teachers. They were more concerned with the education of our souls than academic excellence.

The sisters had a beautiful house and garden, which they shared with their pupils. It was an old manor house with polished wooden floors. There was an inner courtyard with a cloister. The ground floor was for classrooms, the first floor for dormitories, and the second floor for the nuns' rooms. I began to enjoy school because it felt like a family. The nuns, in my eyes, were happier people than my parents or the lay teachers in my old school. Keeping the house clean and washing the dishes was something the pupils participated in with the nuns. Not all the nuns were qualified teachers, but they were all part of the family we called school. They knew us all by name and would talk, laugh, and joke with us. During mass, the whole community would be together in their long black robes without the aprons worn in the kitchen or hiked-up robes as in the garden. I enjoyed the aroma of incense and seeing the nuns worshipping as a community. I enjoyed listening to Latin. It was all a bit mysterious, and as a child I was attracted by that. The religious life began to have a strong attraction for me.

At eight years old, we had already started to learn Latin and French. Catechism was another important part of the timetable. We sang, and played the piano, and sciences played a very minor part. Every lesson began and ended with making the sign of the cross and reciting the Hail Mary. At midday, the whole school gathered to recite the Angelus before lunch. On the various feast days, the daily schedule was abandoned for attendance at mass, a picnic, and, if the weather was warm, swimming in the outdoor granite-lined pool.

The garden was truly a delight. That area of England is renowned for magnolia, azalea, and rhododendron, and because of the mild climate the rhododendron bushes grow into large trees that make wonderful places to play under. There was a magnolia grove, the fragrance of which I can never forget. The white clusters hung on branches stretched out under a blue sky.

The nuns were not rich and lived very simply. They sold bunches of flowers to parents to make some extra money. Sometimes we just ate bread, margarine, and lettuce at a meal. Especially in Lent, the meals were simple. Some children boarded in the convent. I slept there only when my parents were on holiday. A nun slept in the dormitory of the youngest children. She had a curtain around her bed, but we saw her without her veil, her head bound in white. One time I needed to find a sister in her own quarters, and saw that the sisters slept two in a room. The room was very simple, just beds and some holy water from Lourdes. The nuns did not have a car, although the priest did. He was a kind man who liked to play games with the children. On Sundays, the nuns would take us for walks. It was pleasant to walk hand in hand with a nun and enjoy her kindness.

The nun who helped me most with sitting still was Sister Gertrude. She was old and retired from teaching. She would call me to sit at her feet and read some scripture to her. It was in Latin still, and I did not understand much, but there were English texts too. I had inherited the enjoyment of reading aloud from my mother. In order to read to an elderly nun, I might have to miss a class, but no one seemed to worry.

I remember as a child I would sometimes find myself alone. It would feel very quiet and still. I would be standing at the edge of the cloister and the other children were outside playing. It was still enough for me to feel my breathing. These deep moments of stillness were what I would later learn to recognize as *shamatha*, the initial part of meditation, when the mind becomes quiet. Later when I practised meditation with Tibetans, one of my teachers also remarked that I liked to practise shamatha or stopping, bringing peace to body and mind. My teacher, Thay, would later give me the lineage name Tam An, "Peace of the Heart."

The convent is no longer there because the nuns have all died of old age and no young nuns came into the convent to replace them. In the past, it was common in Europe for young men and women to enter the Christian monastic life, just as in Asia today in many Buddhist countries it is not uncommon for young men and women to enter the Buddhist monastic life. Now it is extremely rare for a young person to enter the ranks of Christian monasticism.

The relaxed way of learning with Les Soeurs de la Croix continued until I was eleven. Then we had to take a public examination, the Eleven Plus, and I failed. This was a shock to my parents. They woke up to the fact that my sister and I might not be learning as much as we could. They were alarmed about our education and future career and decided to send us back to the old school in Truro.

In 1961, after three or four years at the Catholic school, I went back to the school I had started in. The discipline was strict. We wore a brown uniform and we had to wear every item correctly according to the season. My parents had to pay for all this and they were not rich. It was difficult to fit into a new class especially when I was sadly behind in many subjects. There was an entrance examination and because of good results in some subjects, I was put in the highest stream, the A stream, when in fact I only excelled in Latin, French, and Divinity. In the classes in which I did well, I would sit in the front and was well-behaved. In the classes with which I had difficulty, I would sit at the back with others of the same ilk and not pay attention. In the words of my teachers I was "diffident" and "retiring." I did not know what the word "diffident" meant, let alone how to transform this characteristic. I had no idea of any career, nor did I have any desire to marry and have a family. Family life was not as happy as convent life, so secretly I dreamt of becoming a nun. Religion was a comfort to me. The idea of something beyond the daily routine, something deeper and higher, attracted me. To kneel and pray in the chapel was a chance to be in touch with this higher, more refined thing. I also had dreams of helping people with disabilities, especially people like my cousin Robin who had Down syndrome. I thought I would start a school for such children.

While I was in primary school I enjoyed Divinity lessons very much; when I became a teenager I found them tedious and irrelevant. When I was seventeen or eighteen and in the sixth form at school, we were taught by a canon from the cathedral, and were able to look more into the mystical side of Christianity. Once I asked why we had to repeat *mea culpa, mea culpa, mea maxima culpa* (through my fault, my most grievous fault) when we had not done anything wrong. He explained that wrongdoing is collective. We confess the wrongdoing of our ancestors and our society. I found this very helpful for my practice of confession during the Eucharist. He also introduced us to the practice of cosmic consciousness, a concept that was first talked about at the beginning of the twentieth century—an awareness of the oneness of all things and of interbeing. It was like being told about the ultimate dimension. I tried to go out in nature and be in touch with everything as one.

It was strange to be in such a large classroom with more than thirty students. The evenings at home gave me a sense of continuity. Mother provided a snack and then we would walk down to the sea. In the summer we went barefoot. After the winter our feet were still tender, but soon they hardened. The path through the woods was cobbles and gravel in the beginning for about one quarter of a mile. But after the first gate, it turned into soft forest earth, the result of many years of composted leaves. What was now a woodland path had once been a road for horse and carriage from the manor house to the pier. When we were very small, before our legs were strong, we had certain resting places on large round stones. Grandmother also liked to rest, when she walked to the sea, where the sycamores were shady.

Every day the sea is different. Depending on the moon, the tide is high or low. Depending on the wind, the sea is calm or rough. Calm sea has its delight, but rough sea was also fun to play in. High tide seashore shelves more quickly, so you could reach the depths easily. Low tide shore has all kinds of beautiful pools hiding in the crannies of the rocks, with varieties of seaweed and shellfish.

When the tide was high enough, we could swim from the granite steps of the pier, which was built out from the shore. It was high enough so that even at the highest tides you could moor your boat to it. At the end of the pier there were steps so that on disembarking from your boat you could climb up on to the pier. One day when I was eight years old, I pushed off from those steps—one stroke, two strokes, ten strokes—I floated, I could swim! It was a day for celebrating. Before that, I had been held in the water by Father or by an inflated rubber tyre.

The water on the south coast of the Cornish peninsula on which we lived was gentle. But twenty miles away was the rugged north coast with its surf. There the sea was dangerous with strong undercurrents. We never used any rubber floating device or rubber dinghy because they were easily carried away on the current with the person on board. We played in the safe places on homemade wooden surfboards, which Father fashioned and varnished in his tool shop. My father and grandfather had spent so much time on boats. My grandfather had his own boat and after his retirement, every fine day in spring, autumn, and summer he would be out sailing. My father did not have his own boat but he was a good sailor and there would always be a place for him in the boats of his friends.

Once we could swim, Father taught us how to sail. Father had been sailing since he was a small child and he was the best teacher. When he saw we were proficient enough, he would let us go out in our little scow alone as he shouted instructions from the beach. One day he went off to Teign-mouth in the car, not saying why he was going. When he returned, he was towing a brand new sailing dinghy. In the summer when there were beautiful long evenings of

Learning to sail in the Carrick Roads (first time sailing on my own).

light, we could go sailing and sometimes race our sailing dinghy. The wind often drops in the evening, and it would take us a long time to return to shore. Sailing is a time to be in touch with the wind and the water. The sailor and the boat can master these elements and use them to travel fast. It is very exhilarating to sail in a stiff breeze and to feel the saltwater splash up against you as you lean out to keep the boat upright.

My father was a very strong swimmer. One day two people in a rubber dinghy were being swept out to sea. They were crying for help but were so far from the shore no one could help. Father ran into the waves, swam out to them, and then pulled them back to the shore against the current. He collapsed on the shore and called for brandy for the two rescued ones, and after they had drunk some he himself took a capful. At the time I marvelled at how Father instructed a capful of brandy be given to the ones he'd rescued before he himself took some. Mother was standing by with hot tea. She must have worried so much. We read afterward in the newspaper how an anonymous man had rescued two people.

Father's life was an interesting one. He had a kind of second sight, which I often relied on. This second sight did not come from rationalization. I could not always rely on his judgment because he sometimes made mistakes, but sometimes he knew exactly the right time to do something and the right thing to do. Although he used to be an angry person, in his old age he had a quiet calm about him.

Later in life I would enjoy very much sitting at table with him, after he had retired from farming and my youngest brother had taken over the farm. He had a wooden chair with arms and would rest his elbows on these arms and join the ends of his fingers while he was thinking or saying something. He knew the right amount to eat, but sometimes Mother served him too much and he never liked to throw food away. He always finished everything on his plate, not a crumb left behind. He was very content and concentrated when eating. You could feel that his mind was not wandering here and there. He was just eating in the way that we in the monastery, where I now live, practise eating in mindfulness.

When I went up to London University I developed anorexia nervosa. I enjoyed the feeling of being hungry and refused to eat. I enjoyed the feeling of floating and being light and I thought I was doing the right thing by not eating. I always thought I should and could be thinner. As a child I had been plump at one time and this brought about much disapproval from my father (my maternal grandmother was fat and maybe Father had disapproved of her for that). But on a visit home, sitting alongside Father on a trip to the Scilly Isles, he offered me some of a chocolate bar, which normally I would never eat; but I ate it without any resistance. Eating a piece of bread without butter or anything else became tasty in his presence. He was completely relaxed when eating, and that alone made the food taste good. This sense of ease when doing something with his hands, like repairing an electrical gadget or some other machinery or being midwife to a cow or a sheep in difficult labour, meant that father was very patient and never became irritated or lost peace and calm when involved in some manual task.

I also used to enjoy going shopping with Father. He would enter each shop as if he were entering a world of treasures. He was never in a hurry to buy something and considered the wares carefully. It was a childlike quality of his, which he had kept from the days when there were no supermarkets and going into a shop was a voyage of pleasant discovery.

In public school he had nearly died from peritonitis, an infection caused by a burst appendix. Not long after, in Leeds Technical College, he lost an eye. While looking on at someone welding, a piece of metal flew into his eye. It meant that he could not serve in the Second World War. Father told us that if he had joined the navy in the war he would most likely have been killed. As a public schoolboy he had been in the Officer Training Corps, and therefore if he had gone into the navy he would have been an officer and had to lead his troops into battle. Most of his friends in a similar situation had died in this way. He had never wanted to be a farmer, but he could not continue as a mechanical engineer

Sailing with my mother and a family friend near Falmouth.

or anything else that might cause the loss of a second eye. It was a shock to me to hear that my father could have been killed. I realised how lucky I was to have him as a father and I felt grateful to the naval officer who interviewed him and did not accept him in the navy because of his one eye. Only later did I realise that if he had been killed I would not be there either.

As a farmer, my father cared about the animals in his care. Although he allowed them to go to the slaughter-house, he treated them all with great kindness for as long as they lived. Living on a farm, a child early on comes into contact with a contradiction. It is the contradiction between destroying and protecting life. It is true that we cannot live without taking life, the lives of other species, sometimes plant species and sometimes animal species. Even though we may say we are vegan, we are not in fact vegan. We eat vegetables, and during the course of cultivating those vegetables, some insects are inevitably killed. Our life as a human being depends on the lives of other species, and sometimes our livelihood is threatened by other species, like the rats that come into the barn and eat and befoul the grain, or the rooks and the pigeons who come and eat the tiny seedlings of grain as they sprout up from the earth.

It is part of the business of being a farmer to protect his crops, and that may involve killing the predators. On the other hand, he lives close to his cows and his sheep, cares for them when they are sick, and acts as midwife when they are giving birth. He does not do that out of a desire to make money but simply out of an instinct to protect life. I agree with Mencius that this instinct is very deep, deeper than the desire to make money (Mencius 6A:6); but the desire to make a living is there and it can take precedence over the instinct to protect life, as when the farmer sends his cow to the market to be sold to the slaughterhouse.

As a child you witness all this: your father taking care of a sick animal and the next day sending an animal to the slaughterhouse. It does not make sense to the child. To the father it is just a matter of overriding certain sentiments as he sends the animal to the slaughterhouse; something that his ancestors have also done over many generations, and so is no longer difficult to do. The cow waits for the lorry to come and take her away to her death. She knows that is where she is going. Cows have not lost what we call their sixth sense. She is crying her heart out, but no one can save her. Tears may even fall from her eyes. As a child I stood in the yard with a cow, singing a hymn, trying to comfort her, but I felt powerless; the whims of adults have to be obeyed. However much I protested didn't make any difference to the fate of the cow. I wondered every time when I next ate some beef whether it was not the flesh of that cow. No wonder it was not difficult to become vegetarian once I left home. I became a vegetarian when I was twenty-one. As a university student I read books by Paul Brunton from which I learned that eating meat made the soul heavy and was not beneficial for the spiritual practice of meditation. Still I feel that my love for animals was a very important reason for becoming vegetarian.

CHAPTER TWO

London University

W HEN I was in the sixth form and nearing the end of secondary school, I decided to go to university and pursue a degree in Classics. When at twelve years old I changed schools again, I had already learned some Latin and was ahead of my classmates. So I found it very easy and did very well in the examinations. This was one of the reasons I chose Classics. Another reason was that I enjoyed Greek Philosophy, especially Socrates, Plato, and the Presocratic philosophers to whom we were introduced in the sixth form. To me these philosophers could show one a way out of suffering, and also Socrates taught that death did not mean becoming nothing, which was proof to me that my grandfather was wrong about that! Not many people studied Classics, so the classes were small and the teacher could give each student individual attention.

My father said he did not agree to send me to the university to study Classics. What a waste of time studying languages that are no longer in use! He thought I should train as a bilingual secretary. That was his dream for me. It was very far from the study of the Greek philosophers. My father wanted only to pay university fees for my brothers. I never knew how, but he changed his mind and I was allowed to apply to read Classics at London University. Maybe it was my mother who persuaded him. My father even drove me all the way to London for the interviews.

It was the first time I had been to London. We stayed in a hotel. In those days London was still very polluted with black smoke from coal fires. London and the Cornish countryside were poles apart. It was rare for me to spend time alone with my father and I noticed how kind he was to me when the two of us were in London together. He came with me to the interviews and sat and waited in Regent's Park and the Westfield College gardens.

I was accepted by Bedford and Westfield colleges. They were women's colleges in those days, but in 1967, the year I came up, they were accepting their first men students. I chose Westfield College. It was a beautiful enough place in Hampstead, not too big, with everything I needed and all the good conditions for studying. Unfortunately, I did not apply myself to my studies and make the best of this environment. Sometimes the courses were too difficult for me and I lacked self-confidence when I saw that there were other students doing better than I was. From childhood, I had learnt to always compare myself with others, and this was the cause of much suffering. One thing about my university education that has remained with me is the study of Sanskrit, which I continue to find useful today.

My roommate was Anglican and, to begin with, we went to the Anglican chaplaincy in Gordon Square together, in the heart of Bloomsbury and the administrative centre of the university. I did not find any solace there nor answers to my questions.

I had questions about ethics: what were the ethics of protests that bordered on violence or actually became violent? It was 1967–1968 and even though I did not take part in the sit-ins, protests, and demonstrations going on in the various colleges, only supporting the actions by going on strike and not attending any tutorials, I was influenced both consciously and unconsciously by my environment and the way the students were talking and thinking throughout Europe. Everything was changing. According to what I had learned before going up to university in 1967, extramarital sex was unethical, but many of the students I met contested that idea.

I needed solace because when, just after my eighteenth birthday, I went up to university, I left behind not only the physical presence of my mother and father but also the way of living in the countryside that I had known. I was in a huge metropolis and could not sleep because of the noise of traffic at night. On the other hand I was exposed to many new and exciting ways of experiencing life, and in a way I had to die to the old in order to be born to the new.

As well as my studies, and discussing philosophy and politics with my friends at the university, I had times when I withdrew into myself and enjoyed just sitting still. I wrote:

> It is good to hear the bird sing
> In the evening,
> To sit still
> And to think nothing.

Since I was a teenager I had written poetry as a way to deal with my emotions. I had discovered that there is a wisdom inside that can be unearthed by writing poetry. You sit down in a calm, not-thinking state of mind and let your pen write. Sometimes the emotion needs to be expressed, like that of fear:

There is not very much at all,
Only a tree, a green tree tall
That reaches to the sky
And of fear we die.

Luckily my other university student housemates had seen that I could not sleep in my room facing Finchley Road, so a student who lived in a quiet room at the back of the house exchanged with me. There I could hear the birds singing and gaze on the tall green trees.

In many ways university was a disappointment to me. To start with, the dons, our lecturers and professors, were not as special as I had expected. They were not very wise people who could impart something deep to me. They were just ordinary people and (I thought) sometimes not even as wise as some of my schoolteachers had been. All students were assigned a "moral tutor" who was supposed to be a mentor who helped the student in a spiritual way. I always felt embarrassed to speak with my moral tutor and never dared to talk about my problems, because I did not think she could help me. So I ended up without any guidance at all, which as an eighteen-year-old student I really needed. I needed guidance on how much time to spend on my studies and how much time to spend discussing politics or going to the theatre. I needed guidance to help me relate better with my father. I needed guidance on how to handle male students who made advances. Without support from my tutor, I had to work out how to navigate student life on my own.

Once in university, I avoided visiting my family. One day my father rang and told me how much my mother missed me. He asked me: "Can you not come home just to make your mother happy?" My mother loved me so much, she would bake cakes for me and send them by post. I was the first of her children to leave home. I had received so much support from my mother during my life—support for going to Communion early on Sunday mornings and to read Classics at University. But I had the desire to shake off my childhood and become independent because I thought my family were conservative and did not care about social change and making the world a better place. Looking back now, I see that I was quite callous to my mother at that time and probably to my father too.

When I first left home to go to university, I thought I would be homesick. London and Cornwall were so different from each other, and I loved the countryside. Actually, I was not homesick at all. The first vacation, the Christmas vacation of 1967–68, I went down like most other students to be with my family. Grandpa Laity, my paternal grandfather, was very ill with liver cancer. He was emaciated, one-third of the size he had been when I last saw him. I did not know if he knew he was dying and I had no idea how to comfort him. It was only later as a nun that I learnt how to be with those who are dying. My aunt, with whom he was staying, and my paternal grandmother did not even tell him that he had cancer. My opinion then was that he should be told, but on reflection I now feel very differently. If someone asks what is wrong with them, how long they have to live, we can answer with compassion, but if they do not ask, they may not want to know. He died soon after. It was my first experience of death in my close family.

When I went up to London again after the vacation, I came into contact with a new group of friends, and this further distanced me from my family. I met up with a group of Catholic Marxists and started going to the Catholic chaplaincy instead of the Anglican one. We all need friends and they became my friends. I began to feel that the sphere I had lived in was too narrow. As a teenager I'd had rebellious moments, declaring myself to be a feminist or refusing to stand up when the national anthem was sung, but ideas about overthrowing the government had never entered my head. Now by being drawn to Marxism, I went in the opposite direction to my parents and family. I still needed religion because it was the spiritual dimension of my life, but at the same time the rebel in me wanted to overturn capitalism. Joining Christianity to communism made Christianity engaged in relieving the suffering in the world—and first of all that suffering was poverty. Looking back on this time now, I realise this period watered the seeds of monasticism in me. Becoming a nun is in itself a revolutionary step. It means going in a different direction from that of society. In 2005, Thay, on his return to Vietnam after almost forty years of exile, told the Vietnamese Communist Party leaders: "We monks and nuns do not own a private car, telephone, or computer. In fact, we are the real communists."

In my second term at university, contrary to my earlier interest in the Classics, I now found other subjects more interesting and able to captivate my budding intellect and thirst for knowledge. I did not immerse myself in the study of Classics because I found it boring and I spent my time reading philosophy and studying my special subject, which was comparative philology. No wonder I only received a II.2, a lower second-class degree. Nevertheless, I was accepted as a postgraduate student at University College, London because I had done very well in my special subject paper on the topic of the philology of Greek and Latin.

As a postgraduate I belonged to the Department of Comparative Philology, which was housed in two rooms in University College at Malet Street and Gordon Square. The faculty had two members, a French woman who was its head and an Irish man who was assistant lecturer. It was here that I learnt Sanskrit and Tocharian. One form of Tocharian, Tocharian A, was used to translate Buddhist texts, because there had been Buddhist monasteries in the area of the Tarim Basin. I remember one text we read about a sculptor who made a statue of a woman, which he liked so much he managed to bring it to life. Although I was not interested in Buddhism at the time, I was struck by this metaphor for the insight that our mind creates the outside world.

One day while walking along Gower Street on my way to University College, a cloud of dust blew up in front of my face. It had a strange effect rather like that of the cosmic consciousness we had heard about in the sixth form from our canon. I stopped in my tracks and saw for the first time that everything is interconnected in a wonderful way, which I had no words to describe.

My French tutor wanted me to do research into

non-Indo-European elements in the ancient Greek language. First of all, I was expected to make acquaintance with as many ancient Indo-European languages as possible—Hittite, Gaelic, Avestan, Sanskrit, Tocharian. Doing this and schoolteaching took all my time. I had a small bursary from a charitable association and did not have to pay tuition fees, but I needed to work to cover my daily living expenses. The first post I held was teaching Latin in a boys' state grammar school in Ewell, which is a short train journey from Waterloo. Ewell is part of the commuter belt of Greater London and its inhabitants are mostly well-to-do. I did not envision myself as a schoolteacher for my whole career and hoped that I should be able to complete my postgraduate studies and teach at the university level.

When I went for the interview in the boys' school, the headmaster did not believe that I was twenty-one years old. He said I looked younger than the sixth form schoolboys. When I produced evidence of my age, he told me that I must never smile in the classroom because the boys would think I was not serious and take advantage of it. It was no easy task not to smile. I enjoyed teaching the boys, especially the sixth form, although in the beginning I was very nervous. I do not remember the boys taking advantage of my being young.

The next teaching post I took to support myself was in a girls' school called the Greycoat Hospital. It was very near Victoria Station and not in the most beautiful surroundings. The headmistress took pity on me as a poor postgraduate student and gave me the post teaching Latin. I made friends with a young English teacher who belonged to the Catholic organization Opus Dei. This well-endowed, conservative organization was much disliked by liberal Catholics, like my Catholic-Marxist friends, who could not accept that it did not use its wealth to support the poor. One thing I admired about this young teacher was that when a mathematics master became friendly toward me and she saw us talking alone in a classroom one day, she had the courage to advise me that this teacher was a married man who had the tendency to befriend young schoolmistresses. When I talked to her about needing somewhere to live, she told me that Opus Dei had a residential college in Sussex for foreign students to learn English and I could come and live there. I was tempted because I liked the Sussex countryside very much, with its peaceful rolling hills. Nevertheless, I stayed on in the inclement atmosphere of Surbiton, a London suburb, to be with people who I felt were liberal. I was living in a household of postgraduate students. At that time in my life there was this dichotomy between what I considered to be the comfortable middle class and liberal socialism, and I felt I had to choose between one or the other.

There was a time when my tutor had to go into hospital and would then have a long period of recovery. She suggested I teach Greek Dialects, Sanskrit, and Hittite to undergraduate students to lighten her load while she was recovering. So I gave up schoolteaching to teach in the university. One time I prepared some notes about the history of the Hieroglyphic Hittite language. I made a serious mistake in these notes, which I left on the teacher's table. My tutor read this and kindly told me about the mistake I had made. I firmly denied having made it until she was forced to tell me she had read my notes. The lesson I learned from this was not to lie, and afterward whenever I lied to a teacher I would always confess as soon as I realised what I had done. Years later, I lied to a Tibetan teacher and, having gone back to my bedroom for the night, I felt remorse. It was already late, but I could not bear to be with my feelings. I made my way to the teacher's room and fortunately he was still awake, talking to his attendant. He was happy to receive my confession.

During one summer vacation I stayed in a Benedictine convent in Normandy in France. Staying there strengthened my wish to become a nun and I asked the abbot what he thought about such a path. He was not very encouraging and suggested that the monastic life was not for everyone and I could always practise as a layperson. It was not long after this that I ceased doing any Christian practice. Since the time I had been a pupil at the convent school I'd had the desire to become a nun because I liked the community life and felt peace going into the chapel to pray on my own; I had the idea that being a nun would make the cosmic consciousness more easily available. But when I was living out in the world, religion had none of these advantages. So gradually my practice of Christianity slipped out of my life and I preferred being in nature to sitting in a church. Church services no longer fulfilled my spiritual need.

Simultaneously, comparative philology was no longer important to me. Without a postgraduate degree I needed to support myself by schoolteaching. I saw there was a post available for a Latin teacher in Plymouth; I applied and was accepted. It was the third teaching post I'd had, and it was a permanent position in a small private school that had been a convent and was now given over to lay teachers. The Classics department there only taught Latin. It was a shame not to be able to teach Greek, but the reality was that fewer and fewer schools had Ancient Greek as part of the syllabus. As I began to teach, I had some enthusiastic pupils. The school saw the largest number it had known pass the O-level examination in Latin, so I suppose my teaching was effective.

When I first arrived, I had nowhere to stay. An elderly lady with a large house took in teachers when they first arrived until they found lodgings. It was early spring in South Devon. The mimosa trees in people's gardens in the neighbourhood were in flower and very fragrant. I walked past them on my way to school as they blossomed. I was happy to have left the university and my research. I had work, I could help the children in little ways, I had food to eat, and a salary that was more than enough to live on. I used to donate what I did not need to the Krishnamurti Foundation because I had read about the kind of humane, spiritual education they provided and it seemed so much more meaningful than the normal exam-focused education. I wondered whether I should join the Krishnamurti School in England and teach there, but I felt that was not exactly what I wanted. I appreciated many aspects of the teaching of Krishnamurti, but in his followers I felt something I was looking for was lacking. There was maybe a lack of direction as far as the spiritual practice was concerned. I enjoyed teaching, being in contact with youth—their high ideals and the infinite possibility for development.

When I began to teach, I was still young. I enjoyed the responsiveness of the young people to what was taught. I did not enjoy the rigidity of the education system and having to fulfil the desires of the public examination boards. However, in my experience in teaching Classics, I found it is possible to work within the examination system and to still be nourished and nourish your pupils with the content of the lessons, as long as we bear in mind that passing examinations is not the goal of education. I was lucky in that teaching was my only career and I could devote my whole time to it. During the long holidays I could plan my lessons. My only recreation was taking long walks in nature or going to the sea to swim. I never felt overwhelmed by the amount of marking I had to do. I would use my spare time. I did not have administrative work to do nor did I have a husband and family to take care of. I just had the room I rented.

CHAPTER THREE

Greece

I HAD BEEN teaching for two or three years in Devon when I saw an advertisement for a cheap flight to Greece during the Easter holidays. As a student I had visited Rome but not Greece. Greek language and literature suited me better than Latin; I especially enjoyed reading Plato and the Presocratic philosophers because these writings addressed some of the ultimate concerns, such as what happens when you die, the nature of pleasure and pain, the essence of wisdom, etc. At that time, in the late 1970s, Greece was only beginning to develop as a tourist destination. It was still a part of Europe where people lived simply and where visitors could feel its closeness to Asia and the East. It didn't take me long to decide to go.

In Greece I walked a great deal, visiting ancient sites in the spring sunshine. The peasants in their customary rustic clothing would stop and stare at me, and one old woman asked me if I were an angel. At that time it was unusual to see fair hair in Greece. I would be invited into people's houses to eat bread with olive oil. The straightforward hospitality that I enjoyed and the Mediterranean climate combined to help me open my mind toward other ways of thinking and being.

For the first eighteen years of my life, I had lived with my family, close to the earth. Then suddenly I found myself in London for six years or so and had lost contact with earth

Thessaloniki

Istanbul

GREECE

Athens

Aegean Sea

Izmir
(Smyrna)

ASIA

MINOR

Mediterranean Sea

GREECE & TURKEY

and sky and the simple joys of life. The trip to Greece put me back in touch with these things, and when the time came to leave, I did not want to go back to England.

That trip during the Easter school break was truly a holiday. I saw that I did not have to cling to ideas that had haunted me in the past, such as the idea that eating was something you had to do to stay alive and it was best to eat as little as possible. Now I enjoyed eating olives and bread. I had lived in a comparatively small world of going to school, teaching, living in the UK, and working with and talking to other English teachers. English people are often described as rather stiff and phlegmatic. The friendliness of the Greek people and their simple way of life, without any intellectualism or pretension, gave me a feeling of freedom, not from responsibility, but from old habits and ways of seeing the world. Greece was a gateway to Asia for me.

So when I returned to England after my holiday, I immediately decided to look for a teaching position in Greece. It was 1976 and I was twenty-seven or twenty-eight. I managed to find work as the Classics teacher in an international school in the suburbs north of Athens. The school was an American foundation school that caterered for the children of Americans who were working in Greece as well as for the children of Greeks who wanted their children to have an American-language-based education. So the children came from well-to-do families and the school was in the prosperous suburb of Kifissia to the north of Athens. I had friends of friends to stay with in Athens until I found a place to live.

I eventually moved into an apartment in Kaisariani at the foot of Mount Hymettos. This quarter was peopled by Greeks from Asia Minor who had come there in 1922 as refugees without anything. They had been given land there by the Greek government where, with their own hands, they built simple homes. They were devout and hospitable people, and as a rather cerebral young woman I learned a lot from them. My neighbour used to sit on the stone steps of her house eating sunflower seeds in the evening. She showed me how to choose oranges in the market and told me what to eat at which season. She showed me how to make various dishes and she never threw anything away; she even used the stalks of aubergines. She was a simple soul who spent several hours in the church every day; she followed all the fasts of the Orthodox church, which are quite complicated. Her son showed me the paths to the top of the mountain, where I would sit and enjoy the views over Athens in my free time. I enjoyed walking on my own up the mountain. On the lower slopes was an old Christian monastery where I would stop off on my way to feel its atmosphere of spirituality. There were wild cyclamen growing out of the rock crannies. It was a dry mountain and on the top lived many poisonous adders, so from April onward I had to be very careful as I approached the summit. Often I would hear them hissing as they heard my footsteps approaching. Like most snakes, adders only bite when they feel you are going to step on them. I rarely saw anyone on the upper slopes and I felt perfectly safe.

The classes I taught in the International School were small, and we favoured Ancient Greek over Latin. I had many Greek boy students whose parents wanted them to learn Ancient Greek. Modern Greek has changed a great deal from its ancient form and I had to laugh sometimes when the boys translated the Ancient Greek words according to their Modern Greek meaning. I even had a chance to teach Sanskrit, and the headmaster even hoped that some pupils would take their official O-level exams in the subject, though that did not happen. I continued for this and the next year to be happy, living in Greece and being much more relaxed in my way of teaching than I had been in England. I worked less hard preparing lessons, partly because I was a more experienced teacher and partly because I wanted to enjoy time relaxing with my Greek neighbours. I felt supported by the school and enjoyed the work of teaching.

Sometimes it is very cold in Athens; I was surprised to discover it even snows there. My first winter came and, coincidentally, our school had to move to a new site. The new building had no heating system. One day when snow was on the ground, the pupils rebelled and said that they could not concentrate in such cold temperatures. We were reading Herodotus, I recall, at the time. Whenever I was teaching, I was absorbed to such an extent in the text that I did not notice the cold until the class was over. You could say that my ability to focus was outstanding, but perhaps I also was sometimes neglectful of my body's messages. Fortunately, this icy spell did not last more than two weeks.

It was while I was in Greece, which many consider to be the birthplace of Western traditions of philosophy, that I had the chance to meet Buddhism as a living practice for the first time rather than as a number of texts in Sanskrit or Tocharian. My neighbours persuaded me to contact the Tibetan Buddhist Center in Athens because to them it was an anomaly that I did not practise a spiritual path. They did not expect me to be a Christian, but they told me I needed a spiritual path and a spiritual community with whom to practise. The reason they suggested Buddhism was because they knew I had studied Sanskrit. It was very true that my life lacked a formal spiritual practice and I needed one in order to transform.

I knew about Buddhism, but it had never occurred to me to *practise* Buddhism, nor did I see the absence of a spiritual path from my life as any great defect or loss. I resisted their encouragement to go to the Buddhist Center. One day they challenged me to go along to find out more and let them know what happened there. Since it was the weekend, I had time, so I took the bus and walked to the address I had been given. Standing in the street in front of the building that housed the centre, I thought about going back to my flat. It looked very much as if no one was at home. Then the door opened and a Tibetan nun about ten years older than myself appeared. She was dressed in a yellow shirt and a long maroon lower robe wrapped around her waist. Her head had been shaved but her hair was now two or three centimetres long. Her skin was dark brown. She beckoned to me in the way that people in Asia do, with the fingers pointing downward. Her English wasn't much and my Tibetan nil. I didn't know it then, but this nun, Anila Pema Zangmo, and I would become good friends.

It appeared that there was no one else in the house. It was an ordinary house, rather dark, not particularly tidy. I was not very impressed. I'd expected something more uplifting for a Buddhist centre. Anila showed me the shrine room and told me how to prostrate before the Buddha and bodhisattvas. She gave me a rosary and taught me to repeat the mantra *om mani padme hung.* She told me that was the extent of what she could teach me, but that at the Tibetan New Year a teacher, "a high lama," she called him, was due to come and lead a retreat. It was important I should come back then. Before then, I should not come again. I was very happy to have met this nun, to have a new friend, someone who was on a spiritual path and wanted to share it with me. But I did not understand or appreciate what she was trying to teach me and I did not feel anything when prostrating to the Buddha and bodhisattvas. It was like doing a gymnastic exercise with no inner content. As for reciting *om mani padme hung* I have to confess that I had no intention to do it once I went back home. It seemed to me to be a waste of time. However, my curiosity was piqued by the prospective arrival of a high lama and I was determined to be there when he came.

I met Anila Pema in early January 1978, about a month before the Tibetan New Year. I was a little surprised by her injunction not to come back before the New Year and also that she didn't invite me to attend their meetings or encourage me to join the Greek Sangha, who met every week at that house.

After a month I returned. I had to teach that day, so I couldn't be at the centre in time for the beginning of the teachings. I could only take the school bus that went to that part of Athens in the late afternoon. When I came into the house, I saw about fifty people crowded into a small room listening to a teaching by a self-possessed Tibetan monk whose words were being translated into English by a young monk. Not wanting to disturb the atmosphere and feeling a bit shy, I first sat in the adjacent room. After ten minutes I felt an impulse to return to the room where the teaching was happening. At that moment, as I entered, I heard the young monk translating what the lama had just said: "It is like when someone is walking on a path at twilight. He sees what he thinks is a snake in his path and is very afraid. He looks again and sees that it is not a snake at all; it is only a rope. His fear vanishes immediately. Just so, as soon as we realise the true nature of the object of our fear, our fear vanishes."

These words touched something very deep in my consciousness, which no one had ever reached before until that moment. It was as if by listening to them, I was remembering something from a past lifetime. I thought to myself, *I have always known that this is the truth, but no one has ever let me know that I know.*

This was the moment of my conversion to Buddhism. No other teachings, I thought, could go as deep as this. Khenpo Tsultrim Gyatso—or "Ocean of Virtuous Conduct"—was to become my first Buddhist teacher. I was twenty-eight years old. Enough causes and conditions had come together for me to hear the Buddhist teachings, which I had not been able to encounter before.

My teacher spent much of his time in Athens surrounded by a group of disciples. We walked together in the park, on the Acropolis, and on the beach. All the while, he taught us, not just through the things he said, but also through the way he was.

It was not the outer appearance of the lama that set him apart, but his presence, which I can still feel now although I have not seen him for nearly forty years. For example, one day I sat behind him in a car and I was struck by how he seemed to be completely empty, or at least I used the word "empty" to myself. His outer form to me was empty. At that time I was not acquainted with the Heart Sutra: "Listen Shariputra this body itself is emptiness . . ." but I imagine the lama had reached that stage of realisation. Another time, he was throwing a pebble up and down, catching it, throwing it, and finally letting it drop. When we were on the beach or in the park, he would throw a little ball to us. When he threw me the ball I held on to it, not knowing what to do. He signalled to me to throw it to someone else. All these little actions I considered to be teachings.

The lama did not speak English, though he appeared to be studying a few simple sentences that he was learning from his attendant. One of these sentences was: "We are walking slowly." He frequently directed these words toward me.

Looking back, I conclude that I must have walked fast in those days. Anila Pema Zangmo, who was the only nun in the group, helped me by taking my hand in hers and walking at a very slow pace. Some years later in London, she had to remind me again. We were walking in Piccadilly Circus during rush hour, and I was being carried along by everyone else, hurrying for no good reason. Anila Pema told me that it was good to go slowly, so we did a slow mindful walk while everyone rushed past us like madmen. Whenever I was with her I could be persuaded to walk mindfully, but once left to my own devices I would go back to my habit of walking quickly.

Eventually the day came when Anila Pema told me that I would have an opportunity to "take refuge." I hesitated; I did not see why I should participate in such a ritual. Anila did not have enough English to tell me what is meant by taking refuge, and even if she had it is not sure that she would have done so. She could not answer my intellectual questions. In the end, perhaps a little impatient, she said, "Forget it. If tomorrow you want to take refuge, take refuge. If not, don't."

As a meditation master, Khenpo Tsultrim Gyatso must

have known that I had joined the path of Buddhism during his Dharma talk some days before. The next morning I watched other lay disciples come up and receive the refuges. "Is there anyone else?" the lama asked. I stood up and joined the group. At the time I thought I knew what was meant by the Buddha, the Dharma, and the Sangha, but what I knew was just a dictionary definition. It was the teacher in front of me and the teachings I had heard him give that I was taking refuge in.

I had a flash of insight, thinking back to a day when I had been travelling on a crowded bus in Athens. There were many people standing as well as sitting. The driver had a bottle of ouzo by his seat and to my horror I saw him taking a swig from it from time to time. He was driving too fast. I was overcome with fear. My first thought was that we might have an accident and I didn't want to get hurt. Then I imagined: "What if I was unhurt and everyone else was injured, could I be happy?" Luckily, we all arrived at our destination unhurt, but I saw clearly that my happiness and well-being lay in the happiness and well-being of others and my path was to help others to be happy.

When I took refuge, the lama cut some strands of my hair and gave me a lineage name. The lineage name is the outward sign of our joining our teacher's lineage. Our spiritual ancestors are important for us because they are in our teacher and if they had not been there, our teacher would not be here. He had some white cards in his hand. Each had a Dharma name inscribed on it. He had taken the cards in the order they were to be given to the other aspirants. When it was my turn, he took some time to shuffle the cards that were left before he took one and gave me the name: Karma Trashi Zangmo. Karma, meaning action, because I now belonged to his lineage, the Karma Kagyu. *Trashi* means "auspicious." *Zangmo* means "good." I was so happy to share this last name with Anila Pema Zangmo, the nun who had introduced me to the practice.

Before the last evening of the Khenpo's stay in Athens, I thought it was still early days for me with the Sangha and that many more Buddhist activities lay ahead for me in Athens.

That day after the talk and the chanting, we had a short period of sitting meditation. We were instructed to dwell for that time in undiscursive wisdom. The lama sometimes gave us only one or two minutes for sitting meditation with the idea that we should practise perfectly for that short time. Most of these short periods of sitting meditation would take place when we were walking in the park or by the sea. That evening, hardly had the meditation begun when the telephone rang. Someone in front of me stood up and hurriedly stepped past me to answer the call. For a moment I felt irritated, I opened my eyes, and I clearly heard a voice saying, "You are on your own now." Whose voice was that?

I thought it might be the lama, but now I think it must have been what we Buddhists call "store consciousness" speaking: the deepest level of the subconscious mind. I felt very sad because I did not feel ready or willing to be on my own. It turned out to be a partly wrong perception, which I can link to another dichotomy in myself at that time: not knowing whether I should be independent or dependent on others. However, I think that it was a message for me about not practising with the Athenian Sangha, which from the beginning Anila Pema had advised against.

I have since learned that it is possible to synthesize the ideas of independent and dependent: to take refuge in the Sangha in order to be diligent in your personal practice and to ask for and receive help when you need it; but true insight has to come from within and cannot be given to us by anyone else, not even our teacher.

As I walked out past the lama, palms joined, a cane by the door leapt into my hands, which at the time I believed was to accompany me on my lonely search to find my true spiritual home, which was not to be among the Tibetans or in Athens. I knew that this teacher had watered many beneficial seeds in me, especially the seed of true happiness. I only have to see him in my mind's eye, standing with the Sangha on the Acropolis, for stability and freedom to be touched in me.

I knew that I had at least one more year in Greece to teach; Anila Pema had invited me to visit her monastery in India and Khenpo Tsultrim Gyatso had approved of this idea, but he had said it was too early for me to go to India and that we should wait another year. After the ceremony, however, I did not return to the centre.

I was indebted to Anila Pema for opening the door for me to the practice of Buddhism and bringing me to Khenpo Tsultrim Gyatso, my first Buddhist teacher, who was someone of no mean stature. She also introduced me to her own teacher, the Sixteenth Karmapa, the head of the Karma Kagyu lineage to which we belonged.

One year later, not long before I went to India, Anila

Pema Zangmo came to Athens again when the Karmapa was scheduled to spend several days there for the purpose of performing the Black Hat ceremony. Anila told me that anyone who sees the Karmapa wear this hat during the ceremony is said to be able to be enlightened in this lifetime.

Before the ceremony, Anila Pema wanted me to have a chance to receive His Holiness's blessing privately. I eagerly followed Anila Pema to His Holiness's quarters in the new Tibetan Buddhist practice centre that the Athens Sangha had acquired. We were greeted by his attendant, who told us that His Holiness was resting and could not see anyone. I felt embarrassed and presumptuous to have come, and whispered to Anila Pema that we should withdraw. She said we should wait.

We waited ten minutes or so. Then the attendant reappeared. I understood that we could now go in. On entering the room, I saw no one; it appeared to be quite empty apart from a couple of sofas. Maybe the light from outside coming into the room blinded me. Anila Pema must have seen His Holiness sitting by the window. "Come and prostrate before His Holiness," she said. I joined my palms to prepare to bow, and suddenly a tremendous feeling of happiness came over me. I felt happy as I had never felt happy before and I smiled as I had never smiled before. All this time I saw no one. Still I touched the earth and as I knelt up was aware of a small, quite old man before me, but it was misty. Then without a word we left the room.

The "Black Hat" ceremony followed a couple of days later. During this ceremony, Avalokiteshhvara Bodhisattva manifests as the Karmapa. The Karmapa was carried in, sitting on a daïs with poles at each side on the shoulders of four monks. I looked up expecting to see the monk before whom I had prostrated and received a blessing. Instead I saw a twelve-year-old boy, so young, so beautiful. He seemed to be sitting near a lake. This puzzled me somewhat. I wondered whether everyone else saw the beautiful young boy I was seeing now or whether they saw the form of an old man I had bowed to before yesterday. The young boy I saw supported on the daïs swayed a little from side to side. I was not sure of the significance of this. I felt the fragility of the human bodhisattva form.

After receiving the Three Refuges in Athens, I had begun to read a book, *Buddhism: Its Doctrines and Its Methods* by the French-Belgian writer Alexandra David-Néel, who had travelled extensively in India and Tibet in the early twentieth century. There were quotations from the sutras in it. The ones I liked best I set to music and sang to myself as I went to work at the school. For example, here is a part of the Sutra on the Example of the Saw:

> "Even though robbers and murderers should be severing your limbs and joints with a saw and you should give way to anger, you would not, my disciples, be following my teachings. Even thus should you behave: your mind should be imbued with loving kindness. . . ."
>
> —MAJJHIMA NIKAYA 21

Another was a part of a Tibetan text by Dharmatreya, "Verses on Friends":

"Buddhas do not wash away sins with water, nor remove suffering with their hands. Beings are saved by the teachings of truth, the way things are."

In this way, working and keeping mostly to myself, I kept up my connection to Buddhism.

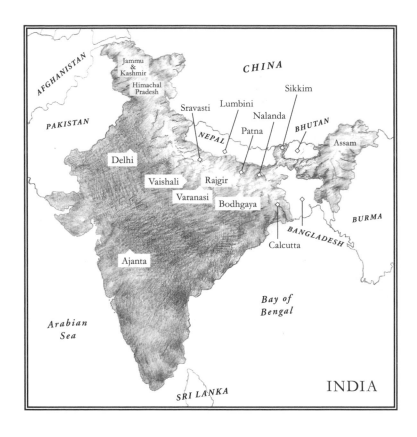

CHAPTER FOUR

India: Tilokpur

ANILA PEMA went back to India and I kept in touch with her by letter. She had a laywoman practitioner who acted as her scribe. After a year, I made arrangements to join her and I flew from Athens to Delhi in the summer of 1980. I had left my teaching post and my secret desire was to remain forever in India in the community of Tibetan nuns.

I had been preparing my trip by learning Hindi from the wife of the Indian Ambassador in Athens. She had told me that in India's northernmost state of Himachal Pradesh, where I was going, "they do not have flush!" On enquiry as to what this meant, she said that they do not have toilets that you can flush with water; you just have to use some open space for relieving yourself. This concerned me a little when I thought about it.

When I arrived in Delhi, I stayed for a few days with a Brahmin family who were friends and supporters of Anila Pema. The young people in the family spoke English and I instantly felt at home. From the roof of the house we watched a glorious sunset. The skies of Delhi would then be darkened by the smoke of countless fires used for cooking, but its parks were beautiful in the evening.

When I saw children playing outdoors in India, I had an uncanny feeling sometimes that I had once been a little girl among them. India felt more like home than England. Everyone seemed to move more slowly and there was more time for everything.

Anila Pema had many contacts in India, as I would discover; she was an Indian citizen who had been born in Himachal Pradesh to a Tibetan family. She had been the attendant and student of the Venerable Karma Kechog Palmo, an Englishwoman and a senior disciple of the Karmapa who, before she was ordained as a nun in the Tibetan Buddhist tradition, had been known as Mrs. Freda Bedi. After Independence, Mrs. Bedi served in the new Indian government, and in 1959 was asked by Jawarhalal Nehru to help Tibetan refugees in India. She set up a school for young Tibetan lamas and so became a practitioner of Buddhism associated with the Karma Kagyu school. She was ordained by the Karmapa as a novice nun in 1966, the first Western woman to take ordination as a nun in the Tibetan Buddhist tradition. (She received the bhikshuni ordination in Hong Kong in the Dharmaguptaka tradition, because there is currently no full ordination for nuns in the Tibetan tradition.) Although her full name and title were Gelongma Karma Kechog Palmo, many knew her simply as Sister Palmo.

Sister Palmo had passed away in 1977, three years before I met Anila Pema. She had known in advance the time of her passing and had remained in the sitting meditation position for a day or so after her breathing and her heart had ceased to function. Anila Pema told me some time later that the nun's continuation or *tulku* had been discovered, a Tibetan schoolgirl living in Darjeeling. Anila Pema had a network of Indian supporters throughout the country, thanks to her having been this nun's attendant.

Our destination in Himachal Pradesh was Tilokpur, the little village in the district of Kangra where Sister Palmo had founded a nunnery for Tibetan refugees. It was a twelve-hour overnight bus ride from Delhi. The bus was not all that comfortable with its seats for three people, and it was crowded. But it stopped frequently for people to refresh themselves. In fact, we did have to go to an outside space to relieve ourselves in some places, but I was happy to find that, when we got there, the nunnery had latrines. There was no running water to flush, but I found the system of bringing water in a bucket perfectly clean and pleasant to use.

Tilokpur is a holy place for both Hindus and Buddhists and there are two caves there where the Siddha (realised person) Tilopa is said to have practised in the tenth century. All I knew was that he had come to Tilokpur (later named after him) as an enlightened wandering monk and that his name was at the beginning of a prayer that we recited with the nuns from time to time. In the valley below the nunnery runs the wide river, whose sound you can hear on top of the hill day and night. When the building of Tilokpur nunnery had been completed, it burnt down. Sister Kechog Palmo was unperturbed and remarked that all conditioned things are impermanent and immediately began the building all over again.

From the bus stop it was a steep climb to the nunnery. During my stay in Tilokpur I came to know that climb very well. Halfway up was a jambu tree. People would sit at its shady base if they needed a rest on the way. If we had heavy things to carry we would need to hire a porter, and then there always seemed to be someone willing to carry heavy loads up the hill for a few rupees. When I first arrived in

India this road below the nunnery amazed me. You would never see a private car driving along; the traffic consisted only of the occasional public bus and trucks.

I settled into life at the nunnery. Sometimes we went to swim in the river, and both monks and nuns in the community enjoyed swimming very much. There were large reddish boulders to jump from, and they secluded the nuns from public gaze. There was also a warmish spring just by the entrance to the monastery to which the nuns could close the gate when they bathed. The village had a public outdoor baths for men and for women. I would sometimes bathe there, but it was not allowed for the nuns.

In the nunnery there was no bathhouse. Every day the sisters would bring water from the village spring for cooking and drinking. I learned how to wind a cloth and make a cushion on my head to carry the water bucket. I never carried a large quantity but I did manage to bring a bucket home. This would have been a wonderful practice if only I had known then how to practise walking meditation. My first teacher had done his best to encourage me to walk slowly, but just to walk slowly was not enough. Walking meditation also has to contain peace, joy, and presence. These things the lama had emanated, but somehow the transmission was not achieved; part of the reason, I think, was lack of words, but the main reason was that I was not ready to give myself wholly to the practice. The teachings I received from Tibetan lamas concerning the practice rather than the insights of Buddhism were limited to bodily actions.

When I was living in the monastery in Tilokpur, without knowing any better I walked without mindfulness as

I fetched water. Although I frequently had the occasion to fetch water, this did not become a cause for awakening for me. I feel happy now when I see that friends who come to the monastery receive clear guidelines on how to practise mindfulness in daily life. The majesty of the Himalayan landscape, the moments of silence sitting on wooded hillsides, the roar of the river, penetrated each cell of body and mind; but I had not yet learned to stop running. I had not stopped searching for something outside of me. The time was not altogether wasted, but let's say it was not put to its best use. I said to myself: "If only I could just stop thinking, running, craving for something, I should fulfil my greatest desire." Knowing that sooner or later all desires come true, I made the vow that one day I would enjoy the sunset without any intervention of thought. While in the nunnery listening to the roar of the river, I wrote a song:

Go very slowly going nowhere,
Go very gently stopping nowhere.
Like a river, deep and wide
always moving, still inside.

The river moves, but not in search of anything, unless it is chasing clouds. The river stops chasing clouds when it sees that clouds are itself. The water that makes the river is also the water that makes the clouds. I wanted to move and be still as I moved. Later I would have the insight that with walking meditation this is altogether possible.

Inside the nunnery, there was the Buddha Hall, the first building in front of you as you entered the gate. The housing and kitchen for the nuns was on your right. A little way down the hill below the nuns' accommodation was the little retreat that Sister Palmo had built for herself. It consisted of two rooms and above it, entered by a separate door, was the room for visiting high monks. At first Anila Pema thought to put me there, but when we discussed it I said I felt uncomfortable to sleep in the place of high monks, and she too thought it would be better for me to sleep below in Sister Palmo's quarters. It was quite a large room. I slept at one end and a sister slept at the other. It was quiet; all you could hear was the distant roar of the river, which easily lulled us to sleep. The room looked out onto the flank of the facing mountain. The bed was hard, wooden boards covered by a carpet. I could not sleep very long because it was too uncomfortable. Food was brought three times a day. I felt happy to be in this environment, but I was not sure I was contributing anything to the work that needed to be done in the monastery. The best thing was the walks we went on in the foothills of the Himalaya.

Since the time I had met Anila Pema, I had been donating part of my salary to her project to build a retreat and an Institute of Buddhist Studies for nuns at Sherabling, a site about seventy kilometres distant from Tilokpur. Khenpo Tsultrim Gyatso had told Anila Pema that she should build a room for me in this centre and, since I was a donor, I was given special treatment. I stayed in my little house and received visitors there. I helped Anila Pema a little by writing letters for her in English, and I began to learn the Tibetan alphabet so that I could read religious texts. However, nobody could tell me the meaning of the words I was learning to read. This was not the way I was used to learning languages. I said that there was not much point in reading a text you did not understand. Such an attitude puzzled the nuns. "Even an ant," they said, "crawling over the pages of a sutra text will benefit, establishing the causes and conditions to be in touch with the Buddhist teachings in a future lifetime." So a human being who pronounces the sounds must receive these good causes and conditions too.

In the little house of the high nun where I lived, there was another nun with whom I became good friends. She had a sponsor and could buy herself extra food. The meals provided by the monastery did not provide enough calories or nutrition. Just by looking at the nuns I could see who had a sponsor and who didn't. The idea at Tilokpur was eventually to find sponsors for all the nuns. Maybe donors are more easily found when they are shown photographs of individual nuns and can choose which nun they will sponsor, they can have correspondence with the nun etc., and that is how this policy arose. In the monastery the same policy was adopted—some monks were well-fed and some looked undernourished.

The nuns chanted the sutra in the Buddha Hall at least twice every day. On special days of the lunar month, there was extra chanting. I liked very much the melodies of the musical chants. These moved me deeply. However, the rather monotonous chanting of certain lengthy texts bothered and even irritated me. I preferred sitting in silence outside, where I could listen to the sound of the river always flowing in the valley below. I could not understand why so many long hours were spent chanting interminable *dharanis* when no one understood what they meant. Anila Pema told me that she chanted the Mahakala Puja every day in order to gain support for her acquaintances who needed it. My Tibetan sisters had a strong belief in the power of chanting, which I did not always share.

One of the people to whom Anila Pema sent support by chanting was her sponsor. He was an American who lived in Oxford with his family. He was certainly a rich man, but he was not self-indulgent and was generous in helping others. He was able to buy her air tickets so that she could travel and raise funds for the nuns' new retreat and Institute for Buddhist Studies at Sherabling. Anila Pema was an accomplished businesswoman as well as a nun. Her teacher had given her the task of coordinating the building of the nuns' retreat centre at Sherabling and she saw it as a difficult task, necessitated by some unwholesome karma she had accumulated in past lives. She had to find the funds, the building materials, organize the nuns and monks as labour, and hire extra labour as needed. It was very hard work. Six years later, in 1986, I had the chance to visit Sherabling again, and I saw the completed retreat centre where some nuns were already in residence. As I beheld the buildings, memories flooded my mind of the different periods of construction. All the worry and anxiety about never being able to finish, not having enough funds, and so on, seemed like a dream. I only wished that the nuns who practised there could have realisations on the path that made them truly happy.

Anila Pema enjoyed staying in the Tilokpur nunnery. For her it was like a holiday. The Sherabling project had not been able to rise off the ground and caused her many an anxiety. While she was away from the building site, she could relax and her mind could rest on more joyful things. She had loved her teacher, Sister Palmo, whose attendant she had been, and to be in the place which her teacher had designed and built watered the seeds of happy memories for Anila Pema. Moreover, it was a beautiful place. The snow on the peaks of the Himalayan range sparkled in the distance, and the wide river flowed below. Little homes hidden among trees could be reached by narrow pathways, while cattle and goats freely wandered around. Many of the neighbours were Anila Pema's friends and they would regularly invite us to lunch: chapati and vegetables cooked with different spices, but not too hot. Houses were built of dark wood with verandas where spices and leaves could be hung from the rafters to dry. Bamboo groves lined the roads, and the paths were of red earth. No cars ever reached these parts.

I had never talked to Anila Pema about how long I should stay. When I did, she shared her idea that I should stay four months and then go back to work in order to have more money to donate to the project. I had a hidden desire to become a nun, but realised that the life of renunciation requires financial support. Anila Pema did care for my spiritual welfare but I knew she valued me as a donor and would not accept me as a nun. Moreover, the nunnery had no money to support any more nuns. Maybe most important of all, it was not the right time or the right place for me to become a nun. Although I felt at home in India, I was European and had little idea of what being a Tibetan Buddhist nun would mean. It would mean being in a very different cultural milieu, of which I had very little understanding.

The Tibetan nuns on the other hand, except for Anila Pema, had no knowledge of Western culture and mostly considered Tibetan culture to be superior to any other. Physically I was not strong enough to live under the conditions in which the Tibetan nuns thrived. My idea of being a nun was then more Christian than Buddhist.

There was a day when the Dalai Lama visited us in our Tilokpur nunnery. His Holiness must have been in the area and because of his position he probably visited as many Tibetan monasteries as he could in order to give instruction and support. Although His Holiness spent only a few hours with us, we needed several days of preparation. The earth on the paths had to be made smooth and sacred symbols inscribed on them in white chalk. The nuns needed to make up an appropriate place for His Holiness to rest in the room for guest monks and set up his throne in the Buddha Hall. At the time when His Holiness was due to arrive, the nuns all wore their saffron *sanghati* robes and lined the road to welcome him. His Holiness was delayed by a couple of hours and so there was a lengthy wait under the blazing sun.

At last an advance party appeared, informing us of His Holiness's imminent arrival. His Holiness was smiling and looked at everyone with compassionate eyes. After a short rest in his quarters, he came into the Buddha Hall to give teachings. He ascended the throne and gave a teaching. I did not understand anything of the teaching since I knew no Tibetan and there was no one there to translate. The final part of the programme was that every nun, myself included, would come up to His Holiness's throne in order to prostrate and receive a blessing. Standing in the queue waiting to approach the throne, I found my mind in quite a turmoil. In order to receive the blessing, I would have to bow down and prostrate myself before the throne. I did not want to do this. In Athens when Anila Pema had first taught me to prostrate, I happily complied because I wanted to please my new friend. However, the more I thought about it, the more senseless it seemed to be. Surely the holy ones did not want us to prostrate to them, especially when we did not have the spontaneous inclination to do so? I was thinking of all the reasons why I should not prostrate before His Holiness, but at the same time I knew my turn to prostrate would come sooner or later. With my mind full of all these doubts I arrived before the throne. His Holiness gave me no chance to prostrate; he bent down from his throne, his hand outstretched to receive mine in a handshake. I was abashed. He also asked me a few questions in English, as to where I was from, what I was doing in the nunnery, and so on. I marvelled at how His Holiness understood my state of mind. So the day passed and life went back to normal, except that all of us had had our happiness boosted by this fleeting visit.

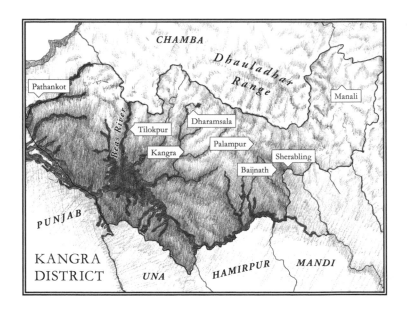

CHAPTER FIVE

India: Sherabling

I T WAS AUTUMN in the year 1980. After one and a half months in Tilokpur, the time was drawing near when we should have to leave the relative comfort of the nunnery for the Sherabling monastery seventy kilometres away, where the abbot had given the nuns some land to build their retreat centre toward which I had been giving donations. This land was on the other side of a valley opposite to where the monastery of Sherabling was. In order to do the building work, Anila Pema and some nuns had to be present. The monks gave these nuns a room at the far end of their cloister. Having ascertained which day would be auspicious for travel, we prepared what we should need. This included a small kerosene stove for cooking, since the monks did not have the wherewithal to feed us.

We boarded the bus to Palampur on the road below the monastery. A shepherd with a sheep at his feet was in the front row. The conductor took our fare. The scenery was beautiful: little streams running between green, grassy mounds, glimpses of towering mountains and, on the outskirts of Palampur, the hilly tea plantations began with their darker green. At Kangra we stopped and Anila Pema had enough time to alight to buy some vegetables in the market. At Palampur we took another bus to Baijnath. All heavy items of any bulk were carried on the roof. Nimble bus conductors glided up and down the small ladder attached to the back of the bus, to take items up and down for passengers. To go in the direction of Baijnath was to go in the direction of mountains, the scenery becoming more magnificent all the time.

Before beginning a journey, we never knew how long it would take. Anila Pema was quite unable to answer a question like: "How long? How far? At what time?" I soon learned not to ask these questions anymore. A journey that I might imagine would take two hours could take two days. This way of living annoyed some Occidentals, but in some ways I enjoyed living in a world where time was not important. After I had been in the nunnery a few weeks, my watch stopped and I was happy to let it stay that way.

When we alighted at Baijnath, I had no idea that we were now beginning an eight-kilometre walk, which would involve crossing streams, rivers, and rice fields, and climbing up steep rocky paths. I was never very strong for carrying things. Anila Pema only needed to look at me to know that. We hired porters when kind friends, usually monks or blood relatives of Anila Pema, were not available to help. A porter would receive five rupees, a mere pittance, but we too had very little money.

Sometimes someone would see a snake slithering in the muddy streams that flowed through the rice fields. We would wait for it to pass and proceed with the utmost care. As we prepared to cross a river, Anila Pema remarked that a woman had been washed away and drowned while making her way across a month earlier. I discovered that it is easier to cross a river with bare feet. Jumping from stone to stone, bare feet slip less easily. Anila Pema insisted that I wear shoes at all other times when walking outside. Seeing Indians going everywhere barefoot, I wanted to do the same. Anila Pema told me that there are worms that can come inside the skin of your feet and cause terrible infections.

When we reached the steep pine-forested slopes, I was feeling tired and wondering how much longer it would be before we arrived, a question I knew it would be useless to ask. The air was very good and fragrant as rice fields receded below us. After some time we came to a clearing, and shining in the distance was a glimpse of a temple roof. Then some minutes later we heard the ritual horns playing. It was music practice time for the novices.

Outside the monastery portal was a sandy place for the children to play. The monastery had a school for children who had already become monks and those who were considering doing so. There were thirty children and teenagers living within the monastery precinct and only seven mature monks: the master of studies, the schoolmaster, two monks who taught the Tibetan horn, and the treasurer, the cook, and assistant schoolmaster. There were also four or five young adult monks who were fully ordained bhikshus.

The Rinpoche Tai Situpa, whose official seat is Sherabling, was only twenty-six years old at that time. He was recognized as a reincarnation of a line of lamas whose name he bears, Situpa. He designed and had his seat built on land donated in Northern India when he was forced to leave Tibet as a refugee. Anila told me his mother was Chinese and that he corresponded with her in Chinese. He also spoke English. Anila and I went to pay respect to him in his quarters built over the Buddha Hall. He gave me some teachings as to how I should live in harmony with the Tibetan nuns but said nothing about the practice of meditation.

The Buddha Hall at Sherabling was only open to monks and laymen; nuns and laywomen were ordinarily not allowed to enter. If a renowned teacher came to give a special initiation he could ask that nuns and laywomen be allowed to attend. I remember this happening just once while I was there. Normally while the monks chanted and meditated inside, the nuns circumambulated the temple outside as a kind of walking meditation. Repetition of a mantra was the usual practice of the circumambulants. My preferred mantra was *om mani padme hung*, but there was a time when everyone was encouraged to chant the name of Buddha Amitabha. It was thought that if the whole Sangha recollected this name together the overall effect would be so much greater. The power of mantra chanting comes from the fact that while concentrating on the syllables of the mantra, you stop the normal confused thinking that goes on in your head. This clears your mind and there is no room for the negative thoughts that cause us to suffer. In fact there are positive qualities of compassion and understanding that are associated with the mantras. When the whole Sangha recites like this together, a collective wholesome energy is sent out into the world.

Circumambulation was an enjoyable practice. As you came around one corner of the building, a towering snow-covered peak would appear in your frame of vision. When the sky was blue and the sun shone upon the peak, it was very beautiful, indeed awe-inspiring. At the conclusion of each circumambulation, you passed through a little door, which was also the entrance to the monastic cloister. As you opened the door, a little bell would ring. The bell could be heard throughout the cloister. It was our bell of mindfulness, a chime letting us know that someone was practising and reminding us each to return to our own practice. It was also heard at night, since there were those who practised meditation and circumambulation throughout the night. In the late-night hours, the clear small ring took on a mystic nature; the surroundings were so quiet.

The room we women had been given at the end of the cloister had two pallet beds and a cupboard. We added our kerosene stove and a saucepan. The bed had enough coverings. There were a couple of flush toilets and there were showers at our end of the monastery. There was no hot water. Behind the Buddha Hall was a spring reserved for washing clothes. The only heating was the sun. Days without sun seemed very cold in early winter. The showers were in a part of the monastery that was out of bounds for nuns. When we really needed a shower, we would wait until midday when the monks were having lunch. Generally, the water was very cold. It was stored in a tank on the roof and, if the sun shone all morning, by midday the water was one or two degrees above icy. Anila Pema's health did not allow her to take cold showers. Occasionally she would ask the kitchen for hot water and use it for a wash. The cook was generous with hot water. He always had a couple of huge kettles on the fire and when we asked, we generally received.

The monastery did not have a refectory. The monks ate sitting on the sunny side of the cloister. They ate in silence. It was a rare period of silence during the normal day. The children learnt to read and write. Committing sacred texts to memory was an important part of their education. When the students gathered in the classroom they would repeat aloud the lessons they had learnt, all together in unison, very loudly. There was also horn playing and chanting coming from the Buddha Hall.

The early morning liturgy took place very early; I do not know how early since my watch had already ceased to function and there were no clocks in the monastery. I imagine it was about 4:00 a.m., as it was before dawn. I tried to rise with the monks and practise sitting meditation on my bed. The Master of Studies at the monastery did not like anyone to be lying down in bed too long. After the liturgy when the sun had risen, the monks would sit in the sunlight to thaw their frozen limbs.

During the afternoon the little boys were sent with their slates into different parts of the cloister to practise writing. I would watch them from the window of our room. They enjoyed playing marbles and other games. One boy would watch out for the teacher to appear and give a warning signal. This worked successfully some of the time. When the monk teacher walked down the cloister, all the boys were engrossed in their slates. Sometimes, however, the teacher appeared unexpectedly from a different direction, and would then administer his stick, but usually without any anger.

One day I witnessed a very angry monk beating a young boy of eleven or twelve. The blows were heavy. I had known the boy from a time when he'd had stomach pains and I had been asked to decipher the Indian doctor's prescription for him. I'd found him to be polite and congenial, and I could not imagine what he had done to deserve such a beating. The monk's brutality shocked me. I wanted to intervene but did not know how to. Most of the monks were very thin, as the monastery was not well-endowed and had many building projects to complete, but the monk who was administering the beating was not so thin. I asked Anila Pema why this was so, and she replied that he had a generous sponsor. I never found out the reason for the beating.

The monastery's Master of Studies came and made our acquaintance shortly after our arrival. Anila Pema said he was very intelligent, but mad. He came to us whenever a monk had Western medicine to take so that I could tell him the dosage. He did not speak or understand a word of English, so we had to rely on Anila Pema's translation. Sometimes I could not make head or tail of the prescription. He seemed to be very annoyed if this happened, especially when I kept repeating one of my few Tibetan phrases, "I do not understand."

Certainly there were monks in the monastery who could walk through walls or walk through a heavy rain shower without becoming wet. One day I was walking along the path that led out of the monastery grounds. The Master of Studies was there by the side of the road. As I came near, he took hold of a large branch of a tree and with great force pulled it down until it touched the ground. Bit by bit he was able to pull the branch down. I did not wonder why he should be doing such a thing; I just knew that it was meant to be a teaching. In the afternoon when I passed the tree again, I expected to see the branch pulled down to the

ground level, but all the branches were high up out of everyone's reach. Moreover, there was no sign of any branch having been broken. I knew then that what I had seen had only
happened in my mind and the mind of the lama, who was
trying to use skillful means to tell me something. Maybe
I needed to pull the energy down out of my head. Maybe
the lama was mad, as Anila Pema had said. This lama told
Anila Pema that I was not an *Enji*—a foreigner, a Westerner,
someone who is not Tibetan. This was to help me, because
to a Tibetan an Enji is always inferior, and it's not easy to be
considered second class. The lama did truly want to help
me, but I was something outside of his experience and without understanding someone, it is not possible to help her. I
was in many respects an Enji with some strong Asian seeds.
The Enji part of me needed to be understood in order to be
trained.

My task as I understood it was to help the nuns in the
building project. One way in which I could do this was by
writing letters requesting funds. Another way was by picking up the pine needles which fell in thousands on the heaps
of building materials: gravel, sand, and boulders. It would
have been simpler to have covered these piles with a tarpau-
lin, but such a thing was not available, nor did we have the
funds to buy it. Someone with an eye for the practice could
have organized us to combine work with practice, but work
began at eight in the morning and ended at nightfall, and
then we were too tired to practise sitting meditation.

For as long as we lived inside the monastery, life was
quite easy. The building had not begun in earnest and my
tasks were limited to removing pine needles. Anila Pema

and I understood each other well enough. Watching the monks was interesting. You could feel that they were a family and that there was brotherhood. I was learning for the first time about living in a community where everyone feels connected to everyone else. Listening to Anila Pema chanting mantras annoyed me a little, as I was not enamoured of repetitive chanting, but I could walk outside out of earshot.

I enjoyed going on little outings with Anila. It was a chance to learn more about how she lived, and I felt attracted to that way of life. Once we had a chance to visit Dharamsala to see a Tibetan doctor there. He took our pulses and gave us medicine to take. He did not ask for payment. If you wanted, you could make a donation. We found a place to stay above a shop where the owner was a friend of Anila. While in Dharamsala we visited the monastery that was the seat of the Dalai Lama. It was lunchtime and the monastery cooked enough food for all the poor refugees to eat. It was very crowded on the veranda where the food was served when dozens of people came to receive a free meal. We took a walk outside of the town and enjoyed wonderful views of the mountains. It was the first time I had been in a Tibetan town. It was crowded and busy, but at the same time there were many people holding a rosary as they walked and recited *om mani padme hung*.

Once December came, the weather turned even colder than before. The monastery was not heated and the monks kept warm by drinking salty buttered tea served from huge teapots. The Sixteenth Karmapa, the head of this particular school of Tibetan Buddhism, was in ill health and people feared he would not live long. Anila Pema told me that there was a disagreement amongst the monks in the monastery. Some monks wanted to spend the whole day in the temple chanting prayers for the recovery of their teacher, others wanted to keep the normal schedule of liturgy and work. I do not know how the matter was resolved but certainly most of the monks spent more time in the Buddha Hall. Only the young boys, who had not yet received their novice vows, and the Master of Studies never attended these services. The health of the teacher depends on the harmony of the Sangha more than on prayers. So how to live harmoniously together is the most important question, not whether we pray or do not pray.

One morning there was a dead mouse in our room. To me it was no serious matter, but for Anila Pema it was a very inauspicious omen. She told me to take the thing out of her sight, but having seen it, she feared that it meant the death of her root teacher, the Karmapa. The next day we did indeed hear the news that the Sixteenth Karmapa had passed away.

At that time we were making plans to travel east and pay our respects at Sarnath and Bodhgaya as part of the pilgrimage Anila Pema had in mind, to visit the historical sites where the Buddha had lived. Now our journey would need to include Rumtek Monastery in Sikkim, on the northeastern border of India with Nepal and Bhutan, where the funeral rites of the Karmapa would take place. We needed to leave as soon as possible, but no one was sure when we would set out because the lama who had to be consulted to find out which day was auspicious for travel could only tell on the same day. He could not predict for the future. Every evening Anila Pema could say, "We shall leave tomorrow if it is a good day." The next morning, however, the lama would say it was not a good day.

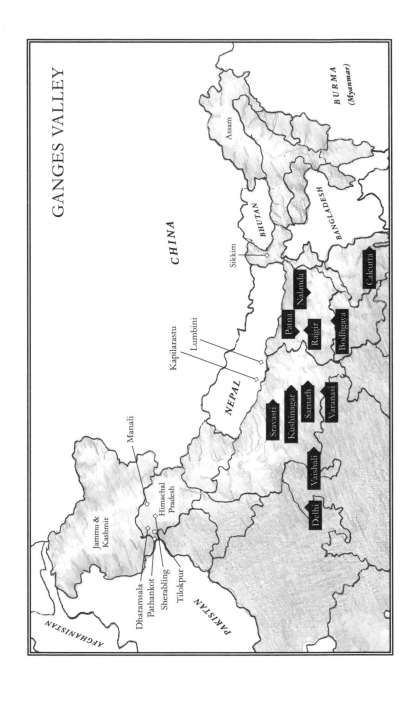

CHAPTER SIX

India: Ganges Valley and Sikkhim

FINALLY, a day that was auspicious for traveling arrived. Without my knowing anything about how or how long we would travel, I set out on the first familiar eight kilometres. This was truly a beautiful walk. The young monks who accompanied us went very fast, almost running, and skipped from stepping stone to stepping stone as they crossed rivers. Anila Pema went slowly, thank goodness, otherwise I could never have kept up.

We left the monastery by the main portal and walked over the sand where the monastery schoolchildren were playing, down the hill to a hamlet where the village children were playing among the five or six mud-walled buildings whose floors were made of beaten earth. The children were poor with tattered clothes, yet they were such happy children, always laughing, staring at my Western face, and cheekily asking "girl or boy?" since my hair was short and I wore trousers and a shirt. The parents who eked out a living from the land also seemed happy.

There were no roads here, no traffic, no mechanization, and hardly any plastic. If a plastic bag did manifest it was treasured and kept to serve some use. In a thousand years or more, nothing had really changed in the lifestyle. I was amazed and I felt happy in the simplicity and sustainability of what I was seeing. If only my mind could be as simple as that. We saw buffaloes and crossed rice fields. It was

December so the harvest was over and there was just stubble in the dry earth. A wonderful fragrance came, and in five minutes we were walking past a hedge of the most fragrant flowers. Then more groves of trees and fields and then the descent began to the river. It was a rocky path, not easy to scale or descend if you were carrying things. The view over the valley was beautiful—a paradise indeed.

Crossing the river, I was always a little apprehensive when jumping from stone to stone in case I might slip and fall in the water. This time that did not happen. Then there was an easy path up to the little town of Baijnath from where we took the bus. Some enquiries were made as to when the bus would leave, and we had time to have a good lunch of rice and *dal*.

Anila Pema was extremely cautious about what I ate, and she must have saved me from many stomach upsets. She preferred restaurants where she knew the proprietor. She would go into the kitchen to observe the cook's hygiene and the food, and she would wash the bowls and spoons herself which we were to use. She would give orders as to what we were to eat and how it should be cooked. Many Indians were somewhat in awe of Anila Pema. This was partly because she had been attendant to Sister Palmo, who was revered and loved by the Indian people in the area.

From Baijnath, we travelled west-northwest by bus until we reached Pathankot. Pathankot is the northern gateway to the Punjab, and from there we took the train southeastward to the state of Bihar, where we would change trains at Patna. Coming from a small country such as England, I did not think of train journeys in terms of successive days and nights; I was impressed by the vast scale of the country we were traversing. Another difference between British and Indian rail travel was that third class had disappeared in England before I was of an age to travel on trains. Always wanting to save money, Anila Pema had bought us third-class tickets, which meant sitting on wooden slatted benches, if you were lucky enough to get a seat. When the train arrived at the platform, hundreds of people pushed their way on to the carriages as others pushed their way off. Those who could not get in through the door climbed in through the windows. Anila Pema pleaded with the conductor to give us a seat in the midst of this chaos. We ended up huddled on a seat with a man who looked rather rough.

The train left the station under steam and crawled through the Indian countryside. Roof travellers would jump down as the train passed through their village and others could climb on because the train moved so slowly. Leaving our seat to go to the toilet was an ordeal. The corridor was blocked by travellers. Vendors were always in plenty on every station platform and they competed with the passengers who were clambering in and out of the windows for a place to sell their wares. This time I dared to ask how long the journey would take but was taken aback by her answer. Anila Pema cordially said, "Two or three days." I wondered if I had heard right. I repeated what she had said back to her. There was no denial; so I steeled myself to being on this slow-moving, crowded train for the next forty-eight to seventy-two hours. It was not possible to sleep lying down, but at thirty-one years old I was young enough to be able to doze off while sitting. I did not dare to drink any water because, although it was described as potable, I had no trust that it was so for my Western stomach. If I had been on my own it would have been an ordeal, but I had trust that with Anila we would be OK. The thing that frightened me most was the man I sat next to, who occasionally put out his hand to touch me. Luckily he did not stay for the whole journey.

We arrived in Patna after dark on the third day and waited for an early morning train bound southward to Gaya. The station was crowded with people wrapped up in blankets and lying anywhere they could find to sleep. It was a great relief to discover that the train to Gaya was less crowded, and from there we took a rickshaw to Bodhgaya, the site of the Buddha's enlightenment, which lay a short distance of sixteen kilometres to the south.

The countryside had a strange appearance with little mounds and craters like the moon. Bodhgaya is a Hindu place of pilgrimage as well as a Buddhist one, to which millions of tourists and visitors come to pay their respects each year. We stayed in a Hindu *vihara*, which was also an orphanage. The two holy men who ran the vihara were good friends of Anila Pema. I appreciated their kindness and politeness and the cleanliness and quiet sacred atmosphere of the vihara after three noisy days on the train. We were given a room on the roof alongside that of a poor child who had typhoid fever. She was skin and bones and so weak that she could not stand up. We wondered if she would live and prayed for her. All the orphanage children were smiling and well-behaved, thanks to the kind treatment they were given by the vihara adults. Here we could drink and eat clean food and water. The children worked in the kitchen and the garden and cleaned the buildings.

We went to the pilgrimage site, and Anila Pema told me on several occasions to prostrate in front of the many icons and statues there. Unfortunately I still did not appreciate the value of prostrating and I disappointed Anila Pema one time when I refused to prostrate before a statue of the Buddha. It was not Anila Pema's fault that she had not explained to me the meaning of prostration. I did not understand Tibetan and she spoke limited English. It would not be until six years later that I learnt to prostrate with the true and deep meaning of prostration. We lit butter lamps, we sat in the shade of the bodhi tree where the Buddha is purported to have attained enlightenment, and I enjoyed meditating until dusk. December is a very pleasant month in this part of India because it is not too hot, and the air was refreshing.

We visited a Thai monastery on the road to Uruvela. Anila was also acquainted with these monks. The monastery consisted of huts built of a dark wood. It was a very simple place where people could practise meditation. Uruvela is the village right next to the Bodhi tree. It is on the banks of the Neranjara river, which you can wade across when it is not the monsoon season. Then you come to the mountains where the ascetic Gotama practised self-mortification, which unfortunately we did not have time to visit. It was here in Uruvela, a peaceful rural area, that the Buddha practised enjoying the fruits of his enlightenment, which was not indulgence but also not self-mortification. Then we went westward to Varanasi and Sarnath. We did not stay long in Varanasi, which is not considered to be a place of Buddhist pilgrimage, but is sacred to Hindus.

In Sarnath, not far from Varanasi, we stayed at the Burmese Buddhist monastery whose abbot was an acquaintance of Anila Pema. The monks served us a kind of tea that was "good for the intestines" and treated us with much kindness. Anila Pema also knew certain officials of the Mahabodhi Society who gave us rice and dal, which I was becoming a little weary of. I marvelled at how wherever we went, Anila had friends. Wherever we went we could stay in the peaceful environment of a monastery. However, I was not always an appreciative guest; I did not appreciate that I was lucky to have food, even if it was always rice and dal.

Sarnath's Deer Park is still very beautiful. It was the place to which the Buddha came some weeks after his enlightenment when he had decided to teach the Dharma. He was looking for an audience and thought about the five ascetics with whom he had practised austerities and who then were practising here in Sarnath. Here the Buddha taught for the first time the Four Noble Truths and the Noble Eightfold Path, which are the backbone of the Buddhist teachings. The tall trees that I saw in the distance, when sitting by the ruins around the Dhamek stupa, made me feel very at home, as indeed do all tall trees I see growing in the distance. Everywhere around the stupa were Tibetan monks with their *pe cha*, (Tibetan loose-leaf sutra books held between two wooden boards and wrapped in cloth) from which they were reciting. Our pilgrimage was short but we spent three or four days in both places we visited and then continued onward with a two-day journey to Rumtek, Sikkim, in the far northeastern corner of India on the border with Nepal and Bhutan, to pay our respects to the Karmapa.

Sikkim, formerly an independent country alongside Nepal, was now part of India, though it still preserved its Tibetan culture. The ruling nobility still had some power, though only in collaboration with the Indian government, and there was even a Sikkim royal family. We took the train to Siliguri, where we were met by some of Anila Pema's friends who took us in their jeep to the capital, Gangtok. We drove along the banks of a wonderfully turquoise river, which was bordered with red-leaved poinsettia trees. The scarlet leaves' contrast against the blue-green water was startling. We stayed in a Tibetan household for a day and night because it was too late to go further that day, and Anila had a chance to spend time with people she had known in the past. We then went to Rumtek Monastery.

Walking on the streets in Gangtok, Anila Pema suddenly told me to turn and face the wall. Afterward she told me that the queen had been approaching, and in the Tibetan culture, it is not permitted to look at the queen.

After the Tibetans were forced to leave Tibet, the Karmapa had been invited to Sikkim to build a seat there, which had become Rumtek Monastery. As a senior disciple of the Karmapa, Sister Palmo had built a small house there and this is where we stayed. The house had two rooms: one room was still full of Sister Palmo's things, which Anila kept out of respect for her teacher; the other room had barely enough space for one small bed. It was very cold at the end of December and Anila Pema and I squeezed on to that bed, I in my sleeping bag and she in hers.

There were many ceremonies connected with the obsequies of the Karmapa. There were hundreds and hundreds of monks and nuns chanting, prostrating, and circumambulating. I saw my Refuge teacher Khenpo Tsultrim Gyatso, sporting a flashy camera someone had given him. He was photographing everything. We saw the flames rise up from the cremation and form a five-coloured cloud, which for most Asian Buddhists is an auspicious sign. The young novice who set light to the pyre had to be someone who had never met the Karmapa.

It was very cold in Rumtek and I could not make myself warm. There was a point when I became so cold that I developed a fever. I did not feel at all well. There was the kitchen with its warm fire where laywomen cooked for invited guests. A woman named Barbara Pettee, who was from the United States and frequently donated money to Anila Pema's project, happened to be in Rumtek for the funeral. She had been a disciple of the Karmapa and also of Sister Palmo and had been particularly devoted to the nun. When Anila Pema introduced me to her and she learned that I was not well, she invited me to stay in her hotel room, which had a spare bed. It did not take me long to decide in favour of material comfort, though I regretted a little being out of the monastic ambience.

In the hotel it was much warmer but I was still a little weak. From the physical point of view, I had probably had enough of India at this time, although spiritually I never wanted to leave. The laywoman invited me to go back to the United States with her. She said I could raise money for Anila Pema's project and help her start a meditation group in her garage, which she had transformed into a Zendo. I accepted because I had no plan for doing anything else and was glad to enjoy more warmth, comfort, food, and water. I had also lost weight because of the shortage of food, and my lack of body fat made me feel even colder. The laywoman would pay the airfare and guarantee all my expenses while in the United States.

After the cremation, it was discovered that the heart and the tongue of the Karmapa had not been able to burn. They were retrieved intact and placed in a reliquary. We were invited to process past the reliquary to pay our respects. Since then I have heard of other great beings whose hearts have not been able to burn even in extremely high temperatures. The heart of Master Quang Duc, who burned himself to death while seated in meditation in Saigon in 1963 to protest the oppression of Buddhism by the Diem Catholic regime, remained intact during the immolation. Afterward, people tried to burn it at very high temperatures, but it would not burn.

This presentation of the relics was the conclusion of the ceremonies. Anila Pema told me that one Tibetan devotee had hanged himself in order to be able to follow the Karmapa to the Pure Land. She said that this was a very misguided act of devotion.

Anila Pema would have to make the trip back to northwestern India on her own. I felt pleased that I would not have to make the same third-class train journey back to Tilokpur, but I also felt regret that I could not continue to be immersed in the spiritual ambience of a Tibetan monastery. Instead Barbara and I were going to take a jeep to the airport and then a flight to Calcutta, and I kept thinking how good it would be to have clean water to drink on the aeroplane. I felt pleased with myself, but there was a nostalgia for the austerity and simplicity, joy and happiness that goes with the spiritual life; with the monastery far away from roads and mechanical transport; the paths that only humans, buffaloes, and the occasional horse could tread. However, these seeds of nostalgia were somewhat attenuated by my seeds of desire for material comfort.

I saw my Refuge Master again in the airport looking as relaxed as he always did, walking and standing in that perfect freedom which you can sense immediately you see it, although you may not know quite how you perceive it. That freedom is not outside of you, but it is also not within. To see someone stand and walk like that was enough to give me faith in the spiritual path and faith that true happiness is possible.

In Calcutta I walked around a bit and saw the dreadful poverty, the great sewage pipes in which people made their bedrooms, and entire families living outside on the street. Then I would be back at our hotel, where I could have a hot bath. It seemed wrong to use so much clean water for a bath when others did not have water to drink.

I had been in India for only four months but what I had experienced made it seem much longer. It had changed my life.

CHAPTER SEVEN

California

W E FLEW to Hong Kong, and the hotel where we stayed was even more luxurious than the one in Calcutta. From Hong Kong we flew to San Francisco. It was January and a little cold the day we landed. The airport was a desolate place, and the air was not clean. In India dirt and decay were always evident in the cities. It was not uncommon to see a sick man, an old man, or a corpse on the streets there, but there is also an underlying atmosphere of spiritual purity and devotion. In the United States, I instantly understood that there is an attempt to have things new and clean on the outside, but underneath the unclean is lurking, ready to push its way out.

We were driven to a house in Los Altos Hills, a lovely place with a nature reserve just a short walk away. I liked walking there very much. The house of the laywoman donor had a large garden and I had my own room with its own separate entrance. As I walked, I absorbed the experiences I had had in India, so different from what I had lived through before. The song I composed while I was in Los Altos Hills was:

> O love where have you been hiding?
> Where did you go so long ago?
> There is no place that I could go
> I'm ev'rywhere, always abiding
> so very far from sorrow.

O thought what have you been making?
Such grief and sorrow.
Why is it that you are always taking
Thought for tomorrow?

Love here refers to the *bodhicitta*, the mind of love, that I had been in touch with in the monastery, in the monks and nuns, and which I missed now, although I knew that it was something I could touch at any time if my mind was properly directed.

Some mornings there was a light frost on the grass, sometimes a gentle rain. The deer would roam into the garden. It was a beautiful place. My hostess liked to be on the move and this meant that I managed to visit many parts of California during my stay. It was rare for us to eat breakfast at home. Having breakfast in a restaurant was something new for me. Although part of me said that this was very extravagant, there was another part of me that enjoyed ordering pancakes and maple syrup for breakfast and was attracted to the abundance. There was a trip to Palm Springs, where the father of my hostess lived on the edge of the desert with an orchard of grapefruit trees. We paid a visit to the Santa Barbara Tibetan Sangha, where we attended Sangha activities, spoke about the nuns' retreat project in Sherabling and received donations for the project. We went to Hollywood to visit the son of Sister Palmo, the Indian actor, Kabir Bedi, who was living there at the time. We went to Santa Cruz with its beautiful beach and the sound of the waves on the shingle made me happy.

While we were in Santa Barbara, we went to a retreat to

learn how to die and be born in the Pure Land. It involved visualising Amitabha Buddha and chanting a Tibetan text. The retreat began with the practice of the visualisation of Amitabha Buddha and the recitation of the name of Amitabha. Alongside Amitabha Buddha, we visualised Avalokiteshvara and Mahasthamaprapta Bodhisattvas. Avalokiteshhvara represents the compassion and Mahasthamaprapta the strength or power of the Buddha.

The two bodhisattvas are visualised as sitting one on either side of Amitabha. Once we had been initiated into the practice of this visualisation, we learned to chant the *phowa* ceremony. We practised until a sign appeared on the top of our head. The presiding Rinpoche said that I had the sign very clearly. Rinpoche said Europeans practised more diligently than Americans. I do not think that is always true. My American friends were good at rejoicing at others' success; they truly practised joy in the achievement of others. I could see they were happy for me having the sign on my head, which meant I would be born in the Pure Land, but we were told that in order for this really to happen we should have to keep practising the chanting and visualisation at least once a month. I have not done that. It would be years later, when I came to live in my home in Plum Village in France, that I would learn how to enjoy the Pure Land in the here and now.

In Santa Barbara we walked on the beach in the early morning. There was a train that had been made into a restaurant, and never moved from its place on a siding by the seashore, where we would occasionally eat ice cream sundaes. I learned to enjoy these simple pleasures.

I was grateful for this first visit to the United States. It was so different from India. It helped me to see that the Buddha can be found in the austerity of a Tibetan monastery in India but also in the comfort and material luxury of North America. What attracted me a great deal about Plum Village when I first went there was that one could practise without too many material comforts and without too much austerity.

✹ PART TWO ✹

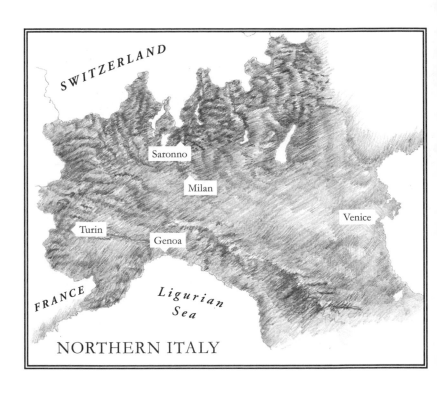

SWITZERLAND

Saronno

Milan

Venice

Turin

Genoa

FRANCE

*Ligurian
Sea*

NORTHERN ITALY

CHAPTER EIGHT

Italy

IN APRIL 1981, after four months in the US, I went back to England at the suggestion of the Tibetan lama who had given the teachings on dying in Santa Barbara. The lama had told me it would not be good to stay in the United States any longer. At the same time, when we returned to Los Altos Hills, my family informed me that my brother Thomas was about to be married. So I told my hostess that I would like to return to England to attend my youngest brother's wedding. To be honest, I was not particularly interested in going to my brother's wedding at that time but I did want to follow the lama's advice. My hostess was not sad or disappointed and she probably felt that I had been with her long enough.

When I went to India in 1980 I had gone directly from Greece, so I had not seen my family since I'd left England four years earlier in 1977. Maybe because I felt myself to be different from the other members of my family, I did not miss my family. My journey had been about following a spiritual path and I felt my family would not understand. So, what I did tell my mother and father was more about material things and this included the physical hardships I had been through in India. It was not a sensible thing to do because, unknown to me at the time, it only caused my mother to worry the next time I went there. It was difficult for them to understand why I should opt for poverty and deprivation when I could have easily continued to enjoy a life of material comfort in Europe.

At twenty-six years old, my youngest brother married a woman he had met while he was at school. My two brothers both enjoyed farming and we wondered which one would take over the farm when my father retired. It turned out to be my youngest brother. Stephen, the older brother of the two, studied aeronautical engineering at university and then went to work for Rolls Royce. When my father officially retired at the age of seventy-five, Thomas and his wife and two children went to live in the family home, the house in which I grew up. Now when I go to see them, I revisit my childhood paradise.

At the time of my brother's wedding, England went to war with Argentina over the Falkland Islands. Disgusted with the jingoistic atmosphere and unable to support my country in this war, I decided to leave for Italy (an ally of Argentina) and teach English there until I had enough money to return to India and live with the nuns again.

I stayed with a friend of my brother's in Milan, a city with virtually no trees, but not far from lakes and mountains. At the weekends I would take the train on my own to the countryside around Turin. When I could find no permanent place to live in Milan, I went to live with a wealthy and well-known family in Saronno. I was to teach English in the evening to the children, who were eight and ten years old, in return for my lodging. I went on the train in the morning to teach mainly businessmen in the Oxford School of English in Milan, which was housed in a large old building. I used to eat my lunch in a park nearby and every day I ate delicious Italian ice cream.

The family I lived with owned a biscuit manufacturing firm. The house they lived in was a former monastery, very well protected by walls, gates, and locks because family members had been kidnapped and held to ransom for the family's money. Sometimes I would eat breakfast or dinner with the family. The father would bring home new varieties of biscuits. The mother was a little lonely and would sometimes engage me in conversation. In this way, six months or so passed, neither happy nor unhappy, living each day with largely neutral feelings because I was not really present. I was not doing what I really wanted to do. The short moments in which I enjoyed any pleasant feelings belonged to the times when I was teaching someone who was happy learning. Sometimes I would sit at the window of my room looking somewhat wistfully over the beautiful garden below. Because the house was an old monastery, I would imagine the presence of the monks walking in the cloister. My stay in Italy was just a means to an end, since my idea was that as soon as I had enough money, I would return to India. I was always dreaming of returning to India, where I hoped to find true happiness sitting on a hillside contemplating the scene below.

I missed the company of other Buddhists and sometimes looked around for a Sangha near where I was living. I made the acquaintance of a young man and his girlfriend who had copies of the Pali Sutras in English. I only had to read a few sentences and I felt I was at home. They lived in a small village among rice fields and we walked together along the paths in the Italian rice fields.

One night the family of biscuit manufacturers had gone away. I was in the large house on my own. Late at night I heard something rattling the glass doors that opened on to the garden. I sat up in bed very afraid, thinking that perhaps the kidnappers had returned. Finally I recognized my fear and overcame it. Without turning on the light I went downstairs to telephone the gardener. In Italian I said, "There is someone trying to come in the garden door. Please come quickly." When I told him that the noise was like someone scratching the door, he said that it was just the dog trying to come in the house; all I had to do was take the dog around to the other side of the house where his kennel was. At this point my fear vanished, just like the fear of the person who realises the object of their perception is not a snake but a rope. I verified that it was the dog and having led him to his kennel, I went to sleep myself.

CHAPTER NINE

Second Time in India

AFTER SIX MONTHS in northern Italy, I had enough money to return to India in 1982. I bought a one-way ticket, because this time I was determined to stay and become a nun. I had had this dream of being a nun since I was nine years old, although then it was to become a Christian nun. I do not know exactly where this idea came from. Obviously there were external causes and conditions, such as the time I'd spent in the convent school and the time I'd spent in the Tibetan monastery, but no doubt there were also memories stored up in *alaya* consciousness from before I manifested in 1949. All the money I had, I would give to the nuns.

From Italy I returned to England by bus, since it was the cheapest way. I had written to Anila Pema to tell her of my return to India, but without saying clearly that I was thinking of staying for good. The communication between myself and my parents cannot have been very good at that time. I did not ask them what they thought about my returning to India, as I was inclined to think that my fulfilment had nothing to do with my father and mother's happiness, and I had the right to do as I liked. So there was no real farewell. I did not dream of sharing with my parents that I wanted to become a nun, because I thought they would never understand. Later on I learned how unhappy my parents were about my going to India.

The first time I went to India I did not have to go through any real hardships, and I remembered the positive things, like the views of the Himalayan mountains and the simplicity of the way of living, more than the drawbacks like the strangeness of the language and the culture or the lack of spiritual guidance. I was happy to share the simple life with the Tibetan nuns, so I did not take anything special with me except a sleeping bag and some tapers to help me light the fire. It was difficult for me to light a fire with a single match.

This time I took the overnight bus from Delhi to Baijnath on my own. The bus journeys I have made in India have never been boring, and this was no exception. One time a bus driver told us to look down into a ravine, as we travelled along a narrow road on the edge of a mountain with no barrier to stop anyone hurtling over the edge. As we looked, we saw a bus upturned in the bottom of the ravine. "Brake failure," the driver said phlegmatically. There were stops in town and in the countryside where people could get down, stretch their legs, and buy something to eat. We relieved ourselves in whatever empty space we could find. It was a warm time of year, and the windows and doors were left open as we travelled. The bus groaned as it went up hills and around corners. It made the noise that only an old diesel bus can make, along with the frequent sound of the horn. The sound of the horn was to tell everyone to keep out of the way. It was not necessary to wait for the road to be clear in order to overtake. It was necessary only to blow the horn louder than anyone else.

After Baijnath, I had to walk the eight kilometres to the monastery as I had learnt to do eighteen months earlier.

When I arrived at the monastery, I learned that Anila Pema no longer lived in the monastery complex with the monks. She was staying in a hut near the building site of the nuns' retreat house. From time to time she would leave to go on a trip somewhere to raise funds when the project had no more money left. The hut where she was staying had been built by a lay practitioner who came from time to time to do retreats in it. When he was not there, he gave it to the abbot, who allowed the nuns to use it. To reach this hut from the monastery you needed to go down a very steep incline and then up a steep hill on the other side. When I arrived I was exhausted. I could eat nothing and my head seemed to be spinning. At night I lay down to sleep and slept for fourteen hours.

On waking, I found the situation somewhat different from before. Building work on the nunnery had begun in earnest. Sometimes, when she had the funds, Anila Pema hired Indian labourers to speed up the process. Anila Pema now had to stay at the building site nearly all the time to supervise the work. Nuns took it in turns to come and help too, but not many liked it. There was very little to eat and the work was hard. I arrived in June before the monsoon set in. We all slept on the floor of the small one-room hut like sardines with no space between us. Our toilet was the bushes on the other side of the hill. We would take a tin of cleansing water with us when we went. Occasionally I would wryly remember the Indian Ambassador's wife in Athens warning me that there was "no flush" in the toilets in Himachal Pradesh.

There was water piped in from a spring two miles away,

but the supply was not reliable and there were times when we took it in turns to sit up at night in case some water arrived so we could put it in pitchers. When no water came, we could not spare water for brushing teeth, washing clothes, or bathing. There was a stream in the forest with wild rhododendrons on the banks where we could wash clothes. It would be a day's outing to go there, wash clothes, then wait for them to dry on the bank, and come home. We could not bathe there since it was in an exposed place. I enjoyed the times we went to wash clothes in the stream. It had large boulders in it, which helped form little pools of clear, clean water. You had to be careful not to make the water soapy upstream of where others were rinsing clothes; the soaping place was downstream of the rinsing place. After the clothes were washed, they were laid out on the grassy bank to dry. I sometimes wondered why we did not take water from the river and boil it to drink. I suppose we wanted to keep the firewood for making tea, roasting barley, and cooking.

From the hut you could see the high peak of the nearest mountain in the Dhauladhar range, which was always covered in snow. The red light at dawn made the peak a splendid rose colour.

What I learned on this second stay in India was the joy of living simply. My happiness did not depend on material comfort: good food, running water, or electricity. My happiness was to be in a place where spiritual practice came first and where the beauty of nature was around me. The air was fresh and good, the moon beautiful. The chanting that wafted across the valley moved me, and the energy of the practice seemed to have entered every tree.

Occasionally there would be a day of rest, which was truly delicious. Every tree seemed to be resting too. The monks would chant the sutra in the early morning and then the rest of the day was free. They looked so relaxed and the younger ones went to the river to swim. We walked in the forest and sang songs to each other. The nuns taught me two songs of Milarepa and I sang to the nuns songs I had composed myself. Khenpo Tsultrim Gyatso liked very much the practice of singing and was a specialist in the songs of Milarepa. One of the songs I learned was about meditation: meditate on the sky without clouds, the ocean without surface and depths, the mountain that is firm, the mind that has no thoughts, and in the next verse to meditate on the sky with clouds and the mind with thoughts. I never knew the meaning of the other song, but I learned it by heart because I enjoyed its melody so much. We would go into the fragrant pine forest to sing these songs and watch the moon or contemplate it as we sat on the roof, waiting for the water to come into the tank.

Sometimes the monks came over to our side of the hill to visit. One day, we nuns were carrying heavy wood planks to build the Buddha Hall of the nunnery. Each plank had to be carried about a mile. I was tired and not enjoying the work. I arrived at the building site with a plank and put it down. I saw a monk sitting on the side of the hill. He had removed his upper robe. Although he did not say anything or even look at me, I was struck by his freedom and happiness. His face and his posture radiated that freedom and happiness. He sat for a long time looking out over the rice fields and the river far below, not caught up in anything.

I never imagined I could be as happy and free as that. I composed a song, which began "O What It Is to Be Happy," inspired by that monk. Twenty years later I found myself sitting on the top of a hill in Vermont looking at the mountains around and I felt that monk's freedom and happiness again.

The thing that made me feel sorry for myself was being so dirty all the time. When I saw my arms blackened by dirt, and I could smell the unpleasant odour of clothes that had been rained on and then dried on my body, which had not had a bath for three weeks, I felt a self-pity that brought me close to tears. When at last the water supply came back on, I went in the early morning before anyone was up to bathe with the help of a hose behind the wall of the main building of the nuns' retreat which had already been erected. It was a discrete enough place at that time of day, as no one was around. That was a very happy moment.

One night we were sitting by the light of a tiny oil lamp on the floor of the hut near the construction site. A large scorpion crawled in front of us. Anila Pema said the week before a nun had had to go to the hospital after being bitten by such a scorpion. This scorpion just crawled nonchalantly in front of us and disappeared out of the door.

Our food was rationed quite severely. The nuns at the building site and I ate together. Anila Pema said she had to keep the money she was donated for buying building materials. Breakfast might be just a bowl of tea. If it was available, there would be a small helping of roasted barley flour to mix with the tea. Tea grew in that region and so we enjoyed the unfermented green leaves, which made a very refreshing tea. Lunch was a small helping of fried vegetables with two small chapati. Sometimes the vegetables were simmered with dumplings. Supper was rice soup, but the poorer we were, the more water would be added, until there was only a little rice water.

There was one time when Anila Pema was away and I had to eat on my own. Before she left I had become very angry with the nuns; I thought they were talking about me and saying how lazy I was. Actually, they were talking about one of the workers but, because my Tibetan was not very good, I misunderstood. So I shouted at them that I was not lazy. After that the nuns did not want to talk to me, although they did bring me food. I knew it was wrong to be angry like that, and I asked the Buddha to let me pay off my bad karma as soon as possible. I felt that being put into Coventry was my way of paying off bad karma. It was very unpleasant, and I was glad when it was over and I could apologize and people would talk to me again.

When we were working there was *chai* to drink, sweet tea with sugar and powdered milk. I was often detailed to make this tea at ten in the morning and three in the afternoon. It involved lighting a fire. Anila Pema said that matches were expensive and I should only use one match. When the wind is blowing and you are not an expert fire lighter, this is no easy feat. I would try to save every little scrap of paper and would add this to dry grass to start the fire, boil the water, add the tea, sugar, and milk powder, and finally strain the mixture into cups. It is very pleasant to drink a cup of this hot sweet liquid when you are hungry. There was a little wooden stool to sit on as I cooked, and three large stones around the fireplace. The saucepans were very black and one day I decided to clean them all. I used ash from the fire to do this, and when I rinsed them with water they had miraculously lost all their soot, which nevertheless had attached itself to my hands.

Our kitchen and washing up place was a patch of dirt at the bottom of the steps that led down from the hut. After our supper of thin rice soup, I would wash the dishes in the dark. I had to feel with my fingers whether the bowls were clean. The only light we had was a small oil lamp. The sisters who liked to study the sutras had to wait for the moon to be bright enough to read. They would stay up late, studying by moonlight for a few days every month.

Another task I had was to keep the bricks wet. For some reason new bricks have to be kept damp. Before they are made into the wall it is easy enough to keep them wet by allowing them to lie in large containers full of water. Once they have been incorporated into a building, for at least two weeks they have to be sprayed with water twice a day. With a high pressure hose or even a medium pressure hose, the work would have been very easy. We did have an ancient rubber hose which was full of leaks and not long enough to reach everywhere it was needed. The leaks were mended with old pieces of cloth, which may have stemmed the leak to a small extent but not enough to make the water reach the top of the walls. I resorted to filling a bucket and trying to fling the water high enough. I had to laugh at myself as the water would fall back, wetting me more than the bricks. In short, the kind of work I had to do at the monastery was completely different from anything I had ever done in my life, and I never succeeded in practising while doing it or feeling I was doing anyone much good. Nevertheless, I was glad to have something to do in repayment for the hospitality I was receiving and to keep my mind out of its mischievous habit of thinking about negative things.

Because of the small amount of food, I would go to bed hungry and wake up hungry. In the colder months of the year, I went to bed shivering and woke up shivering. I was determined to stay and become a nun, but Anila Pema was very discouraging. It would not have been difficult for someone else looking on as an objective observer to see that I was not a suitable candidate for the nunhood in the Tibetan tradition: I did not speak the language; I was not physically strong; I did not have a teacher or a sponsor. My reasons for wanting to stay on were that, although I did not enjoy building work, I knew that it was impermanent and I envisioned myself practising as a nun in the retreat centre we were building. I enjoyed living in a monastery because it satisfied my deep need for a spiritual life and I was willing to undergo hardships in order to fulfil that need.

One day I heard that my Refuge teacher, Lama Khenpo Tsultrim Gyatso, "Ocean of Virtuous Conduct," was leading a retreat for Westerners in Manali, a town higher up into the Himalayan foothills about a hundred miles away. I asked permission to go. Anila gave me money for the bus fare and I was allowed by the retreat organizers not to pay for food and lodging, as I had sponsored the nuns.

The retreat centre in Manali was in a beautiful valley by the river with many apple trees. I was given a room with a bed made of string tightened across the frame. There was a day I found it difficult to concentrate on the Dharma talk.

The scenery outside the window was very beautiful and I was lost in looking at it. At one point I caught the Rinpoche's eye, and after that talk the translator called me into the teacher's room. He questioned me about sitting meditation. For how long did I sit? I replied "a few hours." He told me that as a beginner I should only sit for twenty minutes at a time. Later on, as I became solid in the practice, I should be able to sit for longer. I agreed with him. I was finding the long hours I sat in meditation unfruitful. It was as if I sat for a long time struggling to achieve a sense of calm and then my consciousness would leave my body for a short time. This had no effect on my life as a whole. I was not becoming a more peaceful person. From then on, I obeyed my teacher and only sat for twenty minutes. I asked what other practice I should do. He said I should study. I said I had no books. He said, "The universe is your book."

He was a kind teacher. When I came into the room he had a large bowl of apples. In Manali, apples grow very well. He handed me an apple and a knife to peel it. Later he taught me the verse, "If you have not dreamt of being happy yourself, how can you aspire to make others happy?" That was precisely my predicament. Without dreaming even of my own happiness, I always thought that my task was to bring others happiness. I had misunderstood the practice of *tonglen*, which a different lama had shared with me earlier. I understood that this meant when you breathe in, you breathe in the suffering of other beings and when you breathe out, you breathe out your own happiness to benefit other beings. Although I could do this intellectually, it was not possible for me to enjoy such a meditation. I had the feeling that many of the teachings were for the others and had nothing to do with me. The benefit of this personal meeting with the Rinpoche was that I stopped the wrong kind of meditation I was doing. Now, I just sat for a very short time, imitating the relaxation and happiness of the lama sitting on the hillside.

During that retreat the lama also taught a text of Maitreyanatha or Asanga, which in English was translated as *The Unchanging Nature.* One of the verses of this text reads: "Nothing whatsoever to remove from this, not a single thing thereon to add. Properly regarding the true nature, when truly seen, complete liberation." Later on, after I was ordained as a bhikshuni by Thich Nhat Hanh, or Thay, I could see the connection between this teaching and Thay's teaching on "This is it," and "It's now."

Lama Khenpo Tsultrim Gyatso advised us to memorize it and put it to music. I still sing this verse to this day. In some of the Mahayana Sutras, for example in the Vajracchedika (Diamond) and Lotus Sutras, we read: "If someone recites with respect and confidence just one *gatha* from this sutra, it is worth more merit than making offerings to the Buddhas in the ten directions." I usually recite this verse when I have the kind of insight it is describing and sometimes I recite it to remind myself of the insight it is describing.

After the retreat of not more than a week, I went back to Baijnath by bus and arrived at the bus stop in the late afternoon. The sun set during my walk back, and I had to make most of my way in the dark. I was a little afraid and walked as quickly as I could. I crossed the flooded rice fields, which, unknown to me, were full of leeches. As I walked through the forest it felt as if my shoes were full of water. When I arrived at the nuns' hut, I removed my shoes and walked up the steps. I walked into the hut and was met by a strong reprimand. What I'd thought was water in my shoes was in fact blood, and I had left bloody footprints all over the floor of the hut. The leeches on my feet had removed the clotting agent and my feet were bleeding. I had to sit outside in ignominy. My close companion, the monastery dog, came and licked my feet clean. I felt comforted by the dog, so the next day I gave it a bit of my chapati. Anila Pema was not at all pleased. This food was for me to eat. It was true, we did not have enough to eat ourselves, and it was foolish to give it to the dog who could fend for himself and would receive scraps from the monastery and the monastery guests.

One time Anila Pema and the two other nuns had to go away on business; I was on my own. A Polish student of meditation was doing a retreat in the forest, living in a little hut there. She paid a Tibetan laywoman to bring her food every other day. The lady brought her too much one day, and the Polish woman shared it with me. I was so happy to have my rations supplemented that even though I thought the meal contained meat, I ate it all. Later I learnt that it was not meat but soya protein chunks.

I used this time alone to reflect on my recent experiences. When I was a child I had spent summer holidays in France with a French family, and later when I had lived in Greece, and now with a community of Tibetan nuns in India, I enjoyed my opportunities to learn new languages and to be open to other ways of life. Living in different cultural situations was something very enjoyable for me, as long as I did not feel that I was inferior.

In the beginning it had been quite a cultural challenge living in the monastery in India. There were so many social customs I had to pick up, and I often fell short of the task unknowingly. The first thing I had to learn was always to keep my feet tucked in under me when I was sitting. Then, as a laywoman, I could never sit or stand in a place that was higher than a monk or a nun. For example, if a nun wanted to go under our hut, which was on stilts, to fetch something, I would need temporarily to leave the hut so that I would not be above her. I should never say, even as only a supposition, that something bad might happen, because the very saying of it would make it more likely that the event would occur. I should never wear someone else's shoes or allow someone else to wear my shoes. Seeing a dead mouse or rat was a bad omen; while this never seemed to be so in my own case, as far as the Tibetan nuns were concerned, whenever they saw a dead mouse or rat, it signified bad luck. I should recite the sutras in Tibetan (because the English was not available) and, even though I did not understand a word of what I was reciting, it would be very beneficial for my practice. One time when an ant was crawling over the sutra text I was reciting, I was told not to remove it because this encounter of the ant with the written word of the sutra meant that the ant would be in touch with the Buddhadharma in a future life. The nuns had a devotional faith which was quite different from mine.

The prayer wheel was something else that I did not understand in the beginning. The entrance to the monastery across from us on the other side of the valley had a gate like a turnstile that was in effect a prayer wheel. In order to enter the monastery by this gate you had to turn the prayer wheel. As you did this a bell hanging above would sound, and the words *om mani padme hung* would make one turn inside the prayer wheel.

In order for me to incorporate *om mani padme hung* into my own way of life, rather than recite the syllables I tried to sing them. I sang them to the music of the hymn I had learned as a child in England, "The King of Love My Shepherd Is." One day I was surprised when I stopped singing that the syllables of the mantra came back to me as if from the horizon of the landscape around me. I began to value the mantra more after that. It had helped me clear my mind and be in touch with all that was around me.

Only later did I appreciate the deep meaning of the prayer wheel and the ant crawling over the sutra, and yes, even reciting words that you do not understand. Now I see that every little event can contribute to the awakening that is taking place in the deepest levels of the individual and collective consciousness, especially when we have faith that this is so. However, the effectiveness of reading a text in a language you do understand is immediately recognizable, if you read with concentration and mindfulness. In the Lotus Sutra there is a chapter that tells us that even a child playing in the sand who draws a stupa is laying down a cause for enlightenment. When a pilgrim walks along, turns his prayer wheel, and recollects the words *om mani padme hung*, the seed of those syllables associated with Avalokiteshvara, the Bodhisattva of Compassion, are being strengthened in the unconscious mind.

I spent six months in India this time and it did not go as well as I had hoped. I became ill with diarrhoea and had no money. Little cuts on my hands and legs became infected and wouldn't heal and I had a fever. Anila Pema needed people who were strong and could do heavy manual labour. A large part of the work needed was carrying heavy loads, mixing cement, and digging foundations. I was miserably ill-equipped to do any of these things, being so slight of build. Some tough nuns arrived from Tibet and Anila Pema fed them well in exchange for the hard work they did. As for myself, the rations became smaller. I did what I could. I could carry small stones to make the septic tank. I spent days carrying stones in order to do this.

ENGLAND

SCOTLAND

North Sea

Samye Ling

Isle
of
Man

Ulverston

Manchester

Irish Sea

Chester

WALES

Birmingham

Oxford

Greenham

London

Brockwood
Park

Smarden

Falmouth

English Channel

CHAPTER TEN

Greenham Common

ONE DAY in March, a monk with a radio was passing our hut. He wanted to try out his English on me. He had been listening to the BBC World Service on his wireless and asked me if I knew what was happening in England. When I said no, he said there were thousands of women besieging the US missile base at Greenham Common in Berkshire in protest of the British government's decision to allow American nuclear weapons to be sited there and to stop the weapons from being driven out from the site. The Greenham Common Women's Peace Camp had begun the previous month and would go on to become one of the longest-running antinuclear protests, continuing for nineteen years until 2000.

Why did I not go and join them? Always a committed pacifist, I suddenly saw that there was something I could do in the way of fulfilling my ideals. In India, I was not able to help the world in a concrete way; instead I was becoming a burden to my community.

Suddenly I realised there was a way out, and this was a relief to me. I had been caught in the idea that I should have to stay in India and become a nun in order to realise my ideal. Now I saw there was another way. That young monk was to me like a divine messenger bringing me the news I needed to hear in order to have a way ahead. In England

I could do something to help the world. But how could I return to England? I had no ticket and no money to buy one.

I wrote to my father and asked him to lend me the money to go home. My father had always been very generous. Since we had no telephone I could only communicate in writing and I forgot to tell my father where exactly to send the money. After more than two weeks, I received notice that some money had been sent to me in India, but it had arrived in Bombay. I did not have the funds to take the train to Bombay. I scraped money together to take a bus to Delhi, where I would have to persuade the Delhi branch of the bank to give me the money.

Anila also saw that it was time for me to go, and when we parted I had no idea whether I should ever see her again. There was no special farewell and I no longer had any ideas of coming back to become a nun. I had mixed feelings about leaving: on the one hand I was happy that I should be able to be in England where I now felt it would be easier to follow my ideal; on the other hand I was sad to leave those magnificent mountains and the aura of sacredness that went with them.

In Delhi there was a hostel run by Western students of the Dalai Lama where I could have a bed and some food. I went to the Delhi branch of the Bombay bank where my money had been sent. At first the clerk was adamant that he could not give me the money. I broke down and cried. I was penniless. What could I do? He relented and telephoned the Bombay branch to ask if my money had arrived. They confirmed that it had, and they wired it to Delhi. I bought my ticket and paid for my bed and food in the hostel. I was very grateful to my father and the bank clerk in Delhi.

On returning to England, I wanted to see my parents for a few days before going to Greenham Common. My mother came to meet me at the same bus stop, the Norway Inn on the road between Truro and Falmouth, where she had always come to collect us when we came home from school. She remarked that I was very thin; I weighed about six stone. She and my father had to go away for a few days shortly after my arrival, so I was left in the large farmhouse alone.

At Greenham Common I knew there was no shelter and it was illegal to pitch tents. So we should have to sleep with just a sleeping bag covered by a sheet of plastic to keep off the rain. I wondered how I would fare and decided to experiment. I brought my sleeping bag into the garden on a cold night at the end of March and managed to sleep quite well.

I felt I had no more reason to stay in my parents' house. I wrote a letter telling them that I had gone to Oxford to visit friends. I had told my mother that I was going to join the women's camp at Greenham Common, but she had been extremely afraid that my father would find out and disapprove. I had to promise her that I would not tell Father.

I set out early one morning with a change of clothes and my sleeping bag, wearing rubber boots. I thought I would ask for water from houses along the way as I had been accustomed to doing when I travelled in India. I would walk to the train station nearest to my parents' house to take the train to Oxford and then walk from Oxford to Greenham, just over thirty miles. This meant quite a bit of walking and rubber boots are certainly not good for long-distance walks.

I felt very free as I walked along in the early spring countryside, listening to the birds singing so happily. I was free to walk in the direction of my ideal and I did not need a house or material belongings! I was free of all my fears for material security. As I walked from Oxford to Greenham, however, my feet became more and more painful. I stopped at a house to ask for water, since I was by now very thirsty. My request was not so well received. In India, people walking past our monastery often stopped to ask for water. When I gave them a glass they would say in thanks, "The one who gives water gives life," and they would go on their way. England was not India. If you stop at a house and ask for water, it is likely that the owner will look at you with extreme suspicion and either grudgingly give you what you ask for or refuse outright. My ideal had been to walk freely without possessing anything. I had imagined people smiling and handing water to me, and I soon saw that the world was not as I had imagined.

When I arrived at Greenham Common, I saw that the women had organized themselves into different camps near the gates of the missile base, named after different colours. I arrived at Green Camp hardly able to walk. My feet were swollen and bleeding. The Green Camp campers told me they had enough people already and I should go to Turquoise Camp. By the time I reached Turquoise, I could not walk. It would take a couple of days before I could hobble around.

It was lunchtime. Someone had cooked curry and rice. I ate with the fingers of my right hand as I had done when in Indian houses; I expect I wanted people to see I was well travelled. I asked about the organization of Turquoise camp. How did they have money for buying food? How had they divided the tasks among themselves? They said occasionally a benefactor would give a donation, but generally the women went to the local Department of Health and Social Security office, said they were looking for work, and would receive unemployment benefit, about ten pounds a week. This they gave to the camp for buying food. Unemployment was high and as a Classics teacher, it was unlikely the office would find work for me. For as long as I had no work I could receive ten pounds a week.

As far as the organization of tasks was concerned, everyone did what they saw needed doing. Whoever wanted to cook would cook. Whoever wanted to dig or fill in the latrine pit would do that. If someone saw something that needed to be done and could not do it themselves, they would announce it to the community. It was a free-form, nonstructured, but generally harmonious way of living.

Women camped around the perimeter of the Greenham Common Royal Air Force base to stop missiles entering and leaving the base. If ever a gate was opened, whistles would be blown so that the women could place themselves in the gate and the vehicles drawing the missiles could not come out. As far as I understood it, the resistance was nonviolent: we could stand, sit, or lie down in the gateway and our bodies would block the way, even if they wanted to drive over us.

The task I liked to volunteer for was the night vigil. There had to be a night vigil in case the missiles were brought out under cover of darkness. We posted two people at the gate, one sitting right by the gate and one keeping a fire alight at a distance for us to warm up by if we became too cold. While sitting at the gate I cannot remember ever feeling unbearably cold, but there were times when I needed the fire to warm up. The young soldiers on watch inside the fence would tease me in a good-natured way, saying that I would freeze to death. They asked me what I was doing keeping vigil; I used to repeat *om mani padme hung* to myself. When I was tired of sitting I would walk up and down the path by the fence in the dark, with the fir trees on the other side as my companions.

Recently I was sharing with a group of English lay practitioners that I had spent time at Greenham Common Women's Camp in 1983. One of them said he had been a soldier guarding the missile base at that time. Maybe we had seen each other, he inside and me sitting outside. Now we were both on the same side of the fence, practising to create peace in our daily lives and our environment.

For as long as I stayed at Greenham, no missiles came out of Turquoise gate, so I never had to lie down in the path of the vehicles and I was not arrested.

At Greenham, I missed the spiritual element of living in community as I had with the Tibetan nuns, which had bound us together in sisterhood. While we agreed that we did not want nuclear missiles on Planet Earth and in particular on Greenham Common, a common practice to have peace in our hearts was not something we could share. I asked everyone at the missile base, "Does anyone know about Buddhist practice? Does anyone do meditation? Do you know anybody who is in the peace movement and also is a Buddhist?" Everyone said, "No," they didn't know anyone. Then one day someone said, "Oh yes, I know someone. He is a Buddhist teacher from Vietnam," and they said

Thay's name. The women I talked to were not interested in organized spirituality, and I realised that I needed to find a way to bring together my political and spiritual ideals with others.

After some time at the camp, I discovered there was an organization called the Buddhist Peace Fellowship. Eventually I found an address and wrote to them. They sent me their newsletter and in it was published a poem by Vietnamese Zen Master Thich Nhat Hanh, "Please Call Me by My True Names." This Zen master had been nominated by Martin Luther King, Jr., for his peace activism during the Vietnam War and, banned from his native Vietnam, now lived in exile in France. There was a photograph of Thich Nhat Hanh smiling, holding a teapot to pour tea. The poem impressed me deeply. I had never read such a poem before. Now that I knew that there was a Buddhist Peace Fellowship and a Zen master who was part of the peace movement I realised that, although I had only been in Greenham Common a few weeks, I wanted to go somewhere that I could practise with other Buddhist practitioners and work on my peace activism from within as well as without.

On the whole I enjoyed living out in the open air and, when I returned to living in a house, for some months I always had to keep the window wide open in order to keep that happy memory alive. I had great admiration for the women who lived for years at Greenham for what they were ready to go through in order to protect Planet Earth from nuclear weapons and also for their non-organized and generally harmonious way of living together.

After Greenham I needed to earn my daily bread. I went

back to Cornwall and stayed in an old farmworker's cottage on my father's farm. My father and mother were not very happy about me not working and receiving the dole, but we had no choice. It was not easy to find a job teaching. Whenever I applied, I would be asked why I had left the jobs I'd had before. I could only tell them the truth, that I'd wanted to travel. Heads of schools did not want to employ someone who could not be relied on to stay in a job for very long.

I attended a Sangha called the Friends of the Western Buddhist Order in the nearby town of Truro. We meditated counting the breaths from one to ten and then back down to one again. If we lost track of the counting we would go back to one again. It was not very interesting, but it did clear my mind of a great deal of unnecessary thinking. I would take the bus to the evening session of meditation they held and then stay the night with my godfather and his wife who lived in Truro.

There was also a group of Tibetan Buddhists whom I tried to join, but they were in an inaccessible place and I had no car to drive. Then I discovered that my nearest neighbours were Buddhist and we could meditate with each other. After some months I went to Scotland to seek to live in Samye Ling, the Tibetan Buddhist monastery there, which had been founded by Chogyam Trungpa and Akong Tulku Rinpoche, students of the Karmapa and beneficiaries of Sister Palmo. My request for residency was turned down by the lama in charge. I understood that I needed to be able to pay my way while staying there, and I still needed to pay back my father for the money he had sent me in India.

Although the Tibetan tradition put me in touch with the

teachings of the Buddha, it became clear to me and to the teachers of that tradition that it was not the best path for me. The abbot in Scotland asked me: "Have you ever asked your parents if they are happy with what you are doing?" I had never considered that it was necessary to ask my parents this question. After all, it was my life, I thought. What did it have to do with them what I did? The Buddhist perspective is different. We are a continuation of our parents, and what we do is very much their concern.

So I went back to Cornwall and asked my mother how she had felt when I went to India. We were sitting in a car in the back seat together. I saw my mother cry. She said, "I will never know why you gave up such a good position and good salary to go to India, to a place so remote that there were no doctors, no telephone. What would have happened if you had fallen ill?"

I had thought that my life, my body, was mine to do with as I wished. I had never imagined that my mother cared for my body as she cared for her own. I wanted to cry, too, at my stupidity, my utter lack of understanding and sensitivity.

I flashed back to a time when I had been at university and my mother had come to visit me, and how unwelcoming I had been, how heartless. I used to leave her on her own in order to do my own thing. Looking back, I could have spent so much more time with her, showing her around my favourite places in Hampstead and walking on Hampstead Heath. It was a revolt against what at the time seemed such a narrow way of life, which had nothing to do with the group of friends I now had. How she had cried then. I remembered another time when my father rang me in my second year and asked why I did not come down in the vacation to visit them, and how much my mother missed me. I was a foolish child causing myself and my parents to suffer together. Later on, I would find ways that we could all be happy together. I am grateful my life has been long enough to do this, and my parents' lives have been long enough too.

After India and Greenham Common, I was determined to try and find work as a schoolteacher again to make my parents happy. I had not been able to become a nun, and the next best thing I could do was to teach; I did not know then that, thanks to the great compassion of my teacher, Thay, I would eventually grow into the life of a nun and ordain.

However, it was not easy for me to find work as a Classics teacher. To begin with, Greek and Latin, which used to be the cornerstone of any child's formal education in England, were being taught less and less in British schools in the 1980s. Then there was the fact that I had left three posts without any good reason. Headmistresses wanted to employ teachers who would stay in a post for ten years and provide stability. They did not think that I had the capacity to do that.

I found work in an organic garden in Shropshire, not far from the pretty Roman town of Chester in northwest England. Although I like pottering around in gardens, the heavy work of a hired garden worker was not suitable for me. Once again I was faced with the challenge of my physical limitations. I had never been physically strong or robust. The owner of the garden was Indian and a teacher of hatha yoga. As garden workers, we were invited to the owner's weekly yoga class. I enjoyed this class because it was a chance to be warm. The room had a thick carpet and radiators for heating.

I arrived at the beginning of autumn. The crops we harvested in late autumn and winter were spinach, broccoli, and Chinese cabbage. A Chinese cabbage is quite a miracle. They grew in the greenhouse. From a little seed and organic compost and water, this magnificent being of closely packed leaves would come about and I enjoyed looking after these cabbages. Usually we ate the less handsome-looking vegetables, selling the best. We had a stall in the local market once a week and sent vegetables to organic supply shops.

I suffered badly from the cold because of my poor circulation. The worst thing was picking vegetables in the winter; I remember once picking spinach in a blizzard. When vegetables are ready they have to be picked whatever the weather. First my hands froze, then my feet. It is very painful when the blood circulation cannot make its way through the contracted veins. There was a time when the pain reached its peak in one of my limbs. Then it would ease in that limb or go to another. I tried to run around to warm up. It helped a bit, but then I had to go back to my job of picking.

I had trouble with swelling in my knees and also in my finger joints, so my employer took me to her herbalist. She also was interested in herbal medicine and was in touch with a herbalist in a town near Manchester who came from a line of excellent British herbalists who had handed down the practice of diagnosis and treatment from parents to children. He took just a drop of blood and put it in a machine his father had invented. He asked questions about my health and said there was too much acid in my body—I was to have no more rhubarb, plums, or other acid-forming foods. Oranges were to be eaten only on their own and not in combination with other foods.

The herbalist gave me several different pills and oil for rubbing into my joints. The rubbing, he said, was more important than the oil. The pills had to be taken at the prescribed time. He was very insistent about the time: not too early or too late. He said that I would become quite sick and then the matter of water on the joints would be healed. After ten days of taking the medicine, I woke up with a fever and headache. An orange-yellow liquid poured out of one ear. This was the toxins that the medicine was removing from my body. After that I had to fast for three days. My Indian employer said I should fast for a week, but I became irritable after three days and asked to be allowed to eat fruit. After that, I never suffered from excess swelling in the joints again. At the time I visited this herbalist he was already in his nineties, and his daughter who was in her sixties was preparing to succeed him.

One day my employer hosted a workshop with a healer who taught us total relaxation listening to music. He then told us about the aura he saw around our body as we practised total relaxation. Mine was clear blue. It was the first time I had heard about coloured light around the body. Since then, other people have told me they see various lights or colours around bodies. When we are concentrated on chanting a sutra, people may see white light around our body.

Although I was glad to be introduced to some new aspects of spiritual life in England, my employer and I did not always get along, and I was not really happy in that employment. One night I had a dream that marked a turning point in my life. I had climbed up a green hill and was almost at the summit. There was a huge high hedge, very difficult to scale. I began to tackle the hedge, climbing up and slithering back down. Finally I came to the top and scrambled down the other side where there was a farmer working in his fields. He looked at me with surprise and asked, "Why did you climb over like that when there is a perfectly good gate to go through?" He took me along the hedge to where there was a small gate. I could not believe that I had been stupid enough to put myself through such hardship when there was a much easier way. How to find that little gate? It was not insignificant that the person who showed me the gate was a farmer. I thought it was my father in me.

The day after I had the dream, I received my second copy of the Buddhist Peace Fellowship's UK branch magazine in which there was an announcement that the community that served as the headquarters for the Fellowship had a space for another member. I applied to join the community and was accepted. They lived in a large house in Smarden, Kent, in southeast England. It was comfortable. There was a flower garden and a vegetable garden. Smarden was a beautiful little village in the Kent countryside, and there were plenty of places where we could walk through woods and fields. In the community was a woman of seventy, the Englishman who edited the newsletter, a Dutchman, a young couple, a middle-aged couple, and a single mother with her nine-year-old son. There was also a young woman who enjoyed looking after the vegetable garden. I cannot say that we were an altogether harmonious community. Only two of us called ourselves Buddhist, two were disciples of an Indian guru, two had Christian-Buddhist double belonging, and the other four were eclectic. So we could not practise together and, though we ate together, we could not come to an agreement to eat vegetarian. Nevertheless, the bonus was that I could live very simply in an old van out in the garden. I felt a certain freedom to have the time to study about Buddhism and peace in the world.

I was thirty-four at the time, and my responsibility in the community was to write articles and edit and type up the BPF newsletter. To make a living, I worked in peoples' gardens and homes tidying and cleaning, and I taught an evening class in comparative religion. When I went to tidy up people's gardens they would sometimes like to talk about Buddhism, and I would hardly have any time left to do anything in the garden.

The centre was within commuting distance of London, and I frequently took the train to London on Buddhist Peace Fellowship business, attending meetings of peace organizations or conducting interviews for the newsletter. The computer and word processor did not yet exist and I used an electric typewriter.

Once a year the community went to Brockwood Park near Winchester, the school founded by the Krishnamurti Foundation, to listen to talks given by the famous Indian teacher Jiddu Krishnamurti. We took tents and camped. There were hundreds, maybe thousands of people attending these talks. Apart from the talks, I found it interesting that there were no practice sessions and no instructions on how to practise. Krishnamurti was against practice of any kind because he considered it was a means to an end and not the end. The talks were given every other day. When there was no talk we were left to our own devices, except when from time to time a concert was arranged.

When Krishnamurti gave talks, I would sit on the floor in the big marquee in front of the master, almost sitting at his feet. Listening to him speak, I was inspired to teach like that. One year I was suffering from feelings of jealousy, and it startled me that Krishnamurti talked about jealousy, how we should face it and finish with it. After the talk, I managed to do this. Now when the mental formation of jealousy arises I recognize it as it is and look into its root. During that season of talks in 1985, Krishnamurti scolded the retreatants who played drums late into the night (I am ashamed to say it was our group from the Buddhist Peace Fellowship) and said that this would be the last large gathering at Brockwood. It was true. Early the next year Krishnamurti died and the following year there was no gathering.

CHAPTER ELEVEN

Meeting Thay

I HAD KNOWN about Krishnamurti for many years, but while living in Smarden I learnt more about another teacher, a teacher who had inspired the very existence of the Buddhist Peace Fellowship. It was Thay, Thich Nhat Hanh. I had read his poem "Please Call Me by My True Names" in the first issue of the BPF newsletter I had received. It moved me more deeply than anything I had read before, and then I read the poem "The Old Mendicant." I copied it onto a piece of card and sent it as a Christmas present to my mother—she enjoyed it too.[1]

Some Catholic nuns had published part of Thay's *Miracle of Mindfulness* and made it into a small book they called *Be Still and Know*.[2] The fact that Catholic nuns had published Thay's teachings shows how all-embracing they are. Then I did not appreciate this wonderful book as I do now. Thay has a way of writing from the heart that goes straight to the heart of a reader. As with Thay's poetry, this was the first time that I had read a Buddhist book that was so simple, so heartfelt, and so practical. Nevertheless for many different reasons I did not yet seriously begin to put mindfulness into practice. I did introduce mindfulness in my evening classes on comparative religion, but I still did not have enough faith and confidence in the practice of mindfulness, because I lacked the experience of practising it in my own life. What I needed was to attend a retreat where I could *experience* mindfulness.

The BPF newsletter editor asked, "Why not invite Thay to England to lead a retreat and give talks?" I could help organize that, I thought. Thay accepted the invitation. The editor disappeared on a trip to Sri Lanka, and I was left organizing the tour without any experience of such things. The Quaker Centre off Euston Square in Central London allowed us a room for Thay to give a talk. The Manjushri Institute near Ulverston in Cumbria was available for a retreat. I went by train to check the place out beforehand. The Manjushri Institute had been a castle, a prison, a hospital for tuberculosis patients, and was now a Tibetan Buddhist Institute. This seemed to me good enough since I had already practised with the Tibetans, forgetting that the climates of Tibet and of Vietnam could not be more different from each other. The Tibetans were quite at home in a cold, draughty English castle; I had no idea then how unsuitable it would be for Thay.

It was in March 1986, that I went to the airport to greet Thay and Sister Chan Khong. She was also called Co Chin (Aunt Nine) or Chi Phuong (elder sister Phuong). She had long hair and was dressed in brown. Thay wore the long brown robe of a Vietnamese monk and had a shaved head. This was the first time I had seen a monk in brown robes. It was in contrast to the maroon and yellow with which I was familiar. Brown is such a humble colour, the colour farmers in Vietnam wear. It was also the colour of my school uniform so a colour of dress with which I was familiar. Generally I was a shy person, retiring and withdrawn. Luckily there were Vietnamese people there too who could talk to Thay in the proper way. I felt unsure if I was doing the correct thing in greeting such important people at the airport, but they were so simple and humble and greeted me kindly so that you would never think they were important. At that time I had no idea that Thay would be my teacher, the one to point out the way to overcome suffering, but I felt a closeness to Chi Phuong whose Dharma name was Chan Khong, True Emptiness. I felt I had known her before but I did not know where or how. At that time I had no idea how much Thay and Sister Chan Khong had done together and separately to relieve suffering in the war years in Vietnam, and how she had been Thay's loyal assistant for so long.[5] Thay has called Sister Chan Khong a "peace warrior" to describe her intrepid and untiring work to bring about more happiness and less suffering in the world. I did not pay so much attention to Thay until we started to walk, and then I noticed how Thay walked. The essence of Thay's practice was mindful walking and breathing. Thay walked just to walk, without any idea of needing to arrive somewhere else. He was completely relaxed and in the present moment as he walked. We were walking to the car park and, as we walked through it, I noticed how Thay gently put his hand on the bonnet of a car as if to feel the metal and ground himself. Since Thay walked very slowly I had to hold myself back from my habit of rushing, otherwise I would find myself far ahead of Thay.

While living in Kent with the Buddhist Peace Fellowship, I had met some Vietnamese people through our events. At that time, in the 1980s, Hong Kong was still British, and the government there did not want to accept Vietnamese refugees. They had a policy of sending refugee boats back out to sea, and the refugee camps that did exist were more like prisons. There were groups in England opposing this cruel policy, and through them I met the peace activist Nguyen thi Tuyet Mai who is now a lay Dharma teacher disciple of Thay. I went with her to visit Vietnamese refugees in London, who had been in the Hong Kong camps, to interview them. However, Thay and Sister Chan Khong were the first Vietnamese people for whom I would act as a host.

We took Thay to visit Chinatown in Soho to look at Chinese books and calligraphy brushes, then the next day we had to drive north to Cumbria for the five-day retreat I had organized. It was March and still bitterly cold, and the castle retreat centre in Cumbria had huge rooms that could never be heated. The fireplaces gave out heat to a space of only a one-metre radius in front of them.

Before the retreat began, Thay invited me into his room to ask me what I thought of the daily schedule he proposed for the retreat. I was moved: why would Thay ask me? After all I was a complete beginner; I knew nothing. Still, I said the proposed schedule was very good.

One day it snowed, and one day the weather was fine enough for us to take a walk to the sea. Thay did not complain. He ate the English food that the retreatants ate. He attended all activities on the schedule and led them all, as well as giving the Dharma talk. Gently he encouraged me to practise by saying, "You do not need to hurry, just take one step slowly at a time," because I wanted to run everywhere, doing everything.

Thay had someone bring a "cloud bell" from his home in exile, Plum Village in France, to use to announce activities and summon us to mindfulness. A cloud bell is a flat piece of bronze moulded in the shape of a cloud. It has a sharper sound than the round bowl-shaped bell. In the Plum Village tradition, we say we "invite" a bell to sound rather than "striking" or "ringing" it. The bell was invited in the draughty corridor on the ground floor of that castle over thirty years ago in 1986.

Thay must have felt cold. When I looked at Thay's bed it looked as if it had never been slept in. I imagined Thay seated in meditation all night long. Sister Chan Khong asked me to try to find an electric heater for Thay's room. I do not remember that we paid Thay or Sister Chan Khong any honorarium.

On a sunny day we were able to practise walking meditation to the sea. We sat down on the beach, watching the waves on the shore. I was sitting close to Thay. At one point he asked me, "What is everyone doing?" I probably said something like, "Looking at the waves." Thay said, "They are turning neutral feelings into pleasant feelings."

"How are they doing that?" I asked.

"What do you think?"

"By thinking," I said.

"No, by being aware," Thay said.

Sitting on the beach with Thay and the Sangha, enjoying the fresh sea air, was not a time to lose oneself in neutral feelings. It was a chance to enjoy a happy moment.

One day I sat next to Thay at suppertime, and Thay said when I had finished, "Let's go and take some more." I probably remember this because Thay said it as if we were friends, and also because I thought that spiritual people were not expected to be interested in food, especially not meant to be so indulgent as to have more food after the first helping. In this simple statement, I saw a kindness and generosity that I wasn't accustomed to seeing in my spiritual teachers. One day someone spilt some milk on the floor. I was mopping it up and I saw Thay looking at me very deeply. I wondered if Thay was reading my mind. It was just natural for me when I saw the milk had been spilt to mop it up. It came from a sense of responsibility I had as organizer of the retreat, and I felt peaceful enjoying doing something I had seen my mother do many times. When I felt Thay looking at me, it increased my concentration.

Before I met Thay, I had read his teachings on mindfulness and been in touch with the deep insights of Thay's poetry, but now I could bathe in the teachings much more deeply because Thay was the living embodiment of what he taught.

My aunt had knitted for me a thick brown sweater, which kept me warm as we sat in that draughty castle. It seemed important to me to be wearing brown like Thay and Sister Chan Khong. I felt we were one.

Thay gave a Dharma talk on the last day of the retreat that touched me deeply. The talk was on the Heart Sutra and emptiness. This sutra had until then been a closed door for me; the commentaries I had seen and heard on it had been complex and difficult to understand. In that Dharma talk, I observed Thay closely as he held up a sheet of paper and asked, "When is its birthday? When will it die?" Together with Thay, the retreatants examined all the elements that had come together to make the sheet of paper possible. Was the birthday of the paper when it rolled off the paper machine, or was it when the pulp was put into the paper machine? For the pulp to be there the trees had to be there; for the trees to be there the cloud had to be there. Thay asked us if we could see a cloud in the paper.

I looked at the piece of paper to see the cloud floating in it. The piece of paper was truly empty of a separate self—this the intellect could understand—but Thay transmitted something more than what the intellect can grasp. Thay's own emptiness and my emptiness were in it too.

When the retreat was over, we went to Birmingham where Thay was to give a public talk for Vietnamese people. Only ten people came. Thay did not say anything about the size of the audience and gave a talk as if there were one hundred people. I did not know anything about organizing for Thay. I thought that organizing consisted of hiring a venue and that was it. So I did not do any advertising and consequently only a handful of people turned up. The only time I heard Thay reprimand someone on that tour was when they kept adding more events to the itinerary. Thay said: "If you crack the bell, it will not sound anymore," reminding us that Thay is not a superman, and we could not go on adding more and more events to his schedule.

We returned to London and Thay gave a talk in the Quaker Centre in Euston Square. After the talk, Thay asked me to speak a bit about the Buddhist Peace Fellowship to the audience. Then we went outside to prepare to go home. It was already very late. Thay said, "Thay is tired, cold, and hungry. Let's go and have something to eat." We found a Chinese restaurant where we ate noodle soup and sautéed vegetables for dinner. After that it was time to say goodbye. Thay was going on to the Buddhist monastery, Amaravati, which had been established just outside London by Thai Theravada monks in the UK in 1984, but I had to go to work the next day. When we arrived at my lodgings in Cricklewood, Thay got out of the car and gave me a hug. I was rather surprised and very moved. Thay asked me to come to his practice centre in Plum Village in July and stay for a month free of charge.

How lucky I felt as I went to sleep that night! How lucky to have met Thay, although I was on my own again. I was reinspired. I joined a Tibetan Sangha in London (there was no Sangha in Thay's tradition there at that time). I attended a weekend retreat with the Tibetans. They practised prostrating to a hundred Buddhas. Each Buddha had a name. There was even one Buddha of Mindfulness, before whom I felt much gratitude, as Thay had taught mindfulness to me. I was very happy that, having practised with Thay, I now knew how to prostrate. Before I'd met Thay, I'd had a strong resistance to prostrating myself before anything. For me it was just an outer form. Thay taught me the deeper meaning of prostration—surrendering all ideas of a separate self and touching the qualities of great understanding, great action, and great compassion as being available in the here and now. My practice in that Tibetan-based Sangha was more successful because of what I had learned in the five-day retreat from Thay.

When I left India, Anila Pema had told me that I would meet my teacher in my native land and that he would not be

Tibetan. It was true that since I met Thay in England I have never looked on any one else as my root teacher.

It was time to go back to schoolteaching. I had a post as a "supply teacher," who stands in for another teacher when they're sick, in the East End of London, which was then a poor area with a very high rate of unemployment. I lodged in a Quaker house. It was not easy to teach in the East End because the children knew just how hard it would be when they left school to find employment. Even people who had qualifications were out of work, so they did not have the motivation to study to pass examinations. What I was teaching them probably did not have anything to do with what they encountered in their daily lives. One time a girl hit me, not very hard, but all the same it upset me. I don't remember having made friends with any of the other teachers, but that wasn't the most difficult thing. The difficult thing was that I was teaching subjects that I was not expert in because I was a supply teacher. I did not teach what I was used to teaching, and above all the children did not want to learn. Before I had taught in private schools or grammar school. This was my first experience of a secondary modern.

I was glad I had been to the retreat with Thay. In the early morning I would practise ten minutes of sitting meditation before going to work. I decided that from now on instead of taking the bus to school I would practise walking meditation at least half of the way to the school and back, so I could be in touch with the flowers growing in people's gardens I passed and experience some peace of mind. It watered seeds of joy in me to see that even in this poor neighbour-hood people had found time to plant roses. I also practised deep relaxation as taught to me by Sister Chan Khong. As soon as I came home, I would take off my coat and lie on the floor. I let all the perceptions and memories of the day fall away from me into the floor beneath. Only in that way did I have enough strength to face the next day.

CHAPTER TWELVE

Plum Village

A T THE BEGINNING of July in 1986 in my thirty-seventh year, I took advantage of the summer holidays to respond to Thay's invitation to go to Plum Village. I went on the hovercraft to Calais and then travelled down to southwest France by train, to Sainte-Foy-la-Grande. French provincial stations were familiar to me from childhood, the long, often deserted platforms stretching into fields under sunlight. I did not have to wait on the platform. Sister Chan Khong had arranged for me to be met by Ellen, a North American laywoman who had joined us for the retreat in England and was now staying in the Upper Hamlet of Plum Village. She took me to an old yellow Renault Quatrelle and drove me the eighteen kilometres to the Upper Hamlet of Plum Village.

We drove along small winding roads passing through villages, forests, and agricultural land with sunflowers and ripening fields of wheat. At one point we left the Sainte-Foy to Eymet road and climbed the hill toward Thénac. Then we turned down a narrow track with vineyards on one side and an oak forest on the other. It was rocky soil with rocks appearing from the earth everywhere. As the track ended to become a forest path we turned again and saw the buildings of the Upper Hamlet; a farm house and farm buildings that had housed several families who had worked the land here. There were so many rocks I wondered what the farmers

could have cultivated. Eventually the younger people in the settlement had decided to look for an easier way of earning a living and left for the towns. This farm, as well as the farm that now constitutes the Lower Hamlet, were for sale in 1982 at a very low price. What better place could there be for Thay and Sister Chan Khong to come and build a Pure Land? Their aspiration was to establish a place where people could come and experience a spiritual life, where you can do one thing at a time with full awareness of what you are doing. When my mother came to stay in the Upper Hamlet some years later, she enjoyed so much the views from there across the fields of plum trees, vineyards, and wheat fields down to the valley and the forests on the other side. I have been able to practise sunset and sunrise meditation from the Upper Hamlet to enjoy these magnificent scenes without thinking about anything.

When we arrived, Thay was sitting on a hammock in a grey monk's robe. In England I had only seen Thay in brown. It was a very hot day and the grey short robe was more suitable for the weather. As we approached, Thay looked at me and his first words to me were, "Here is India, India is here." I thought at first that Thay was referring to the weather, meaning it was as hot here in France as it is in India. His statement was deeper than that. To me India was home, at least my spiritual home, and I believed my spiritual home could not be found anywhere else. Perhaps I had told Thay when we were in England how much I missed India and "Here is India" meant "You have arrived; you are home." Everything I was longing for was here.

It was the first day of July. Thay was in the Upper Ham-

Newly arrived in Plum Village.

let to prepare for the Summer Opening, Plum Village's major annual retreat when people of all ages from all over the world gather to practise together.

Thay showed me to the room I would be staying in. It is now the bookshop in the Upper Hamlet and was then called "Young Moon." I was touched that Thay would do something like that himself and not ask someone else to do it. Although many things needed overseeing for the preparation of the hamlet, Thay did everything in a very relaxed way as if he had nothing else to do but be there for you. I liked the room and its name, the small slither of a moon that you see in the western sky, very much. It could not have been more simple and uncluttered. There were no shelves or cupboards. There was a bamboo cane suspended horizontally from the ceiling to hang your clothes on, a lamp, a bed, and a chair. It felt very relaxed, like home, though it was very different from the home I had been brought up in.

There were three main buildings in use. One was the stone house where Thay had his room. Another was the meditation hall, which had rooms on all sides; my room was one of these. The other was the kitchen. There was an old cow house, which had been left as a cow house. Ellen had bought some avocados and found me something to eat.

Sister Chan Khong was in the Lower Hamlet, preparing for the Summer Opening there. Over the next few days some Vietnamese children arrived. Thay took good care of them and they enjoyed being in Thay's presence. You would often see Thay walking with them.

I helped prepare the rooms for the Summer Opening. We made the beds out of four large bricks and a board. On top of the board we placed a thin foam mattress covered by a sheet and a sleeping bag. Everyone slept on these beds. There were two bathrooms; one in the stone house and one attached to the stone house on the outside.

I couldn't help comparing Plum Village with my stay in India and, although it sounds spartan, I felt the accommodations were luxurious. What was more, there was hot water in the showers and three proper meals a day. I realised that the spiritual life did not have to be one of such material hardship.

What a few years later would become the Transformation Hall was still a cattle stall. The meditation hall we used then was much smaller and was called Yen Tu, after the sacred mountain in North Vietnam where many renowned Buddhist masters had lived and practised; there was also the Buddha Hall, the place for ceremonies. Yen Tu Meditation Hall had also been a cattle barn, and you could still see the wooden posts that had been worn away in places by the cattle rubbing their backs. So at that time there were just two small meditation halls, the Yen Tu Meditation Hall and the Bamboo Forest Buddha Hall. Now they have both become offices and we have two much larger halls, the Transformation Hall and the most recently built Still Water Hall.

Thay had asked me to come to Plum Village in order to be able to deepen my understanding of the Buddhist practice in the Plum Village tradition, that is what we call the Plum Village Dharma Doors. Dharma Doors are ways into the practice of Buddhism. That summer Thay taught the Anapanasati Sutta (Majjhima Nikaya 118). Anapanasati, the mindfulness of breathing, is the most basic and essential Dharma Door. Mindfulness of breathing means that we are aware of the in-breath and aware of the out-breath. Our awareness naturally makes the breath deeper and slower and at the same time brings our mind and body together and makes them more peaceful. We can be mindful of our breath at any time and in any place. During the sitting meditation we practised:

> Breathing in, I know I am breathing in.
> Breathing out, I know I am breathing out.
> Breathing in, I calm my body.
> Breathing out, I smile.

It was as simple as that.

For the sessions of sitting meditation, we would sit close to and facing the stone walls. One day Thay came and sat next to me during the sitting. I felt the power of Thay's concentration and joy of meditation straight away.

I began better to master the Dharma Door of walking meditation. Observing Thay walk made me feel peaceful, and by following my breathing and feeling the ground under the soles of my feet I found I could walk as Thay did. In Plum Village we can walk as slowly as we like and walking slowly with awareness of every step is the best way to take care of a strong emotion and, if we are outside, to be in touch with the wonders of nature.

The Yen Tu Meditation Hall was very crowded during the Dharma talks, and people who could not fit in the hall sat in the doorway to listen. It was here that Thay taught some of us to invite the bell. He would take our hand in his to show us how to make a rounded movement as the inviter touched the rim of the bell. Thay told us to practise one hundred times, so that we could be ready to sit at the bell for sitting meditation. It may sound very simple to ring a bell, but it takes a long training to make the sound not too harsh nor too soft. The sound of the bell that we produce reflects the state of our mind. A peaceful mind of a well-trained bell master can bring peace to a whole congregation.

There was sitting meditation in the early morning and in the afternoon. We sat for eighteen minutes, then practised slow walking in a circle in the meditation hall, then sat for eighteen minutes again. Thay came to all the activities: tea meditation (when we come together to enjoy a cup of tea and a biscuit in silence and in mindfulness), and Dharma sharing (gatherings when we would share insights about our practice), as well as giving the Dharma talks.

Every week there was a recitation of the Fourteen Mindfulness Trainings. They are precepts created by Thay in

Saigon in 1966 based on the Ten Wholesome Practices, which are both Mahayana and Theravada practices. The recitation was either in English or Vietnamese and took place in the Yen Tu hall. I, like many others, was and still am very moved whenever I hear these trainings, because they encapsulate all that is so precious to me about the Buddhist practice and at the same time they are not "Buddhist" in a sectarian sense. Thay's niece Anh Huong, who was about twenty-five years old at that time, would help Thay by reading the trainings during this ceremony. The ceremony began with offering incense and the practice of prostration to be in touch with the qualities of Buddhas and bodhisattvas. Thay had put to music the English and French versions of the chanting of touching the earth as well as the opening and closing verses, which are chanted before and after the sutra is recited. But the Heart Sutra had to be be read in English; only the Vietnamese version could be chanted.

On one specific day during the retreat there was a transmission of the Fourteen Trainings. At some time toward the end of July, I was standing next to Thay when the bell was invited. After standing together and breathing for a while Thay asked me if I should like to become a member of the Order of Interbeing. In those days Thay knew all his disciples personally and would invite them as he saw fit to be ordained as core members of the Order of Interbeing, Tiep Hien, the order that Thay had founded in Vietnam in 1966. Up to this time that Order had consisted only of laypeople. I thought that Thay was asking me if I wanted to become a nun and as a visiting Vietnamese nun was standing nearby I asked, "Dear Thay, do you mean to become a nun like this nun here?" Thay said: "Sister Chan Khong (the Dharma name she had received in 1966 when she received the Fourteen Trainings) is a member of the Order. You would practise the Fourteen Mindfulness Trainings as she does. It would not mean becoming a nun."

The date was set for our ordination and I eagerly awaited it. For some reason it was cancelled at the last moment. I felt disappointed. I was looking forward to the ceremony. Then another date was set, and some time in August I received the Fourteen Mindfulness Trainings along with Joan Halifax (Chan Tiep, True Connection), who would later found Upaya Zen Center in Santa Fe, New Mexico; Cynthia Jurs (Chan Nguyen, True Source) the director of the Earth Treasure Vases project and her husband, Marlow Hotchkiss, and two Vietnamese ordinees, Nguyen thi Bich Thuy and Nguyen van An, Chan Dinh and Chan Minh. I was given the name Chan Duc, which means True Virtue. My lineage name was Peace of the Heart, Tam An. As an ordination certificate Thay had made a calligraphy in Chinese characters of my Dharma name (True Virtue) and my lineage name (Peace of the Heart, 心安).

Receiving a spiritual name is part of most Buddhist traditions and I had become acquainted with this custom when I took refuge in the Tibetan Buddhist tradition. It is said that your teacher gives birth to you in the spiritual life, so with that birth you also need a name. The lineage name links you to the lineage to which your teacher belongs. It also links you to the lineage of the teacher who founded your teacher's lineage, since before he founded his lineage he had belonged to a different one, the lineage of his own teacher.

Just after OI ordination. Left to right: Joan Halifax, Nguyen thi Bich Thuy, Marlow Hotchkiss, Cynthia Jurs, True Virtue, Nguyen van An.

Thay belongs to the Lieu Quan lineage, which began in the eighteenth century in central Vietnam from the master Lieu Quan. The Vietnamese tradition is that when a master founds a lineage he writes a poem and each word of the poem is used for the first part of the name of the successive generations. Thay belongs to the eighth generation of the Lieu Quan line so the first part of his lineage name (Trung) is the eighth word of the poem. Thay's disciples belong to the ninth generation so the first part of the name is the ninth word of the poem, "Heart." Lieu Quan belonged to the Linji school from China so Thay and his disciples also belong to that school. One of Master Lieu Quan's teachers was Chinese. The idea of a lineage is that there is an unbroken transmission of the Dharma from the time of the Buddha until now.

The name Peace of the Heart was easy to understand although it may not always have been easy to practise. I did not know what to make of the name True Virtue, Vraie Vertu in French. I tried looking to see if I could find some virtue in myself and I could not find very much. Some days later as Thay was sitting in his hammock in the Upper Hamlet, he told me that it was a good name. This helped me to be more interested in the name. I wanted to know why it was a good name. A Dharma name is an opportunity to practise. A Dharma name is telling you that you have this seed of true virtue but it needs to be developed. Thay says that a good teacher is someone who helps you find the teacher in yourself and I wanted to find out about this name rather than ask Thay to tell me more.

There is virtue and there is also true virtue. Virtue may just be something that is visible on the outside, like being present at all the practice activities, but there is no real content inside. Virtue in the first place means quality. People talk about the quality of life, and the quality of my life is living deeply each moment of life—what I have a chance to do as a nun. Virtue can also mean morality: to live in such a way that I do not make others suffer and that I am able to bring more happiness into the world. The Buddha once said that people praised him for his virtue of eating one meal a day, not going to shows, not receiving gold and silver. But there was virtue that went deeper than this: the discovery of teachings that go very deep. Thay taught me on many occasions to manifest a quality of truth and authenticity. One look, one word from Thay would let me know when I was not being entirely authentic.

Toward the end of the summer retreat I went down to the Lower Hamlet and stayed in the Plum Hill building, a building that had once served as the place for drying tobacco and had now been converted into a dormitory. Lower Hamlet, as its name suggests, is in a valley from where you can see the hill where Upper Hamlet lies. There were farmhouses and farm buildings of stone. The two huge centenarian oak trees were a focal point. Under them was a wooden kiosk where you could buy Vietnamese sweet dishes, and a wooden platform where you could sit and look out over the then–newly planted plum trees and fields stretching down to the forest. The path for walking meditation was very inviting. It began at the Plum Hill building and curved down to a couple of ponds joined by a little stream. A bridge had been made over this stream and crossing it you found yourself in a forest. The walking meditation would pause there and people would find a broken branch or tree trunk to sit on, or even some bricks that had been brought down there, and sit in silence turning neutral feelings into pleasant feelings. Later on, when I came to live in Lower Hamlet, I would spend many hours in this place. The walk would continue through the forest and then leave the forest by a little path which joined the path we had walked down on.

The Lower Hamlet was the more Vietnamese of the two hamlets. Though there were Vietnamese retreatants in the Upper Hamlet too, most of the European and North American retreatants were in Upper Hamlet. Sister Chan Khong had overall responsibility here. The atmosphere in the Lower Hamlet was like that of a large family reunion. You could feel the delight of the Vietnamese refugees who for

After OI ordination with Sister Chan Khong.

one month could return to a small version of their homeland. Large greenhouses sheltered the tender Vietnamese
vegetables and you could hear Vietnamese spoken wherever you went. Once the schedule was not well commu-
nicated between the two hamlets and the Upper Hamlet
residents arrived unexpectedly for an activity which the
Lower Hamlet did not know was happening. Sometimes
activities would begin a little late or run over time but no
one worried. By the end of the day we had done everything
we wanted to do.

We would have sitting meditation first thing in the morning. Then there was breakfast, which consisted of *biscottes*
and jam. A Vietnamese practitioner owned or worked in
a *biscotte* factory and we received offerings of many *biscottes* from him. There was a Dharma talk or consultation
in the morning. Thay did not give a talk every day; some

mornings there would be a personal consultation with Thay. We practised walking meditation outside down to the two ponds and then sitting by the ponds for a while before returning through the forest. Then we had lunch. The first twenty minutes of the meal were in silence and I noticed that many of the children practised this too. I asked one boy if he enjoyed eating in silence and he said that the food tasted better. There was a children's programme for learning Vietnamese language, culture, and history. Vietnamese lay friends and Sister Chan Khong volunteered to give these classes. For adults there were Dharma sharing and tea meditation sessions.

Thay would come down twice a week to give a Dharma talk in the Red Candle Meditation Hall. It was quite a formal occasion; the senior layman Anh Le Nguyen Thieu would formally invite Thay to come to teach the Dharma and would lead Thay from the Persimmon Building, where Thay was waiting, to the Dharma Hall with a bell and incense. Thay continued to teach the Sutra on the Mindfulness of Breathing that year.

As the end of the month-long Summer Opening retreat grew near, I was beginning to think about having to go back to England to teach. Sister Chan Khong told me not to think about leaving just yet, because maybe Thay was going to ask me if I wanted to stay on. One day when we were in the Upper Hamlet, Thay asked me if I would come for a walk. When we had been walking for a while Thay stopped and asked, "Would you like to stay on as a resident of Plum Village?"

"Yes," I said, but after thinking a bit I said, "Dear Thay, what do you want me to do here?"

"You can just be yourself," Thay said, and then after a pause, "If you like you can plant a few green vegetables for the autumn and winter."

I had enjoyed the Summer Opening so much that I was very happy to be able to stay on in that wonderful atmosphere. I was also relieved that I did not have to go back to London to teach.

Soon after that in the autumn of 1986, Thay and Sister Chan Khong had to leave for Australia to teach and to help the Vietnamese refugees in the refugee camps in Hong Kong and the Philippines for some months, and things were very different without their presence in Plum Village. So far I had only really been in touch with Thay and Sister Chan Khong and other friends and retreatants I had come to know during the summer retreat. Now I found we were a community of twelve living in the Lower Hamlet in the building that is now the kitchen and refectory—myself, four young Vietnamese men newly arrived from the refugee camps who were former boatpeople escaping Vietnam, and in the adjacent Persimmon Building, a refugee family: father, mother, four children, and their uncle. The eldest child was twelve and the youngest less than two. They made a living by growing Asian vegetables and selling them in Bordeaux, the largest provincial city of southwest France where there was a sizeable Asian community about an hour-and-a-half drive away. The father was an ordained member of Thay's order, the Order of Interbeing. He was Anh Le Nguyen Thieu, the Elder of Plum Village, and he would organize the recitation of the Fourteen Mindfulness Trainings every two weeks. Apart from him and one other refugee who had received the Fourteen Mindfulness Trainings at the same time as I had, no one in Lower Hamlet was interested in the practice. There was no more sitting meditation, walking meditation, Dharma discussion, tea meditation, and so on.

Sister Chan Khong had told me she wanted me to be an elder sister for the four young men, but I was not up to the task. To begin with I did not speak very much Vietnamese. True, I had learnt to sing Dharma songs and started to read Thay's books in Vietnamese but as far as everyday conversation was concerned, I did not know much. So this was an opportunity for me to learn more just by listening and speaking as well as I could. I never used other teaching materials to learn this language, just listening to Vietnamese people talking and Thay's Dharma talks and books.

Having spent many years in refugee camps, the young men needed help to adjust to a new situation. I understood that in the refugee camps there is very little to do. It is like a prison where the refugees are just waiting to be accepted to go to live in a third country, and they become used to having nothing to do other than playing cards. They cooked meat and smoked a large amount of cigarettes. I tried to help them stop smoking so much in the house but to no avail. One brother would go shopping for us, and since I ate on my own, I would often eat instant noodle soup.

That winter it snowed heavily and since in that part of France there was no equipment to clear the roads, we were not able to leave Lower Hamlet. The wild animals were very hungry and wild boar came nearby looking for food. We had collected just enough wood in the months before to keep ourselves warm, but the pipes froze and so we collected snow to melt and use for drinking water. Later Thay would teach us using the metaphor of preparing wood for the winter. We live deeply and appreciate the times when things are going well so that we nourish ourselves and have spiritual strength when things do not go well. Once the snow has fallen, it is too late to go and collect wood. Life has its wonderful message of impermanence that encourages us to practise and helps us be grateful for everything that is available for us in the present moment.

The half-cylindrical clay tiles of the roof were not cemented into place but cupped into each other so that they could slip and leave gaps that allowed the rain, wind, or snow to come in. The people of the neighbourhood climbed onto their roofs at least once a year and replaced the tiles that had slipped out of place. In the past, not many tiles needed to be replaced, but with the invention of the supersonic aeroplane this changed. Planes would break the sound barrier just over Plum Village and the resulting boom shifted the tiles. Nowadays people prefer to cement their tiles into place.

In 1986 that aeroplane had only recently been invented, and none of us knew about repairing roofs and we were subjected to numerous leaks. The attics of our buildings were full of buckets and tubs to collect rain before it penetrated the ceiling beneath, but we never managed to cover all the leaks, and if the rain was heavy enough it was sure to come into your bedroom. I would move my bed to the other side of the room but the leak would follow me.

Not only rain came in but snow too. In the first two years I lived in Plum Village it snowed significantly and the snow stayed for many days. There was enough room between the tiles for powdery snow to blow into the attic. The snow in the attic could reach a depth of six inches and it was important to clear it because its weight could break the ceiling of the room below. Clearing snow in the attic was very cold work. We filled rubbish bins with snow and hauled them out, but they were very heavy to move. There was no heat up there and the bitter wind blew in through the tiles. Soon my hands and feet were frozen stiff.

Each bedroom had a small ceramic and iron wood-burning stove. We would buy these second-hand from local people who no longer needed them. There was a hole in the wall for an aluminium pipe to take the smoke outside. The stove did not hold much wood so after an hour or so, if you did not replenish it, it would go out. We found the wood on the Plum Village land of the Lower Hamlet, which consisted of twenty-one hectares. I helped the four young Vietnamese refugees who lived in Plum Village at that time by splitting logs and sawing branches to put in the stoves. These young men went out and cut down trees for us.

Our neighbour, Monsieur Mounet Père, was a bodhi-sattva. One day he came into the kitchen where we were sitting and said that in France you cannot cut down trees on other people's property. It seems that the young Vietnamese refugees did not know where our property ended. To put right this ignorance he took us to the Mairie (the town hall) and showed us the plan of the different parcels of land that had been purchased for the Lower Hamlet. He then took us on a tour of the boundaries, showing us exactly where Lower Hamlet territory began and ended.

M. Mounet Père was a good man. He promised Thay he

would not go hunting during the annual Summer Opening retreat in Plum Village. He taught us many things about gardening and cultivation of the land. He baked *tartes aux pommes* (apple pies) and sold them and when his oven—which he had made himself—was hot, he allowed me to bake our bread in it. Whenever I needed help in practical or administrative matters and Sister Chan Khong was not there, I could go to him.

M. Mounet, with his dog, Kiki, would visit us almost every day to find out how we were doing and to offer us any advice or help we might need. I was truly grateful for his presence in those early days. His home, the large stone farmhouse at the entrance to the Lower Hamlet, is now a part of the Hamlet and is called the Cherry House after the cherry trees he had planted in his garden. After about five years, he died unexpectedly one night. We prayed and sent spiritual energy for him. Sister Chan Khong went to his house to send energy over the body. She had not witnessed undertakers washing a corpse before, since in Vietnam it is always the family that washes and clothes the body of a loved one, and she was shocked by what she saw as a disrespectful way of treating the body. We went to the burial in the local cemetery, and every year on All Souls' Day we place flowers on his grave and offer prayers and incense for M. Mounet and other local friends who have passed away.

Sister Chan Khong has always encouraged her younger monastic sisters to perform a ceremony of sending energy on that day to those who have passed away in the neighbourhood, and we did this practice when we opened our centre in Vermont as we do now in Germany. I was always moved when I saw how Thay and Sister Chan Khong included whoever they met, whether Buddhist or not, within the embrace of their spiritual concern.

I used to spend time with one of the four children from the refugee family. His name was Nhat Tam, "Sun Heart" after Thay's book *The Sun My Heart*.[4] Tam was then four or five years old and is now a monk in another Buddhist tradition. When his parents would go to Bordeaux to sell vegetables, I took care of him. He liked eating fruit very much, but it was difficult to persuade him to eat rice. One day we had beetroot and its juice made the rice red. He ate it all. So I used the trick of making the rice red. In the autumn and summer we would go on fruit-eating walks. At that time there were many old fruit trees in the Lower Hamlet: plums, greengages, pears, apples, peaches, grapes, and many blackberry bushes. He would pick a blackberry from each bush and evaluate its taste and sweetness, then he would give me one.

Later on one of the Vietnamese refugees bought a clothes washing machine. Up until then we had had to wash everything by hand. Tam would draw a chair up in front of it and watch the clothes wash from beginning to end. There came a time when Tam had to begin to go to the school in Loubès-Bernac. He did not like it at all and it was hard to get him on to the school bus in the morning. It must have been difficult for him at school because his parents did not speak French and neither did he.

At that time, we could not yet call ourselves a Sangha in the strict sense because we did not all share the same spiritual discipline as does a Sangha. Thay and Sister Chan

Khong loved us all and held us in their embrace of care and affection. They wanted us to practise mindfulness every day as part of our ordinary daily living but somehow we were not there yet.

Thay was very patient with us. Sister Chan Khong had instructed me to teach French to the four young men. This was not too easy for one of the young men who was not confident in his ability to learn French and enjoyed above all playing volleyball just at the time when the French class was happening. Thay had asked the young men to, in his absence, prepare a meditation hall for the winter in what is now the registration office in the Lower Hamlet, because the Red Candle Hall was too big to heat for our small community. Just before Thay and Sister Chan Khong returned, the young men suddenly had to start working in order to complete the task, which they had until then ignored.

When Thay came back from the Southeast Asia and Australasia tour, he shared with me that Plum Village would become a practice centre and the people who lived there would be united by their practice. I was very happy and reassured when I heard this and wondered how it would happen. When they were not travelling to teach the Dharma, or during the one-month Summer Opening for families, Thay and Sister Chan Khong lived in a small building not far away that we called a hermitage. They would visit us from time to time. Sometimes the visit was unexpected and sometimes Sister Chan Khong would call us in advance to say that Thay would come and give a teaching. Everyone knew that Thay did not want us to drink wine or eat meat, but there was no formal regulation against it. When they knew that Thay was coming, the Lower Hamlet residents would hurriedly hide away all traces of wine and meat. I never drank alcohol or ate meat myself but I did not need to tell tales to Thay; he seemed to know what was happening whether we told him or not.

Growing vegetables and other crops such as soya beans, oats, and rapeseed was a way of making a living for our small community. The local farmers were very supportive and lent us their machinery to cultivate the land. They also transmitted to us their way of farming, which was not organic. Unlike other members of my community, I had experience in organic gardening. To me it seemed the only sane way to produce vegetables and fruits. To the others it seemed a crazy idea. I had been sure that Thay would support this idea but he was firm that there should be a consensus in the community. We all know how much Thay cares about the environment. Long before coming to Plum Village, Thay had organized the Dai Dong conference in Sweden one year as an alternative to a governmental conference on the environment organized in South Africa. Many delegates to that official conference had a vested interest in not protecting the environment and that is why Thay and his friends saw the need for an alternative.

Under Thay's guidance, I began to learn the practice of living in harmony in a community. Thay said that all of us must sit together, discuss, and agree on how we were going to cultivate the land. During this discussion I was a minority of one. Thay suggested that I take a small plot of land and cultivate it organically. Others would see the results and then we could increase the size of the organic garden.

This is entirely in the spirit of the Fourteen Mindfulness Trainings—we do not force others to accept our views by any means, including authority. Since Plum Village has become a practice centre, Thay has always encouraged the monks, nuns, and lay friends who live in Plum Village to grow their own vegetables so that we can eat organically at little expense. Plum Village now has three very large, organic vegetable gardens called "Happy Farms" in the Lower, Upper and New Hamlets. Working in the garden is a way to practise mindfulness in the open air.

One of the young men in the community had made and sold tofu and bean sprouts in the refugee camp where he had been in Hong Kong, and he taught me how to do this. We grew the bean sprouts in a large old wine barrel—our region is part of the Bordeaux wine-producing land—nearly full of sawdust. The tofu we made by soaking the beans overnight, then pulverizing them in an electric grinder; we put the ground beans in a muslin sack and pressed them. The first milk, which we pressed out by kneading the sack, was thick and creamy. Then we added more water and the milk was less creamy. The first milk was made into tofu and the second, when cooked, was kept for soy milk. When the creamy milk for tofu came to the boil we added a tablespoon of calcium carbonate, or salt or lemon juice and miraculously the liquid gelled. Then we pressed it into shape in a mould for several hours under a lid held down by heavy stones. It was not always successful. Sometimes the gelling didn't happen and there was little we could do with the resulting liquid. I never knew exactly why it was not successful, but there must have been causes and conditions.

Mustard greens grew well in Lower Hamlet. If you dropped seeds on uncultivated land they would germinate. If the plants were left to go to flower they would seed themselves. With so much mustard green we could make pickle. Pickles also need to have the right conditions in order to be successful. Thay taught me how to make mustard green pickle. To make pickles all we needed was mustard green leaves, salt, and water. First we sterilized the ceramic or glass pots we used to make the pickle in, because the presence of the wrong kind of bacteria will stop the proper pickling process and lead to a bad-smelling, mould-covered result. You do not need to cook the mustard greens; you just pour boiling water over them, having put a tablespoon of salt in the pot first. You press the mixture down with a heavy lid and leave it for three or more days, depending on how cold the weather is. We learned not to look at the pickle too early, because opening the lid could also cause foreign bacteria to come in.

The first time I made mustard green pickle, it did not work. I was disappointed just as when tofu failed to gel. Somehow I learned from my mistakes. At first I would think, "What a waste of material resources and time!" Then I would look back and discover at what stage the process could have gone wrong, and the next time I would do something differently.

In May 1987, I was joined by another sister whose name was Thanh Minh. She was a former refugee whom Thay and Sister Chan Khong had met on the tour of the Southeast Asian refugee camps and sponsored to come to France. Sister Chan Vi (Thanh Minh) was the first member of my Sangha that I lived with twenty-four hours a day. Sister

True Emptiness was also one of the first members of my Sangha, but she didn't live with me twenty-four hours a day. When I'd lived in India I had already learned about living with people of a different culture. I knew that things which might seem quite natural to me might be offensive to someone from another culture. When we live with people from other cultures we need to practise mindfulness and be aware of our actions of body and speech because we can easily offend someone without meaning to. I remembered in India when we lived in the little hut on stilts, and underneath was kept the rice and other things, and from time to time a nun would have to go under the hut to bring something out. When I was sitting in the hut it was my duty to leave the hut and stand outside for the nun to be able to go underneath because it would be disrespectful to sit on top of the nun going under the hut. That is not something I learned in England. At first I was very offended if, in the pouring rain, in the middle of the monsoon, I was told I had to leave the hut so they could go underneath and fetch something. But I learned that this is part of politeness, a way of not offending people and keeping people happy; so after a while I managed to do it without feeling any resistance in my heart. With Sister Chan Vi, I also tried my best to learn about what is considered correct in the Vietnamese culture.

One thing we shared in common was that we both liked gardening. She loved being in the garden. When she had been in Vietnam, she had spent time in a temple in the mountains, and she had looked after the garden there. In our little garden we grew quite a few Vietnamese vegetables. Actually, our garden was under plastic because they wouldn't have grown outside. Whenever you went into that garden you could smell the fragrant herbs. Every morning we would rise early and go straight out into the garden because there were many slugs and they would eat everything up if you were not careful. We would pick up the slugs and take them out into the forest in a bucket. We pulled up any weeds. Once we had looked after the garden a little we would go to the meditation hall and practise sitting meditation together.

It was very different from the organic farm in Cheshire where I had worked four years earlier. In a practice centre one has time for this kind of activity and it becomes a meditation in itself. The garden is a wonderful place to practise. The greenhouse is like a meditation hall. The aroma of incense is the aroma of coriander leaves and mint and celery. The mind is the greenness of the plants and the discrimination of what is weed and what is vegetable; somehow the mind needs to discriminate between what is a positive and what is a negative thought.

If it was summertime we would go into the Red Candle Hall. In the winter it was too cold. We didn't have any heat, so we would go into the little room next to the Red Candle Hall. Fortunately someone very kind saw that we wanted to practise and offered to give a donation to fix the roof so that snow and rain wouldn't come in anymore. That was the first time we had a big donation. Before that we were really quite poor. In the winter we heated the rooms with some wood stoves. But in order to have the wood we had to go out and saw it in the morning. We had a saw with handles on two ends. Sister Chan Vi held one end and I held the other, and

Gardening in Lower Hamlet, early 1990s.

we sawed the wood together. She said that in Vietnam she used to do the same. She would go into the forest, saw the wood, and sell it to help support her family.

I was very happy when Sister Chan Vi came. To be able to live together with even just one other person in a Sangha twenty-four hours a day is already wonderful. When you have a sister who also wants to practise with you, you receive a lot of energy in the practice. The energy to practise was not doubled, but it increased ten or a hundred times. She supported me very much. She had often wanted to be a nun when she was in Vietnam, and she really liked the practice. She wanted to practise sitting meditation, reciting the Fourteen Mindfulness Trainings, and chanting the sutras in Vietnamese. She chanted very well. She taught me how to chant the sutras. Sister Chan Vi was also a very good cook, and she showed me how to cook Vietnamese food.

Sister True Emptiness also supported me, and Thay was always patient. I don't think I was an easy younger sister to have. I think I have transformed quite a bit since then, but I haven't transformed everything since you can still see some of the weaknesses I had then. Sister True Emptiness was very patient with me and very open. She never showed any kind of discrimination at all. No one had any kind of strong racial discrimination, though sometimes we find it a bit easier to be with people of our own culture. But Sister True Emptiness is just as easy with people of different cultures as she is with people of her own. She used to ask, "Oh, would you like to eat some muesli? Would you like to eat some brown bread?" and things like that.

We also took care of the orchards of plum trees. The 1,250 plum trees planted in the Lower Hamlet are what gave Plum Village its name. That region of France is famous for a variety of plum trees called Pruneaux d'Agen, which are dried to make prunes. The trees had been donated by lay practitioners, many of them children who donated a plum tree from their pocket money. They knew that when the plums were harvested, the proceeds from selling them would be sent to Vietnam to support the poorest families. I and another lay practitioner who came to live in Plum Village in 1987 whose name was Duc and who is now a monk, learnt in a class for local farmers how to prune the trees and remove the suckers that sprang up around the base of the trees, sapping the energy that was needed for the higher branches.

Sister Chan Khong also had work for us to do that we all enjoyed doing: sending parcels of medicines to Vietnam. She always wanted to find ways to help her countrymen who were in distress. At first she tried to send money to the various social workers or to the people who needed it, but it never arrived. So she had the idea of sending parcels of medicines so that the recipient of a parcel could sell the contents—Western medicines were very valuable in Vietnam at the time—and have money to buy rice to eat. Each one of us had the responsibility of a certain number of recipients of these parcels. I would call myself Chan Duc, pretending to be a relation of the recipient. From time to time I would receive a thank you letter from the recipient. I felt moved reading these letters and the recipient believed I was Vietnamese living in France and shared with me the hardships they were going through and also their joy at receiving the parcel. We needed to receive these thank-you letters in order to know if the medicine had really arrived. It arrived sometimes but failed to arrive at others. Nevertheless, I understood that the cost of a stamp was very high and they had to sell the medicine before they could buy one and send their thank-you letter. I never met them personally and they had no idea who I was, but still I felt a very close connection. Now this kind of activity is no longer needed. Our monastery has a Love and

Understanding programme that raises funds for the poor and the distressed in Vietnam. Sister Chan Khong and the social workers who help her in Vietnam and the monks and nuns in our monasteries now have more reliable ways of bringing the resources to the places they are needed most.

A few months after Thanh Minh's arrival, Thay began to develop his idea of having Plum Village as a residential mindfulness practice centre. He asked me to draw up a "Constitution" for Plum Village, which would lay down the way ahead for practice. Residents of Plum Village would no longer be allowed to eat meat, drink alcohol, or smoke cigarettes. Those who felt they did not want to stay under those conditions could leave and Plum Village would help them find work and a place to live elsewhere. Without bearing any grudge the four young men agreed to leave.

After that, we began to take steps in making the plum orchard organic. We tried to find out about organic fertilizers. The sales representative told us about bone meal and dried blood. We asked him where he acquired such materials. He said that the local *abattoir* sold it to him. We did not feel we could participate in supporting the slaughter of animals, so we relied on planting nitrogen-fixing plants between the rows of plum trees, and using compost and cow dung. Plum Village has now been cultivating the trees organically for many years.

My conscious mind did not realise it, but deep down, the seed was sown. Soon after I had come to live in the Lower Hamlet, I realised I was home. It was a feeling of being at home that I had not felt since I was a child. Looking up at the hills of the Dordogne to the north, I was home.

Contemplating the white knobbed stones that made up the walls of the Red Candle Meditation Hall, I was home. These things had always been part of me and I had always been part of them.

When I talk about home, it's not just a spiritual sense of home—it's everything. The thing that made me feel spiritually at home was the feeling of being like a family in Plum Village. Thay and Sr. Chan Khong were really very kind and treated me as if I were a blood relation, their daughter or their niece. I remember one time early on, when I was in the kitchen in the Upper Hamlet, Thay and Sr. Chan Khong came in with an *ao ba ba*, a loose, brown shirt worn by Vietnamese peasants. And Thay said, "Try it on! Try it on!" So I tried it on. This gift made me feel I was part of the family of Plum Village from the very beginning.

At first Thay allowed me to dream of my Indian home, perhaps because India was part of Thay's dream too. Thay once said to me, "Although you cannot be in India you can dream of being there. For instance there is the little hut you make of bamboo with its banana leaf roof and there is the little garden you plant with mustard greens." Then later Thay would ask, "Have you ever felt that India is in London?" To which I answered a definite "No." Somehow I knew that India is not a place on the map. India is a place in my mind.

✳ PART THREE ✳

CHAPTER THIRTEEN

India with Thay

IN 1988 Thay announced a trip to India. I was very excited about this. One night in October we were practising a full-moon meditation while walking on the road in Lower Hamlet, and Thay said, "Next month we shall see the full moon in India."

One of the reasons Thay wanted to go to India was that he had just finished writing his book on the life of the Buddha, *Old Path White Clouds,* and Thay wanted to verify some things about the map in the book.

Thay had an Indian disciple, Shantum Seth, whom I had already met in Plum Village. He organized this pilgrimage for us to all the sites that are connected to important events in the Buddha's life. Thay, Sister Chan Khong, Thanh Minh, and I flew to Delhi at the beginning of November 1988. We stayed in a hotel and on the next day I had the chance to go to the airport in a taxi from the hotel and meet people coming on the pilgrimage with Thay, as they arrived from many parts of the world. There must have been at least thirty-five of us on that pilgrimage. For me it was exhilarating to be back in India—the sounds of people shouting in mixed English and Hindi, the sight of the flowering trees alongside the roads and the different scents brought back many happy memories.

From Delhi we must have taken the train to Lucknow and then the bus to Varanasi. We had quite a tight budget and stayed in the simplest of accommodations, sometimes sharing our room with the rats. After arriving in Varanasi we went everywhere by bus. I enjoyed the bus journeys very much, looking out of the window at the Indian scenery. Sometimes I could sit next to Thay. Someone had recently put to music the poem "In, out, deep, slow" in English and in Vietnamese. We would sing this in the bus. From time to time a bell would be invited to bring us back to the present moment. I took it upon myself to remind people to board the bus and became known for the phrase I used, "Thay is on the bus," to do this.

After visiting Varanasi and Sarnath we stayed in a Vietnamese monastery in Bodhgaya. The construction was not completely finished but it was comfortable. From there we could go to practise walking and sitting meditation under the Bodhi tree for two days. I walked behind Thay holding an umbrella to protect Thay from the sun. We sat at the foot of the Bodhi tree and Thay had the famous Vietnamese singer Ha Thanh, who was on the pilgrimage with us, sing the song "Tram Huong Dot" ("The Sandalwood Incense Has Been Lit").

We then had a chance to visit Uruvela and cross the Neranjara River on foot, feeling the sand between our toes, to visit the mountain where Prince Siddhartha (the Buddha to be) had practised self-mortification. In Uruvela Thay had asked for a tangerine meditation to be organized for the children. A certain number of children were invited but when others learnt what was happening, they flocked to the site so we had many more children than we had expected. We sat on the ground under the trees and Thay told the children how to eat a tangerine in mindfulness. As they were completely new to the practice it was difficult for some of them to sit still. Nevertheless it must have been a memorable occasion for all of them.

Throughout the trip children often came to join us. In the Bamboo Grove, near Rajagriha (Rajir), some children had breakfast with us.[5] It was a delight to watch how peaceful a child, who knew nothing about the practice, could become by sitting or walking next to Thay. We never gave money to the children who were begging or to adult beggars either, but made a collection that went to a charity that cared for poor children.

The mountain near Uruvela where Siddhartha had practised asceticism was very moving for me. Our visit there reinforced how much the Buddha was a human being. We came to the cave where a few Tibetan monks were living. Since we were the only visitors the monks let us spread our sitting mats and practise sitting meditation and chanting. It was the first time we chanted the Refuge Chant, which Thay had recently composed.

Only just before we arrived in Delhi had I learned that Thay was going to ordain Sister Chan Khong and Thanh Minh as nuns. I immediately thought: "Why not me too?" After all I had wanted to be a nun since I was nine years old and had seen how the nuns at my school lived; but that wish had never been granted. The path to being accepted as a nun had not been straightforward. When I heard Sister Chan Khong and my sister in Lower Hamlet, Thanh Minh, were to be ordained nuns in India I wanted to be part of that ordination too. After all, I was thirty-nine years old; I had waited long enough! I was very sad when I thought that maybe I couldn't become a nun with Sister True Emptiness and Sister Chan Vi. I thought, My goodness, if we come back to Plum Village and they are both nuns and I am not, I don't know if I could bear it. Thay said that is not a good reason for becoming a nun. But I don't think that was the only cause. The main cause was my bodhicitta, my deep desire to love and serve. I think that was there somehow. Maybe an additional cause was Sister Chan Khong, who intervened on my behalf. Thanks to her, Thay agreed.

In Bodhgaya I asked Thay if I could be ordained too. Again Thay told me that lay practice was quite sufficient. I should not feel that I had to become a nun just because two other members of our community were becoming nuns. If it were not for Sister Chan Khong's support, I would have given up then and accepted no as the final answer. She suggested I ask again. Thay said something like: "I don't believe it." Which was a way of saying Thay needed more time to think about whether his disciple was ready for ordination and also for his disciple to reflect on the question, "Are you sure?"

It was only when I asked the third time that Thay finally said: "Ask Sister Chan Khong to show you how to wear the sanghati robe." Without Sister Chan Khong's unwavering support, I should never have been ordained a nun; she showed great kindness toward me in allowing me to become a nun alongside her, seeing as she had been Thay's most loyal disciple for many years and I had only recently met Thay.

On November 15, 1988, Sister Chan Khong, sister Thanh

Chan Duc, Chan Khong, and Chan Vi in India right before their ordination.

Minh, and I were ordained on the Gridhakuta Peak (Vulture Peak) not far from the town of Rajagriha.[6] Thay had a special fondness for this mountain peak where he felt the presence of the Buddha as he expressed in the poem "The Old Mendicant." "The mendicant of old is still there on Vulture Peak, contemplating the ever-splendid sunset." When Thay had visited the mountain on an earlier visit with the venerable Mahaghosananda, Thay could feel he was watching the sunset with the eyes of the Buddha and he taught us that we could do the same.

We arrived very early in the morning so that we could watch the sunrise. A bus brought us monks, nuns, laymen, and laywomen to the mountain from Bodhgaya. We had a policeman to escort us because bandits live there and it is not safe to walk on the mountain in the dark. The moon had set and stars were brilliant against the black sky. It was

beautiful. The air was cool. We practised walking meditation on the path of dried mud, sand, and, in places, loose
stones up the mountain and we stopped from time to time
to sit down, and enjoy our breathing and the quiet surroundings. We reached the summit in time to practise sitting meditation before a beautiful sunrise.

Before we'd left France, my two sisters had already asked
for ordination and their request had been granted. Thus
they had come to India already equipped with the necessary robes. As for me, I had nothing because I had only been
granted my request at the last moment. Sister Chan Khong
lent me some of her own robes to wear.

When it was time for our ordination on the site of the
Buddha's hut on Vulture Peak, I knew I had nothing other to
do than to be present. I had complete confidence that Thay
could help me to receive monasticism. I was only a little
nervous because I had not quite recovered from a stomach
upset and I hoped it would not cause problems during the
ceremony. Once the ceremony had begun, I felt light and
at ease and could concentrate on dwelling in the present
moment. We had mats to kneel on but the rock underneath
was still quite hard and just before we had to stand up I realised that my legs had become numb. Somehow I managed
not to fall over.

On that beautiful morning in the presence of the fourfold
Sangha we were all three ordained in the simplest kind of
ordination ceremony. As witnesses we had the abbot of the
Vietnamese temple in Bodhgaya and an elder Vietnamese
nun who lived in India and a nun from Switzerland who
was on our pilgrimage. Sister Chan Khong and I were

Ordination on Vulture Peak, November 1988.

ordained bhikshunis (fully ordained nuns). We received the bhikshuni precepts and Thay explained a little about them. I had asked Thay if I could be ordained as a novice along with Sister Thanh Minh, who would take the name Chan Vi and receive the ten novice precepts, but Thay said I should ordain as a fully ordained nun with Sister Chan

Khong. Thay explained that the time I had already spent in Plum Village was a kind of novitiate. I trusted that Thay felt I was capable of being a bhikshuni.

After the ordination, we left the site of the Buddha's hut on the peak, which now is marked by a low wall, to allow other pilgrims who were beginning to arrive to come and worship and we went down the hill to a more secluded place to shave our heads. I was wondering what I would look like as a nun. Before I could use my hair to screen what I had always believed was a not very beautiful face. Now I could no longer do that.

When I was ordained I was very happy because I felt very light. I thought I had cut off everything that had bound me—the past and all the fetters—and they were all gone. The next morning when I woke up and put my hand on my shaved head, I felt very light, happy, and free and I thought, *This is the end of all attachment.* But when I came back to Plum Village, I realised that I hadn't at all cut off all my afflictions and fetters. I still got angry, I still became sad, and I still had a tremendous amount to transform. But I don't think I can ever be shaken in my aspiration, in my determination to realise as fully as I can in this lifetime my own transformation and my desire to help others to transform. I was thirty-nine when I ordained. It was a little bit late. I already had built up many worldly habit energies. Maybe my transformation is not as fast as other people's. It is slow, but it is there. Later when we were sitting in Jivaka's Mango Grove to eat lunch, Thay said that as a nun I looked much more beautiful than as a laywoman.[7] This was quite a relief because I had no mirror in which to see myself.

It was not until the evening after the ordination that we returned to Rajagriha. Thay wanted us to sit and enjoy the sunset just as the Buddha had done and use the Buddha's eyes as Thay had done in a previous visit. So we returned to the peak again. In 1988 the number of visitors to Vulture Peak was much smaller than it is now, so we could enjoy the silence and uncrowded atmosphere. We also had a police escort arranged by Shantum so we could enter and leave the mountain before and after official opening hours. We walked slowly down the mountain as the moon rose. The following two days we came back to enjoy a continuing practice in the wonderful atmosphere of that mountain. Thay also transmitted the Five and Fourteen Mindfulness Trainings to some of our party on the Vulture Peak.

The days were light and happy and I felt as if we had been transported to the Pure Land or paradise. The ordination had imposed a certain feeling of purity upon me, as if the weight of all my past suffering had been lifted. During the first few days after, I would wake up in the morning and make my accustomed movement to push the hair back off my face and discover there was no more hair to push back. Then I would remember I was a nun. My hair, my robe, and my precepts were different but I continued to practise in much the same way as when I had been a layperson. The practice of mindful breathing and mindful walking for a layperson is also the practice of a nun. The Chinese Zen Master Guishan Lingyou (771–853) says that being in the monastic Sangha with good spiritual friends is like walking in the mist: gradually your clothes become wet without you noticing it. Wearing the monastic robe you are more aware that you need to walk, sit, and stand in mindfulness. It would look funny to run when you are wearing a robe. Thay would say it is easy to be ordained a monk or a nun, but to continue the monastic practice is not so easy.

After Rajagriha we went to Nalanda. Trained in Classics, I always enjoy archaeological sites. They help us to be aware of impermanence and at the same time help us to be in touch with what was happening so long ago. Yes, thousands of monks once studied and practised here. The chief student of the Buddha, Shariputra, was born and died here. We wandered between the ruins of the buildings that had housed the enormous monastery and university, climbed over the rubble and felt very grateful for all the great masters of Buddhism (Shilabhadra, Dignaga, Xuanzang and many more), teachers of this university whose works we had read and studied.

We were driven by bus from Nalanda to Vaishali where the Buddha had ordained his aunt and stepmother Mahapajapati and many other women of the Shakya clan as nuns. When we arrived near Vaishali we were booked into a comfortable hotel. On the second day some members of the party said that they were tired and still needed a little more comfort. Thay wanted to go and stay in very simple accommodations nearer to the ancient Buddhist sites and said whoever wanted could go with him. I opted for another night in the hotel.

While in Vaishali, Thay gave a Dharma talk. Thay mentioned the acceptance of Mahapajapati and the Shakyan women as Buddhist nuns. After the talk Thay allowed questions. A woman asked why Buddhism was so discriminative against women. Thay said, "I do not discriminate against women. I want to make Sister True Virtue into a good Dharma teacher." Indeed the first three monastic disciples ordained by Thay in the West were women. In Vaishali we looked at some land where Thay thought we might establish an Indian Plum Village one day.

When we visited Kushinagar we laid our cushions out for a tea meditation and then followed Thay on a walking meditation. Looking behind us some people saw monkeys come, pick up the cushions, and run away with them very fast. Their owners ran after them but could not catch up. Luckily, after a while the monkeys grew tired of carrying them and everyone managed to retrieve their cushion. We enjoyed the practice of circumambulation led by Thay around the Nirvana Temple. We circumambulated the temple three times as a slow walking meditation. We took only one or two steps with each in-breath and out-breath and realised that we had nowhere to go and nothing to do other than to enjoy every step. We saw sala trees, the descendants of the two trees between which the Buddha had died. It was the full moon day that Thay had told me about one month earlier in Plum Village. It seemed that we had been in India longer than two weeks because so much had happened. In Kushinagar there was a Chinese temple, which had been founded by a nun but was now in the hands of Vietnamese monks, and Thay gave a talk there as we sat on the cool tiled floor. We visited the huge mound over where the Buddha's body had been cremated.

We crossed the border into Nepal to visit Lumbini, the place where, according to Buddhist tradition, Queen

Mayadevi gave birth to Siddhartha Gautama in 563 BCE, and the town, no longer inhabited, of Kapilavastu where the young Prince Siddhartha had been brought up.

Lumbini was much colder because it was further north. Visible in the distance, the Himalayan range was covered in snow. In the morning we walked out of our lodging to the very loud sound of hundreds of birds singing. It took us some time to discover the exact place where the Prince Siddhartha was said to have been born and the water source where he had received his first bath. At that time Lumbini had not been developed as a World Heritage site and there was only the old and very small Mayadevi Temple. We then went on to visit two nearby temples. The first was a Nepalese Theravada temple. The monk who was the abbot of that temple had the family name Shakya and I was surprised to learn that there were still identifiable blood descendants of Buddha Shakyamuni. He introduced us to other Shakyans. One was a young boy who wanted to become a monk and Thay offered to train him in Plum Village when he was old enough.

Just a few days after I had been ordained, seeing my shaved head and brown robe, a Nepalese laywoman came and prostrated at my feet. I did not know what to do and, out a sense of misguided humility, prostrated at her feet in turn. Thay scolded me. He told me that doing as I had done deprived the laywoman's prostration of any merit. She was not prostrating to me but to the ordained Sangha of the Buddha, which I was just representing. I should sit upright and enjoy my breathing when someone prostrated to me.

In Asian countries, laywomen often prostrate to nuns

to receive their blessings, and I have to be very clear with myself that this person is not prostrating to me, she is prostrating to the Sangha of the Buddha. I have to follow my breathing in order not to forget that I am not the object of that person's admiration. I also practise to see that I am one with the person who is prostrating.

After Lumbini we visited Kapilavastu and were guided by an archaeologist who showed us burnt grains from more than a thousand years ago. Kapilavastu had been burnt down several times. Now it is just an archaeological site and no one lives there. Two places claim to be the place where Siddhartha had lived; one is in India and one in Nepal. We were inclined to favour the one in Nepal.

Last of all in the Gangetic plain we visited Shravasti (Sahet Mahet) in Oudh in order to be able to pay respects in the Jeta Grove where the Buddha had led so many Rains' Retreats and given so many teachings to monks, nuns, laymen, and laywomen. When the Buddha left Shravasti to go on tour, the local people would miss him and Ananda had a sapling bodhi tree brought from Bodhgaya planted there in order for the people to be able to come and meditate. The descendant of that tree is still there today.

In that place there was a monastery with a stupa that belonged to the Chinese tradition but all the Chinese monks had left; there was just one English monk. Thay and another Vietnamese monk invited the Prajñaparamita drum and bell, much to our enjoyment. Listening to this bell and drum responding to each other, you can silence all your thinking and realise the wisdom of emptiness. Our pilgrimage had many light moments like this. Thay gave

Dharma talks and we visited the excavated sites of very ancient monasteries deep down in the earth below.

Then we flew to Bombay. We were to visit Pune and give a retreat for the Ambedkar Buddhists, the untouchables who had taken refuge in the Buddhist Three Jewels after their teacher Dr. Ambedkar, in order to be free of the Indian caste system. At our lodging, Thay asked for water and I went into the kitchen to ask for boiled water. However it cannot have been boiled. I realised later that I should have stood there and watched them boil it. Thay became quite ill and could eat nothing. However the next day he still managed a long trek across the hills to the house where the retreat was to be held and then led the retreat. The house had no electricity and the nights were very dark. We had a strange tea meditation with servers walking along the rows serving everyone with tea as in a Chinese monastery. In Plum Village no one stands up during the tea meditation. We sit in a circle and hand the tray of tea cups from one person to another, rather like in more innovative masses in which, after the priest has blessed the bread and wine, they are handed around in a circle from one person to another. The retreat was successful and people departed happy.

We visited the Ajanta caves which are not natural caves but monasteries carved out of the rocks, dating from the second and first centuries BCE. When I saw these "caves" I was amazed and could not imagine how people could have carved such beautiful temples decorated with frescoes and with statues that had been carved out of the rock. Thay particularly liked the Padmapani fresco, a painting of Avalokiteshvara holding a lotus flower. Thay allowed us to go and meditate in the cave we chose. I chose the cave with the *parinirvana* statue, the statue that depicts the death of the Buddha lying on his right side and his attendant Ananda standing at the Buddha's feet; I sat below Buddha's attendant also at the Buddha's feet. Then I sat in one of the monks' cells. At the entrance to each large cave, which had served as a meditation hall or place for reciting the scriptures, were a few monks' cells. Each cell had two stone benches, which had been beds for the monk and his attendant and an aperture carved out of the wall for the begging bowl of the monk. The entrance to the caves is closed at dusk for the night and normally everyone has to leave. Thay told us that on a former visit Thay had escaped the notice of the guards, staying for a whole week in the caves and living on bananas. The river in the valley below the caves is beautiful and we sat there on boulders in the river with some Thai monks who chanted in Pali for Thay. We listened to the chanting and the water flowing by.

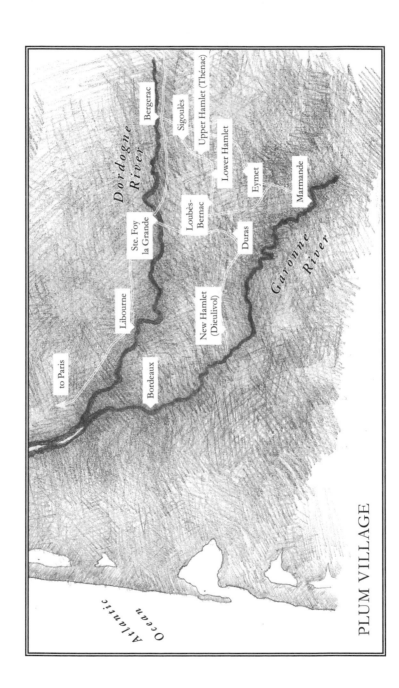

PLUM VILLAGE

CHAPTER FOURTEEN

First Years as a Nun

O N OUR RETURN to France, Thay led the first three-month Winter Retreat ever given in Plum Village, from December to February 1988–1989. From then on, a Winter retreat would be given every year. The subject was the Thirty Manifestation Only Verses of Vasubandhu, a Mahayana text on the nature of consciousness. That winter Thay taught in the Persimmon building in the Lower Hamlet in quite a small, cold room. Thay taught in Vietnamese and Sister Chan Khong translated simultaneously into French as there were just one or two Europeans and they understood French. We were a small audience of the three nuns who had just been ordained and six or seven long-term lay residents. There was a wood stove in the corner and a small whiteboard. Thay allowed me to teach the Sanskrit version of the Thirty Verses. This is not an easy text and I cannot imagine how I could have done anything more than translate word for word relying on what Thay had taught. If I found the text difficult, how much more so people who had never studied Sanskrit before. I complained that no one really wanted to learn Sanskrit and it was difficult to teach people who did not want to learn. In those days I did not hesitate to express my afflictions. Thay skillfully encouraged me by suggesting that I give a piece of chocolate to whoever managed to translate correctly a line of Sanskrit.

Thay encouraged me to learn how to offer incense in Vietnamese. When I did so, people could not help laughing because I sang the words to the wrong tones making the meaning quite other than what it should have been. Being laughed at made me very angry!

During that Winter Retreat, Thay had his ten or so disciples act out excerpts from the life of the Buddha or the patriarchs. These little performances would happen at the end of the Dharma talk. We also had to give unprepared mini Dharma talks. Thay would suggest a topic and have someone come up to present that topic for a few minutes. This is Thay's way of including his disciples in what he is teaching. From the days I first met Thay, I always felt that Thay saw my awakened nature and would therefore include me in what he was doing.

Fifteen years later when we had a large monastic Sangha in Plum Village, Thay began a new tradition that continues to this day. Before giving a Dharma talk Thay would always have the monks and nuns come up and chant before those who have come to hear the talk to show that it is not just Thay who shares the teaching. This was also a way of training us by giving us an opportunity to become used to standing in front of a large crowd.

Even in the first year after we were ordained, Thay began to teach us how to prepare a Dharma talk. First of all we should write down all we intended to say and then we should read it over. Then we should close the notebook and repeat from memory what we could remember. We could record ourselves and then listen to ourselves speaking and we could sit in front of a mirror to look at ourselves speaking. In my room there was a full-length mirror. I sat in front of it as I spoke to see how I looked.

In succeeding years Thay would have us organize a "Dharma Festival" where monks, nuns, laymen, and laywomen resident in Plum Village at the time would take turns as they were chosen to come before the Sangha, draw from the bell a topic written on a slip of paper, and give a ten-minute Dharma talk. In this case they had no time to prepare beforehand.

Thay taught us by means of Dharma talks and at the same time Thay taught us with his body. Every action of Thay could be received as a teaching. This kind of teaching is not something intellectual. It is received on deeper levels of consciousness like the mist soaking your clothes without your being aware of it. One day Thay told me to come to his hermitage to help print the annual Plum Village newsletter. I arrived eager to begin the work, which I knew would take the whole day. Thay told me that Thay had lit the stove in the printing room but the room was not warm enough to begin. (In those days we had no central heating.) Thay said that we would practise walking meditation and we went for a beautiful walk on the hill outside the hermitage. On our return, instead of going straight to the printing room to begin, Thay said we should drink tea. Thay as teacher made tea for his disciple. something that would never happen in a traditional monastery. Every action of Thay during this time contained mindfulness, concentration, and insight. Only after that did we go to begin the printing.

Thay had to teach me how to make a template. Thay told me that the printer was Thay's buffalo, just as a farmer needs a buffalo to help him plough his land. Every buffalo has its own particular character and a farmer needs to know the character of his buffalo in order to be able to work with it. Thay's buffalo had three speeds: fast, medium, and slow. One time Thay had tried the medium speed but Thay realised that when something went wrong, you might not notice it straightaway and you could not stop the printer in time to save wasting paper and ink. So after that Thay only ever used the slow speed. In that way you could observe every sheet of paper as it rolled out of the printer. This day of working with Thay was a lesson I shall not forget. It was not like anything I had experienced out in the world. Whenever I have a task to do it is a model for how to approach it. The work was done efficiently without any sense of rushing or needing to finish. Actually by the end of the day we still had two more pages to print but Thay said it would be easy for him to do the next morning.

As for collating the magazine, many people would help. Thay would put the pages in numerical order on a table and we would walk around the table picking up one page at a time adding them up until we had a complete magazine.

In 1989 Thay was given a video camera and we could see ourselves clearly, thanks to Thay's filming. He would film us walking, eating, talking and singing and we came to know how we looked from the outside and how firm our mindfulness practice was.

In May 1989 Thay allowed me to join him in the United States for part of that year's US tour. I arrived in Virginia and stayed with Thay in the house of Thay's niece, Anh Huong, the daughter of Thay's elder brother. I should have been happy to be included on the tour, but instead I was miserable. I remember one day that I was grumpy to the extent that Thay's elder blood brother commented on it. Thay was very patient with me. He just let me be miserable and suggested that I have a hot bath.

I felt left out because I did not understand much and I was not sure if I was in the right place at the right time. Thay was there to lead a retreat for Vietnamese retreatants, refugees, and others who had settled in the United States. There were forty or so attending and most communication occurred in Vietnamese. Naturally, I would miss important details and then let these small errors bother me immensely. We left Thay's niece's house to go to the retreat centre without my realising that we were going to a retreat and when I was shown my bed in a dormitory with rows of bunk beds, it occurred to me that we were not just going for a few hours but for four or five days. I had not had the sense to ask clearly before we left where we were going, and since I did not know that we would not be coming back to sleep, I had not taken my sanghati robe. In consequence, I was inappropriately dressed for the Five Mindfulness Trainings Transmission and had to sit at the end of the line of lay members. I was very new at that time and so it did not bother me too much where I sat. Moreover the energy of the retreat penetrated me and I felt much better than I had before the retreat began. Still, I couldn't help feeling disappointed in myself.

This was the first time I had heard Thay lead a total relaxation meditation as we all lay on the floor. I especially liked

Thay's encouragement to let go, let go of everything. Then he played a tape of the sound of waves on the shore. Everyone felt very spoilt by Thay.

I met Thay Giac Thanh, who was to become Thay's most realised disciple. When he passed away Thay wrote a gatha for him, saying that he had done what needed to be done.

> People know well you are a true practitioner
> Who has done what needs to be done.
> Your stupa is erected on the flank of the mountain.
> The laughter of children has rung out.

Although Thay Giac Thanh was a much more realised practitioner than I was, I like to think of him as an elder Dharma brother, just as sister Chan Khong is an elder Dharma sister. I practised alongside him in Upper Hamlet, Plum Village, and in Green Mountain Dharma Center and Maple Forest Monastery, Vermont. On meeting him I enjoyed his sense of humour, and he drove Thay, Sister Chan Khong, and myself to his temple in Washington, D.C. He did not seem to be afraid at all as we drove along the highway but quite a few horns were hooted at us and I kept an anxious eye out for the cars around us.

We visited a Vietnamese temple in Virginia after the retreat. There were many mosquitoes so we lit incense as we sat outside in the dark eating ice cream and listening to a monk chant *tan,* a special kind of chanting with bells and cymbal. This was the first time I had heard *tan* and I found it very moving. The next day laypeople arrived and Sister Chan Khong taught them walking meditation under the tall trees in the garden. I received my first grey novice robe which is fastened up the front, because some Vietnamese nuns thought it was not correct for such a newly-ordained nun to be wearing the brown robe, which is usually only worn by high nuns.

Looking back today, I am sorry I was not able to be more appreciative of these wonderful moments I could spend with Thay and the Sangha. I am sorry that I looked miserable and that I often complained. I still do not understand all the reasons why I was like this. I do believe I felt left out, not good enough, and needing everyone's attention. I was also afraid of being incorrect. I didn't realise that, in the end, the clothes I wore were not important. When I think back, I remember the wonderful atmosphere of love and relaxation. I wish I could have contributed more to it or at least been more appreciative of it at the time.

We went to the Omega Institute, a yoga and meditation centre in upper New York State. It rained every day and everything was very green. I walked very slowly behind Thay to the session of sitting meditation in the mornings holding an umbrella over him to protect him from the rain. That was a moment when I felt I was being of service, which made me happy. But I also had to practise handling my anger. For example, at breakfast time I made up a tray for Thay of what I thought were good things to eat: porridge oats, rice milk, and so on. I was amazed at all the different foods that were offered for breakfast at the Omega Institute; never in my life had I seen such an assortment of dishes to choose from for such a simple meal, but Sister Chan Khong told me it was all wrong. Thay could not eat any of the things I had chosen. I was to procure another tray and she would choose for Thay. I felt overcome by a wave of anger and put my hand on the wooden counter and breathed. I said nothing. Then I walked outside following my breathing: "breathing in I know I am angry, breathing out I know I am still angry." My mind quietened down and I saw that it was not such an important matter and hardly worth being angry about.

During my very first month in Plum Village, Thay had shared about the practice of mastering anger. Thay had asked each one of us to compose a short poem of four lines to use when we felt angry so that we could avoid expressing our anger in ways that would harm the other and harm ourself. The key thing is to close your eyes, follow your breathing, and not look at, listen to, or think about the person who is making you angry and then withdraw from the situation and practise walking meditation until you are calm enough to be able to look into the roots of your anger.

Also at that retreat was Joan Halifax, who three years earlier had been ordained together with me as a core lay member of the Order of Interbeing. She remarked to Thay that I seemed to have no energy and she wanted to take me walking in the mountains. Thay asked: "I wonder who will arrive at the top of the mountain first?" We did not reply. We did not have a chance to walk together in the mountains. After the retreat in Omega we had to go to Canada; it was only when we went together to Vietnam in 1992 that we could have climbed to the top of Mount Yen Tu, but at that time Joan was not in good health.

At the end of the retreat, we were driven to Boston and Sister Chan Khong left for France and I became Thay's official attendant. Poor Thay! Sister Chan Khong had done her best to teach me how to cook for Thay, but I still did not know how to flavour the food properly. Many Vietnamese laywomen wanted to cook special dishes for Thay, but these dishes often contained ingredients Thay was not able to eat, so he was stuck with my cooking.

From Boston we flew to Montréal and drove to the Village des Érables, Maple Village, about an hour and a half east of Montréal. Maple Village was founded by Thay's Vietnamese disciples who lived in Canada. Some of them had been ordained as members of the Order of Interbeing before I had. I immediately felt at home in Maple Village and later on would go there to lead retreats once a year. It is situated in the Montérégie mountains and forests with excellent quality air and spring water. I often wished I could go and live there to meditate and to write in a little hut that was built for Thay in the middle of the forest just above a lake.

In Maple Village it became more apparent that Thay could not eat the food I cooked. One of the senior members of the Order of Interbeing who was there, Anh Chan Co, had to buy Thay biscuits to eat and I thought why not let the Vietnamese laywomen cook for Thay. It would give them a great deal of pleasure, and I could tell them what Sister Chan Khong had told me about what Thay could and could not eat.

I felt at ease in Maple Village and with the Vietnamese French-speaking Sangha there. The Vietnamese practitioners who live in Canada consider Canada to be their homeland. They have integrated themselves into Canadian society without losing their Vietnamese heritage. They are, like Thay and Sister Chan Khong, people of two cultures. Many of them are fluent in French and during a retreat someone will always be there to translate everything that is said into and out of Vietnamese and express gratitude to Canada. In other countries like the US, France, and so on, Vietnamese immigrants who feel perfectly at home in two cultures are more difficult to find.

I did not yet have the proper outfit to wear under my long robe so I had to make do with wearing the Vietnamese-style brown trousers and blouse I had owned since being a lay-woman. The mother of the lay OI practitioner Chan Lac kindly made me two suits. I was very content with this new clothing and thought I did not need to wear the long nun's robe as well when we went on the flight to Toronto. I did not know that nuns normally wear long robes in Vietnam and it is considered very inappropriate to be seen in public without the long outer robe.

When we were about to leave Montréal for Toronto, I packed my long robe in my suitcase and checked it in at the airport. When we were approaching Toronto, Thay instructed me to wear my long robe, but I could not because it was in the hold of the aeroplane. The Toronto welcoming party came to meet us before we could collect our luggage so, unfortunately, I was not properly dressed to meet them. I felt very sorry for Thay. How must he have felt having a monastic disciple who did not know how to dress properly? I never received a reprimand. From the airport we were driven to the retreat centre. I had the back seat of the van to myself so I lay down to sleep. Thay had to remind me that it was not correct for a nun to lie down in public. There was so much I did not yet know about being a nun, and only Thay was there to teach me. I had to find it out as we went along, usually through making mistakes.

It was cold in Toronto and I did not have enough warm clothes. When it was time for walking meditation a lay-woman practitioner lent me her coat to wear. It was a bright blue colour. I wore it on top of my brown robe. When Thay saw it, he exclaimed, "What a beautiful coat you are wearing!"

I knew what this meant—nuns are not supposed to wear bright colours—so I returned the coat and I felt happier to be cold rather than to be incorrectly dressed. Later on I had a chance to study the Fine Manners (etiquette) for nuns. Thay was kind enough to correct some of my mistakes, but Thay never lost patience and always made his comments in a very gentle way. The Fine Manners help us to live in a way that brings more peace within and without. Fine Manners are not exactly rules but reminders for us to act in a seemly way that helps everyone to feel comfortable.

In Toronto I was assigned to look after the children of the lay practitioners who had come to take the retreat. Thay would give a short Dharma talk for the children and then I would leave the hall with them and teach them more out-side while Thay continued his Dharma talk to the adults. One child asked why nuns shaved their heads and wore brown robes. I replied that a nun is like a nurse. A nurse has to wear a uniform so that people know she is a nurse and can ask for help. I wondered if this was the right answer. Thay said that it was all right. Thay had taught me to invite the traditional wooden fish drum, so I was happy to be able to do that for the Vietnamese chanting.

After Toronto we flew to California and retreats were organized at Kim Son, a Vietnamese Buddhist monastery in the Santa Cruz Mountains. Here we would hold a monastic retreat for monks and nuns as well as a retreat for laypeople. I had only been ordained for less than one year and I did not know anything about sitting in order of ordination whenever we were gathered together. At mealtimes, the elder nuns who had been ordained for decades were always very humble and allowed me to sit at the top of the line with them. This was a serious breach of monastic protocol. Thay came up and asked me what I was doing sitting with the senior nuns and sent me to my proper place with the newly ordained bhikshunis. Fortunately I met two Vietnamese nuns who had lived for a long time in the West, Sister Dieu Ngoc and Sister Hue Hao, who took me under their wing. I shared a room with Sister Dieu Ngoc, and I was very happy to make the acquaintance of these elder nuns who could teach me more about the Fine Manners.

Sister Dieu Ngoc was the one who told me that whenever I left our bedroom, I should be wearing my long robe. Now at last I knew how to dress properly as a nun! They told me that in Vietnam it is only in the north that young nuns wear the brown robe, and in the south and centre, only very senior nuns wear brown and all the nuns on the retreat were from south and central Vietnam. I was always wearing my brown robe and it looked very strange to them that I, in a sense still a novitiate, was wearing the garb of an advanced practitioner. Then I remembered the grey *ao nhat binh*, the novice robe I had received in Virginia, and I was very happy to be able to wear it. At Kim Son in the lay retreat I had another opportunity to be with the children in the children's programme. One of the things that is always appreciated about our retreats is the possibility for children to attend along with their parents. The Dharma talk begins with a teaching for the children, which the parents also enjoy very much. Then the children leave for their own programme. I would sit with the children and talk to them or we could walk around and play games. There were not that many children so I did not need to organize very much and our programme was impromptu.

After our West Coast retreats, we returned to Paris on a ten-hour flight from San Francisco. It was late at night and the San Francisco airport was quite deserted. We never heard our flight called and we nearly missed the plane! Luckily, Thay looked at the time and saw that it was about time for the plane to depart. We were the last to board. Sitting next to Thay, I noticed that his eyes were always closed. For ten hours he sat perfectly still in meditation. We then took the shuttle between the two Paris airports, Charles de Gaulle and Orly, and I took the chance then to confess some things to Thay that I felt bad about. Thay listened deeply and did not say anything.

It was June, 1989 and time to start thinking about the Summer Opening. Since the end of 1987, Plum Village had become a real practice centre. Our dream had been realised. In the Lower Hamlet at that time were living Sister Chan Khong, Chan Vi, and long-term lay friends Huyen

Chau (now a nun in Plum Village, Thailand), Duc (now a monk in Plum Village, France), Doan (now a nun in Plum Village, France), and Eveline (now a lay Dharma teacher in Amsterdam), who all helped with the family retreat. Duc was quite shy and did not like large crowds, so when our retreats became popular he would take refuge in M. Mounet's house.

In those days, the summer retreat for families was not as well organized as it is today. There were many things that had to be organized at the last minute. All the same, there was plenty of good energy and fun. It was never boring and you could feel we were like a family.

As far as the practice was concerned, Thay was in charge of both hamlets. If Thay saw a lack of mindfulness in the permanent residents or retreatants, he would call the permanent residents together in the Lower Hamlet library and reprimand us gently but firmly. Every week there was a meeting for all Order of Interbeing members since they were also responsible for the running of the retreat. Thay would be very active in the retreat, attending sitting meditation with everyone else. Thay also dropped in on Dharma sharings, when we sit in a circle to share our experience of the practice. There were three sharing groups in each of the hamlets: one French, one English, and one Vietnamese.

Visiting children were expected to be present for the first sitting meditation but because they found it difficult to sit still, we would sit alternating adults and children so that every child was flanked by two adults. One time during the morning sitting meditation, an elderly woman's stomach was rumbling. Every time the children heard the sound they started to laugh. Then we heard Thay's voice in Vietnamese: "Will the person whose stomach is rumbling please leave the hall." Obediently the laywoman left and the children settled down in silence. After that we allowed the children to leave the meditation hall after the first ten minutes when a small bell was rung for them to stand up and quietly go outside.

In 1986 Thay had said to me that the West was not ready for Buddhist monasticism, but by 1988 Thay was ready to begin to give ordinations to monks and nuns from the West. As the first Westerner to be ordained a nun in our tradition I can see how much I have benefitted. Thay could see how much we need the mindfulness trainings in the West. As Buddhism spread through Europe, Australia, and North America, there was much confusion about the best way to practise. There were practitioners in the West who said there was no connection between ethics and meditative concentration. Thay saw how our suffering comes largely from our failure to observe ethical guidelines. Our culture and even aspects of our education speak against moral guidelines. Buddhist ethics is not imposed by customs or religion or authority. Our moral training has to come from our awareness of suffering and how suffering can be avoided. So Thay introduced the practice of the Five Mindfulness Trainings as guidance for laypeople.

This first year of being a nun was not easy for me and I often felt angry, lonely, and out of place. I was not familiar with monastic rules and the Vietnamese culture and language. I had to learn and Thay also had to learn how to instruct his disciples. He was faced with the new situation of having monastic disciples, nuns to be precise, one of whom was European. There was a Vietnamese language class which I enjoyed very much because it consisted of singing Vietnamese songs. This was a skilful means because Vietnamese is a tonal language and you can remember the tones much more easily with the help of music. This class was held in the kitchen in the Lower Hamlet, part of the present-day dining hall; it was the place where most informal gatherings happened. Thay also taught Classical Chinese in the library. I found Chinese very difficult. One day Thay asked me if I was enjoying the class. I said "No" in front of everyone. People laughed. but still I felt it was a gauche way to reply. Vietnamese people tend to have a natural feeling for Chinese as both Chinese and Vietnamese are tonal languages and much of the Vietnamese vocabulary is made of Chinese loan words, but to me it was utterly strange and I could not keep up with the others. We studied a text called Sam Quy Mang ("Repentance and Refuge for Life") which we also learnt to chant. I found the chanting very beautiful and not difficult to memorize, but to read and write the characters was another matter.

When I was ordained a nun I did not tell my parents I had ordained. In fact, Thay advised me not to do so, saying that if I asked my parents whether I could become a Buddhist nun or not, whether they said yes or no would not have much meaning since they did not know what being a Buddhist nun meant. Thay told me to wait for a couple of years and then, when my practice was stronger, to go with Thay to lead a retreat in England and invite my parents to attend.

When the time came for me to write the letter to my parents inviting them to come to a retreat Thay was leading, I did not say anything about being a nun. My mother agreed to register; she had already been to Plum Village and knew a little about the practice, but my father was busy and could not come. I remember catching sight of my mother at the end of a hallway on the arrival day. I recognized her before she recognized me. As we drew closer to each other, she called me the name she had called me since I was a child: "Annie!" Poor Mother! She was taken aback to see me in a brown robe and with a shaved head. The first thing she said was, "Thank goodness your father is not here. He would be shocked to see you with a shaved head." She was also expressing her own shock. Later, if someone happened to take a photograph of me in Plum Village that I considered to be a good photograph, as long as I had my head covered, I would send it to my mother and she would display it along with the photos of my other siblings.

As the retreat proceeded, my mother felt more and more at ease. She saw how I interacted with the retreatants, leading the Dharma sharing and giving a presentation on the Five Mindfulness Trainings. She saw that the retreatants had respect for the nuns. She praised me for the way I facilitated the Dharma sharing. My mother came to all the practice activities although it was her first retreat and completely different from anything she had experienced before. I took my mother to meet Thay. Thay said my mother was easy to get along with, and after that my mother would send a jar of homemade marmalade to Thay from time to time. Thay ate the marmalade on its own with chopsticks to show me how much he appreciated it.

During walking meditation, I held my mother's hand. My mother told me one practice she took home was the practice of total relaxation. She would practise as she lay in bed on waking in the morning.

When Thay went back to Plum Village after the tour, he allowed me to go home to visit my parents and family. I remembered the words of my mother when she first saw me as a nun, and I did not dare uncover my head for the whole length of my stay for fear of shocking my father.

The greatest good fortune of my life was meeting Thay and learning from him how to meditate on my parents as five-year-old children in order to understand them better and gain insight into their difficulties. After I was able to meditate on my father as a five-year-old child, I began to feel deep gratitude and love for my parents and I related to them in the way that they deserved, with more respect and understanding. The meditation goes like this. First you visualise yourself as a five-year-old child. You see how fragile and vulnerable you were at that age and you feel compassion for that five-year-old child that is still alive within you. Then you meditate on your mother and father successively when they were five, and you see that they too were fragile and vulnerable at five years old, and because of this you develop compassion for them. You learn to recognize your mother and your father in yourself and see how their difficulties are also your difficulties, and you make the aspiration to develop mindfulness, concentration, and insight to liberate your parents and yourself from suffering.

In 1989 my mother and father came to visit me in Plum Village where I was living as a nun. I wanted to teach my father walking meditation, but I did not do it too well. From this experience I realised it is often more difficult to teach one's own close family than strangers. However I am glad my father came to Plum Village twice and enjoyed the atmosphere and the community there. Even though he was not interested in the practice, he was interested in the way the Sangha lived and worked. He was interested in the plum trees and he offered to send us a cow so that we could have milk (at that time we were not yet vegan in Plum Village and we went to the neighbouring farm to buy milk). Thay thanked my father for the offer and said he thought we would not have time to take care of the cow and milk her. My mother, on the other hand, was very open to trying out the practice. Her walking meditation was so natural and unforced that people would comment that it was a pleasure to see her just walking.

As a Buddhist nun we say that we "leave the home," but in fact we *are* our father and our mother. Even though we may only see our parents for a few days every two years, they are always there inside us. Thay has taught us: "If you are angry with your father or mother, you are angry with yourself, because you are your father and mother." From a scientific point of view our parents are in us because 50 percent of our chromosomes are our mother's and 50 percent our father's. As we go on the spiritual path of transformation and healing our parents go with us; even if from the outside they continue to live far away, from the inside they begin to have more peace and understanding in their lives.

In 1990 Thay sent me to live in Upper Hamlet to direct the practice activities there. There were newly ordained novice monks up there and a number of laymen. Being in the monks' hamlet I needed to have another sister as my "second body"—a nun always has another nun go with her for her protection. From a physical point of view it is always good to have another sister in case of accident or illness. From the point of view of Fine Manners, when we have another nun with us it reminds us of our practice as a nun and we can avoid doing anything that would not be seemly for a nun to do. Laypeople also feel better when they see two nuns in the town together because in the Christian monastic tradition nuns do not go out on their own. The nuns took in turn to be my second body in the Upper Hamlet, so we were just two nuns in the Upper Hamlet. The other nuns were in the Lower Hamlet. I took my position of practice coordinator quite seriously, and this was not too well received by the young monks.

I placed particular emphasis on the early morning sitting, expecting everyone to be present. I felt very sad sitting at the bell in the meditation hall on my own, although we cannot have been more than ten people in all. When it was well into the sitting meditation time and still no one had appeared, I went to the novices' rooms and knocked on the door; when this received no response I would open the door and say loudly that it was time for sitting meditation. When that had no effect, I did on a couple of occasions pull back the sleeping bags from the sleeping novices.

Whenever it was the Winter Retreat, some visiting novices from Kim Son Monastery in the United States would come to join. One or two of them particularly resented having a nun tell them what to do. Traditionally a nun is the younger sister of a monk and seeks his direction rather than directing him. For the monks from a traditional Vietnamese temple this was a complete turnaround.

Later on, I was joined by Thay Giac Thanh in Upper Hamlet. We both had rooms in the attic of the Stone House in Upper Hamlet. Thay Giac Thanh was the most easy-going monk I have known, but he also had a sharp mind and when he spotted a mistake in someone's practice, he did not hesitate to point it out in order to help that person. He was a poet who deeply enjoyed nature and the wonders of life. At first the novices were not accustomed to Thay Giac Thanh's ways, but he grew into his position of the eldest monk and was later appointed as abbot of the Fleurs de Cactus meditation centre (now Maison de l'Inspir) in Paris. Thay had a hut built for Thay Giac Thanh not far from Thay's hut in the Upper Hamlet. Thay Giac Thanh came back to live there and enjoyed receiving visitors and offering them a cup of tea. He was first and foremost a tea master. He said that since he had been diagnosed with diabetes he could no longer enjoy all the foods he used to enjoy, so he took to enjoying serving and drinking tea instead. He was able to offer solace over a cup of tea to many monks, nuns, and laypeople when they were going through difficult times. Thay Giac Thanh's diabetes was serious and in 2001 while we were travelling in China with Thay we received the news that he was dying in Escondido near the Deer Park Monastery where he was abbot. Monks and nuns were there with him to offer spiritual support and when he died the doctors and nurses were kind enough to leave the body undisturbed for many hours. We were sitting on a bus with Thay when we heard the news of his death. Thay took out his small bell and led us in the chanting of the names of Buddhas and bodhisattvas. There were tears in the eyes of many of us, but we practised walking for him in the Chinese monasteries we were visiting and felt his presence.

One of the joys I had when in the Upper Hamlet was that my mother came and stayed. She was very open and accepting of everyone, and my second body at the time, Sister True Practice, liked my mother very much. Together they made cakes and Sister Chan Tu said that my mother was much easier to get along with than I was. This was because I often reminded Sister Chan Tu about what she should or should not be doing.

Another joy was that Thay allowed me to make a one-week solitary retreat in his hut. Thay's hut in the Upper Hamlet is a wonderful place to make a retreat. To begin with the peaceful energy of Thay's practice has permeated the hut and everything around. Then there are wonderful views over the hills in an eastern direction, so that every morning you can sit on the veranda and watch the sunrise. Thay recognized my tendency of always wanting to be doing something, translating or preparing teachings for a retreat, and a solitary retreat was just to be able to sit or walk and do nothing but enjoy the sitting and the walking. Of course difficulties can come up and you have to stay with them and look deeply to transform them.

Sometimes I thought that my behaviour and practice were so bad that I wondered if Thay was going to ask me to leave. So I was extremely surprised when one day Sister

Chan Khong said that Thay was thinking to transmit the authority to teach the Dharma to her and to me.

The official Lamp Transmission took place in August 1990. It was the first of its kind to be held in Plum Village. Thay said the unofficial transmission had taken place in May. In June Thay organized the first 21-Day Retreat. It was the time when Sister Jina (Sister Dieu Nghiem) came to Plum Village. She was of Irish and Dutch nationality and had practised as a nun in Japan. Thay told me that he "loved Sister Jina too," which sounds strange in English but natural in Vietnamese. It meant that Sister Jina is part of our family. We shared a room in the Lower Hamlet during the 21-Day Retreat. When Thay was about to ordain Sister Jina into the Plum Village tradition he was not sure whether to give her the name True Wonder Adornment or True Adornment with Joy. In the end Thay chose the former. She was able to relate well with everyone in the community and always looked happy.

The 21-Day Retreat is a very special event in Plum Village, organized primarily for members of the Order of Interbeing. In twenty-one days Thay had time to give teachings that went deeper than in the shorter five-day retreats. The official Lamp Transmission was in August so that all the people who came for the Summer Opening retreat would be able to witness and know to whom Thay was transmitting the lamp. Thay explained that as part of the ceremony we should need to write an insight gatha. I did not feel I had any insights that I could put into words. When the ceremony drew near, it happened that a lay practitioner who

Sr. Chan Duc and friend in Lower Hamlet.

had been diagnosed with cancer asked me to write a gatha for her to practise with her illness. Being unable to write any other gatha I asked Thay if he would accept this gatha I had written for the laywoman as my insight gatha. With great compassion Thay accepted. The gatha read:

> I am not the cancer in this body,
> The cancer in this body is not me.
> Taking its hand I practise and play with it,
> So that all beings from the pain of cancer can be free.

They gave me the transmission gatha:

> Suchness shines out radiantly as the full moon,
> When virtue is developed it can transmit the
>   ancestral lamp.
> The practice of transformation will reveal the
>   true nature
> And the wonderful Dharma will continue always
>   to be expounded.

Thay's gatha so skillfully expressed my capacity and the way I could develop it, that even today I marvel at how well Thay was able to see my heart and mind. One fellow Dharma teacher who received the lamp at the same time said that his gatha was for ease and relaxation and mine was for the hard work of transformation. I agreed.

Nine of us received the lamp that first year: two nuns and seven lay practitioners. Each new Dharma teacher had the chance to give an eight-minute Dharma talk. Alongside Thay's daïs was a lower daïs for the new Dharma teacher to sit and give her short talk. When people heard my insight gatha and talk, they thought I had cancer and many came up afterward to express their commiserations. Sister Chan Khong said that she was moved by the short talk I gave.

At the end of the year in 1991, I went back down to live in Lower Hamlet again because Thay Giac Thanh was in Upper Hamlet to look after the young monks. Lower Hamlet had developed in the one-and-a-half years that I had been gone. There was now an organized community of nuns and laywomen and even central heating in the Plum Hill building.

Thay had arranged for Sister Jina and me to go on a tour of North America to lead retreats. We visited many places where meditators would gather, including Chicago; Barre, Massachussetts; New York City; Canada; Los Angeles; Berkeley; Kim Son Monastery in Northern California, Texas, and Montana. When we were not leading retreats we had rest days when we could walk in the California hills or the forests of Massachusetts. Arnie Kotler and Therese Fitzgerald, Thay's publishers in English at that time, were the main organizers of this trip. We had the opportunity to stay in the houses of lay practitioners and learn more about the North American people.

Being a nun in our tradition does not mean staying in the monastery. There is an obligatory period of three months when we have to stay in the monastery to consolidate our practice in the Sangha but for the other nine months we often find ourselves travelling to many countries. As far as I was concerned, going out and leading retreats was something very new. I took it upon myself to give the Dharma talks. Sister Jina was very good at relating and talking to the retreatants. Leading retreats is a wonderful opportunity to learn more about the practice. Whenever a party of monks and nuns asked permission to leave the monastery to lead retreats, Thay would remind them that he was sending them as an offering of Thay and Plum Village. We were expected to maintain our practice of mindfulness at all times (in the airport, the railway station, in laypeople's houses, while sightseeing) and not just practise during the retreat times. This tour was a beneficial experience for learning how to organize retreats and to practise giving Dharma talks.

CHAPTER FIFTEEN

Vietnam

AFTER THAY LEFT Vietnam in 1966 in order to go to North America to call for peace, he was told by the Vietnamese authorities that he was not allowed to return to his native land. He remained in exile until 2005 when, probably for reasons of world trade, he was allowed to return as a visitor. The practice of Buddhism in a communist country is not easy. Since a communist government is not elected by the people, it is always afraid of being overthrown. Buddhism posed a threat to the communist leaders because it could become a very powerful, if nonviolent, force in the country. So the government has to find ways to keep Buddhism within the bounds that it feels safe for itself. Not only was I a disciple of Thay, the Buddhism taught by Thay has a great appeal to young people and intellectuals. It poses a threat for this very reason. Thay has renewed Buddhism to make it relevant to our times. The traditional Buddhism in Vietnam is mostly Pure Land Buddhism which involves chanting and devotion to the Buddha Amitabha. There may be a small amount of Zen with short periods of sitting meditation. Thay's Buddhism is basically the teaching of mindfulness in daily life with periods of sitting and walking meditation during the day and other practices of mindful communication and sharing.

Thay had no hesitation in sending his disciples out to teach the Dharma. As for myself, I was still very young in

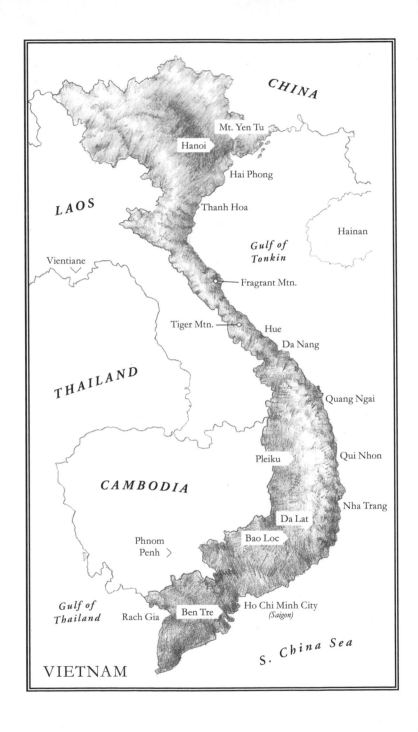

CHINA

Mt. Yen Tu

Hanoi

Hai Phong

LAOS

Thanh Hoa

Hainan

Vientiane

Gulf of
Tonkin

Fragrant Mtn.

Tiger Mtn.

Hue

Da Nang

THAILAND

Quang Ngai

Qui Nhon

Pleiku

CAMBODIA

Nha Trang

Da Lat

Bao Loc

Phnom
Penh

Gulf of
Thailand

Rach Gia

Ben Tre

Ho Chi Minh City
(Saigon)

S. China Sea

VIETNAM

the practice but very eager to go to Vietnam and see for myself the homeland of my teacher. In the autumn of 1992, Thay sent me as his first western monastic disciple to Vietnam to go with some Western laypeople on a pilgrimage of the Buddhist holy places in North and Central Vietnam. We would stay in these places to practise meditation and I could explain a little of the history that I knew about them. Thay and Sister Chan Khong had very carefully organized the trip. At the time, Thay was still in exile from Vietnam. It would be my first visit to Vietnam. My spoken Vietnamese was improving and since I had been translating Thay's book *The History of Vietnamese Buddhism*, I had a little knowledge about Buddhism in Vietnam.

We arrived in Hanoi, the capital city in the north. Chu Hung, one of the few Vietnamese who had been able to visit Plum Village, and his wife took care of us, and she had made some Vietnamese cakes for us to eat when we arrived. As foreigners in a communist country, we had to have a government tour guide but I still managed to go around quite a bit on my own. As I walked in Hanoi, I was surprised to see that nearly everyone dressed the same: usually in khaki or dull green with a mortar hat, and the women students had the traditional long white tunic and cone-shaped bamboo hat. The most common form of transport was the bicycle. Some of the streets were very crowded but at that time of year it was not too hot. Many activities, like the barber cutting hair, or the typist typing up an article for his client, took place outside on the pavement.

We were taken to a hotel where the staff were surprised that I spoke Vietnamese. Thay had instructed everyone to

228/ T R U E   V I R T U E

eat vegetarian food during the trip. Finding vegetarian food actually turned out to be quite difficult. Because North Vietnam had been under Communist rule for so long, people had forgotten about their Buddhist traditions and very few were vegetarian. When I told the hotel chef that I needed him to cook vegetarian meals for me, he said he did not know how to cook vegetarian dishes and I should go to the Quan Su Temple for my meals.

Later on I discovered that even in this temple the monks ate meat. I told the chef it was not difficult to cook vegetarian meals. He should buy some tofu and boil it and I would eat that with rice and mustard greens or whatever greens they had available. They also gave me some North Vietnamese soya sauce, which is very strong and smells of fermentation. So I ate that every day. The rice was unlike any rice I had seen before. It was fragrant and quite delicious. It was not wholly white and not wholly brown, but somewhere in between. Other members of our party were not very happy with that menu and went in search of hotels where Westerners stayed, and ate there.

Sister Chan Khong had given me some gifts for the famous poet Hoang Cam and he came to the hotel to see me. Thay and Sister Chan Khong did their best to support in anyway they could writers and artists in Vietnam who were harrassed, imprisoned, and whose poetry was censored by the communist government. Hoang Cam was one of these. He was about seventy years old at that time. He told Sister Chan Khong afterward that I was like a woman from Bac Ninh. This means to me that I was not like other Western women he had encountered. My Vietnamese accent was certainly not the accent of Bac Ninh. It was also possible he had never before met a Western Buddhist nun wearing the habit of the nuns of North Vietnam.

I wanted to buy fruit to eat and the shoes I had were too small and very uncomfortable, so I went out shopping alone. I must have looked strange: someone with a European face wearing monastic robes. Children were very surprised to see a Western nun and shouted out "Su Tay!" ("Western monk") whenever I passed them.

As I waited in the queue I heard the price of the merchandise I wanted to buy as the customer in front of me talked to the vendor. I was surprised when my turn came that I was asked to pay twice as much. I thought they were trying to cheat me so I said I wanted to pay the price the others were paying. The vendors were most surprised that I understood their language, but explained that because I was not Vietnamese, I had to pay more. I was offended at the time, but when I look back I can see the logic. If I had been in Europe I should have had to pay more so why should I not pay that price in Vietnam and help the poorer people there?

From Hanoi we visited the temple at the foot of the Fragrant Mountain, Huong Tich, and we organized a two-day retreat there. The Fragrant Mountain can only be reached by water. The scenery is very beautiful and quite extraordinary. Mountains rise straight up out of the water. Now they have some motorized boats, but at that time all the boats that plied the waters were rowed by hand, usually by women, so the only sounds then were natural ones, and very peaceful. It was quite a long journey, more than an hour, but very enjoyable. We only worried that the ferrywoman might be getting tired.

The mountain has several ancient temples, which have

been abandoned, as well as beautiful caves and springs of water in many places. Since we were staying on the mountain for several days we could walk around and visit these temples. The most famous temple is the cave where Avalokiteshvara of the Southern Sea is said to have become enlightened.

Avalokiteshvara of the Southern Sea is a female emanation of the bodhisattva Avalokiteshvara. According to Vietnamese folklore she came to practise in a cave there when she had been rescued from the executioner who had been ordered by her father to kill her. Later on when her father became very ill, she had gone from there to cure him by plucking out her eyes and cutting off her arms to make a medicine. Then her father, mother, and sisters had come to visit her here in the cave in gratitude for her father's cure. Pilgrims come to this place in the first three months of every year in order to venerate the great compassion of this bodhisattva, a compassion that leads to transformation of violence and hatred. In recent years superstitions have risen up in connection with the temple and people believe that by touching a certain rock there, childless women will be able to bear children; but the real reason for making the pilgrimage is to touch the compassion in our own heart.

When we visited the cave there was a very young novice who stood by a bell and invited it for people from time to time. I asked him if he would allow me to invite the bell because the invitation of the bell is such a beautiful practice that I had learned in Plum Village and I thought he might like to know about it, especially since the verses we say to ourself while inviting the bell are in Vietnamese (not Chinese). It was lucky, I thought, that I had learnt these verses in Vietnamese and I could now share them.

After that we had a few days visiting the mountain called Yen Tu. This mountain has for a very long time been sacred for Buddhist practice. In the early thirteenth century there were already realised Buddhist masters living on the mountain as hermits. Although it is only 100 kilometres from Hanoi, it took us five hours to drive there. The road was so bad in places that we had to have a truck pull us with a rope over some sections that were rivers or streams. As the truck pulled our van, the passengers crossed the river or stream on foot. We were pleasantly surprised when we saw that we had arrived at the foot of the mountain and the rest of the journey would be on foot. There are many small temples or hermitages on the mountain, but according to the archaeologists, the Hermitage of the Sleeping Clouds is in a very inaccessible place on a different flank of this mountain range. Before I'd left France, Thay had shown me a map. The famous Hoa Yen Temple is one of the temples on the route that Vietnamese pilgrims and tourists take to the top of the mountain. In 1992 some wild people lived on the mountain who made their livelihood by hunting and raising pigs. They thought they owned the mountain and they had the right to say who could stay on it. I heard that they harassed the nuns who had come to live in the Giai Oan (Resolving Injustice) Temple.

We began to climb the mountain on what was quite an easy path, and our first stop was the Resolving Injustice Temple. You may wonder why the temple has such a name. It is said that when the thirteenth-century king Tran Nhan

Tong abdicated the throne to become a Buddhist monk he went to the Yen Tu Mountain to practise meditation. His consorts came to summon him back to the palace. When he refused, some of them drowned themselves in the small lake at the foot of the mountain and the king built this temple in order to resolve the injustice they felt had been done to them. The practice of meditation, chanting the sutra and the precepts in the temple would help the souls of the consorts to be at rest. The Resolving Injustice Temple is the gateway to Yen Tu and it is the place where we are said to leave our worldly concerns behind before we enter the sacred precinct of the holy mountain. From this temple there is an easy path of ascent to the Hoa Yen temple. (In 1992 there was no cable car on Yen Tu Mountain as there is now.) Some pilgrims liked to make their way to the summit and back in one day, but we were to enjoy the ascent in stages, staying the night at the Hoa Yen temple. We could walk slowly and savour the beauty of the mountain paths.

We continued our walk up to the Hoa Yen Temple. Coal mining had scarred many of the mountain flanks we saw below us and as we climbed we could see the cloud of coal dust and smoke below. We stayed that night in the Hoa Yen temple and I slept in a small dark room with one of the two sole occupants of the temple, an elderly nun. The other occupant was a young novice monk. The nun allowed pigs to be raised in the monastery precinct, probably in order not to be terrorised by the wild mountain inhabitants, and she kept a packet of cigarettes in a drawer in her room. She smoked only in the seclusion of her room and in mindfulness. She smoked in the same way as she drank a cup of tea: joining her palms in respect before she lifted the cup,

then taking a sip and, after putting the cup down again joining her palms once more. When she smoked, she would
join her palms then lift up the cigarette, inhale the smoke,
replace the cigararette on the ashtray, and before picking
it up again she would join her palms. I was so fascinated
by this procedure that I was not irritated by the smoke.
Together we drank the tea in mindfulness, truly present in
the here and now, our minds fully focused on drinking our
tea. This peaceful encounter, drinking tea with the Vietnamese nun, was a memorable moment on my first trip to
Vietnam.

We went to sleep early and woke at three o'clock in the
morning to drink tea. As soon as it was light I began the
ascent to the top of the mountain. I let a young Indonesian
man who was in our party know and left on my own. There
was a path, but it was narrow and very steep in places with
rocks to climb over. Later, when I returned to Vietnam with
Thay in 2005, the path had been made into steps and was
much easier to climb. I did not meet anyone except a few
soldiers in the military post near the summit. I enjoyed the
wildness and the beauty of the mountain very much and
I kept imagining the Zen masters of the past walking on
the path I was now walking on. There was a cracked bell
at the summit which could no longer sound as you invited
it, although it was the custom for anyone who reached the
summit to invite that bell. I enjoyed resting undisturbed
on one of the large flat rocks on the mountaintop, watching the leaves of the forest below fluttering in the breeze.
I felt a lightness, a sense of how beautiful Vietnam is. The
Vietnamese people themselves see nature as an artist, and
I could see why.

After North Vietnam, we went to Hue in the centre of Vietnam. Hue is also a centre of Buddhism; the home of the root temple of Plum Village and of the stupa venerating Master Lieu Quan who was the founder of the lineage to which Thay and his disciples belong. Chu Hung, our Vietnamese friend, had booked us into an hotel owned by a Buddhist who would be able to cook vegetarian meals for us. The other members of our party did not like the hotel much and booked themselves into a fancier place, but this caused our Buddhist hosts trouble as they had bought vegetarian supplies specially for our visit. Chu Hung let the elder nun Nhu Minh, the abbess of the Tay Linh temple, know that I had arrived and she came to the rescue, pacifying the irate hotel owners. I had already met this venerable nun in Plum Village. Although she was abbess of her own temple in the traditional Pure Land school, she had studied and practised the teachings of Thay and handed them on to her disciples. She was an assiduous poet, sometimes writing several poems in one day. She has not been afraid to support Thay, even when he was being opposed by the government in Vietnam.

The breakfast in the hotel consisted of bread, peanut butter, and banana. but the Venerable Nhu Minh said that we should not ask the hotel to cook for us any more and she came every morning with boiled banana and rice and mung bean congee, riding on a scooter driven by one of her lay disciples. Since my childhood I had never been able to eat bananas, but these Vietnamese ones were something special and from then on I have been able to enjoy them.

On the first day I arrived in Hue I went straight to the

post office to ring Thay and Sister Chan Khong and let them know where I was. As I walked into the post office a man came up to me and asked if I were a disciple of Thich Nhat Hanh. This was something I had been told not to let anyone know because Thay had been exiled by the communist government. So I remained silent and pretended I did not understand. Sister Chan Khong had told me that when I arrived in Hue I should call her but I should speak in English in case the telephone was tapped. I spoke in English as if I were ringing my blood family, with Sister Chan Khong as my sister and Thay my uncle. Sister Chan Khong said: "Your uncle says you should go to the Tu Hieu Temple right away." The Tu Hieu Temple is our order's root temple because our teacher is the lineage holder of that temple. It was the place where Thay was ordained a novice monk and practised for the first years of his novitiate. Thay is the abbot in absentia of the temple. She said I should go "right away" because before long they were sure the security police would catch up with me and I should not be able to go anywhere I wanted to go.

I wanted to take a rickshaw, but the driver did not know the way. He said we could go to another temple and he would ask them the way. There are many monks and nuns in Hue. It has been a centre of Buddhism since the beginning of the seventeenth century. The Nguyen lords, who made Hue their capital, supported Buddhism in the nineteenth century and it has remained strong there ever since. After we had gone a little way, we met a nun who said she would take me to her temple. This was the Kieu Dam Temple. As we were going there we came to a hill and the nun said we should walk to spare the driver. I was glad she suggested this because if I had been on my own it would not have entered my head how difficult it would be to pull a passenger uphill on a bicycle. By the time we arrived at the nun's temple, it was time for the late afternoon meal. The nun asked for a meal to be given to the rickshaw driver. I realised how poor these fellows were. I was also given soup made with sweet potatoes and other dishes.

I was asked to introduce myself to the whole community, which was headed by an abbess who was senile. I was touched by the fact that although she was not compos mentis she was still accorded the position of abbess and enjoyed the unfeigned respect of her Sangha. The nun then took me to the Dong Thuyen Temple and from there the nuns took me to Tu Hieu, the root temple. At that time the security police were already following me, although I did not know at the time. I was eager to visit Tu Hieu, the temple most connected to Thay, who had told us many stories of the time he had lived there as a novice monk. We passed around the outside of the main entrance on a path of red mud (no one walks through the main gate) and were greeted by the Half-Moon pool. From there we walked up through a terraced garden, with paths of red earth, to the main shrine room to pay our respect to the Buddhas and bodhisattvas. Then we sat in a building behind the shrine in the place where Thay's teacher had eaten and taken tea and we remembered to bow before we walked past his empty seat. The star fruit and the persimmon trees which Thay had told us about were still there in the courtyard. I met the abbot, the Venerable Thich Chi Mau, who spoke in a friendly way, although it was difficult for me to understand all he said because I was not familiar with the Hue accent. I was told to come back the next day to meet the laypeople who were helping with the Love and Understanding programme under the direction of Sister Chan Khong. I did my best to share with them about the practice of mindfulness. I could not stay overnight in Tu Hieu. For one thing it is a monks' temple and for another the security police made it clear that as a foreigner I had to stay in a hotel.

Dong Thuyen Temple is a beautiful temple for nuns, which has a thatched roof. It was founded by the founder of our lineage, Master Lieu Quan in the early eighteenth century. Master Lieu Quan had helped to give the Linji school a Vietnamese flavour in architecture, liturgical music, and way of teaching. The abbess of the Dong Thuyen Temple was the elder nun Dieu Dat, disciple of the late Venerable Dieu Khong. I spent many days in that temple, coming and going to and from the hotel to sleep. I also helped transmit the Five Mindfulness Trainings there in the name of Thay. Someone recorded the ceremony and the security police heard about it and came and confiscated the recording.

The Long Tho Temple for nuns asked me to organize a Day of Mindfulness there. A Day of Mindfulness is like a one-day retreat. People gather in the morning, usually from nine o'clock on, and then they are introduced to the practice of mindfulness. There is a guided sitting meditation followed by a teaching, then there is a walking meditation outside. Lunch is eaten in silence and there is a total relaxation to take the place of a siesta. Everyone lies on the floor and is guided in how to relax and let go of all the tensions of body and mind. Everyone is divided into groups after that in order to share with each other about their lives and spiritual practice. We really wanted to do it, but the security police found out about it and told us we had to cancel. Some people wanted to do as the security police ordered and some wanted to go ahead with the Day of Mindfulness. We ended up just organizing for a small number of people, about 30 instead of 300. The nuns of the Long Tho Temple were very disappointed because it was rare for someone to come from Plum Village to offer the teachings of Thay, who, along with Master Thanh Tu, is the most famous of Vietnamese Zen Masters and of whom the Vietnamese people are extremely proud.

We visited the Hong An Temple of the most Venerable Dieu Khong, founded by the Venerable nun in 1949. It is in the same village as the root temple Tu Hieu. Venerable Dieu Khong was an outstanding elder nun in Hue. She came from a noble family and had had to marry. When her children were old enough she became a nun. The charitable work she had begun as a layperson she continued as a nun. She expended much of her time and energy founding nunneries and teaching nuns in the 1930s until the 1970s. When I came to visit her, she was not in good health. She was sitting informally on a box bed with some nuns and she insisted on putting on her long robe to greet me. It was a way of showing respect for my teacher Thich Nhat Hanh, who was in exile and who had sent me. I was impressed by her presence and humility and felt connected to her instantly. She spoke to me for quite a bit and she told me that although she was not in good health she was going to live on for quite a bit longer. I was glad because I should have liked to visit her again, but she passed away in 1997, before I was able to visit Hue again in 2001.

Next door to this temple was the hermitage of the most Venerable Cat Tuong who also impressed me very much. She was a small and vital nun who remained in contact with Thay and sister Chan Khong, and when sister Chan Khong could not go back to Vietnam the Venerable Cat Tuong could use funds sent from Plum Village to bring relief to the poor. She gave us *banh xeo,* a kind of pancake, to eat and talked to us. She then allowed me to attend her precepts class in the nuns' Institute of Buddhist Studies. However she said I could not go to the class wearing my brown robe. She lent me a grey robe which was too small. Nevertheless it was better than nothing. I enjoyed the class very much. She talked about the hard life of the monks in the time of the Buddha: how they would go on the almsround sometimes and receive no food, and how they had to walk barefoot over rough ground. She mentioned my practice of mindfulness, the practice I had received from Thay, as a practice of purity and commended me for it.

On the memorial day of the death of the Most Venerable The Thanh [d. 1988] we visited the Dieu Duc Temple for nuns. This is the most famous nuns' temple in Hue and serves as an Institute of Buddhist Studies for the nuns. There I met the Most Venerable Dieu Nghiem who was abbess of a temple right next to the root temple. She lived there alone in the beginning, before she had her own disciples, and spent her time with the young aspirants (including Thay) in the root temple. She took care of them as an elder sister takes care of her younger brothers and Thay always addressed her as his elder sister and himself as her younger brother. She showed me the stupa of the Venerable The Thanh who had translated the Bhikshuni Vibhanga of the Four-Part Vinaya of the Dharmagupta school (the precepts which nuns in the Chinese, Vietnamese, and Korean tradition of Buddhism practise) from Chinese into Vietnamese and added a commentary.

The Venerable The Thanh had had a very close connection with Plum Village. She had always wanted to go there and practised diligently the Plum Village Dharma doors, in other words the teachings of Thay. This venerable nun had always remained in close contact with Thay and Sister Chan Khong. She was tireless in doing charitable work, distributing the funds sent from France for the poor. She had to go through many difficulties in doing her charitable work with the security police always trying to stop her. She died completely at ease with a smile on her lips. She enjoyed the practice taught by Thay of "Breathing in, I calm my mind; breathing out, I smile'" so much that she practised it as she was dying. She asked her disciple to take a photograph of her still smiling after she had died and send the photograph to Thay so that Thay would know she had practised his teachings successfully. She was confident that having died she would be free to visit Plum Village without having to pay for an air ticket. An altar was set up for her in the bamboo grove in Lower Hamlet and in the garden in the New Hamlet.

The Most Venerable Dieu Nghiem told me to circumambulate the stupa, which I was very happy to do. Then there was a ceremony of chanting. Many monks had come to attend and lead the ceremony. After the chanting there was lunch. The monks were sitting at tables on a raised platform in a hall which had walls on three sides. The Venerable Dieu Nghiem instructed me to prostrate to the monks at each table. This was the correct thing for a nun who has just arrived to do. Wearing my sanghati robe, I walked the length of the tables prostrating at the foot of each table. I was not very happy about doing this at first, especially when I saw that cigarettes and beer were part of the fare enjoyed by the monks, but as I did the practice I realised that it was helping my humility and I could do it wholeheartedly praying for the transformation and success in the practice of the monks. Then it was time for the nuns to eat. They had a very crowded dining room into which we all squeezed and enjoyed our lunch very much without all the ceremonials accorded to the monks.

Since we were visiting the temples in Hue, the Venerable Dieu Dat said that we should also visit the monks and nuns who were jokingly known as "government" monks and nuns, because they acted as spies for the government on other monks and nuns or were in the pay of the government. I had negative feelings toward these monks and nuns but on meeting them I felt sorry for them. I saw that they were not bad people; they were just suffering and afraid. It did remind me that we were lucky in Europe to be able to practise Buddhism without the government feeling that we were a threat. We went to the Tu Dam Temple, a large and important temple in the history of Buddhism in Hue, where some government monks were to be found. They had a copy of Thay's book *The Sun My Heart* and asked me if I was one of the translators. They had connected Annabel Laity with Chan Duc, the Vietnamese for True Virtue, which Vietnamese people call me by.

The Venerable Nhu Minh gave a Dharma talk there one day which impressed me. She prostrated to the monks present before she began to speak and spoke simply and clearly. The Venerable Nhu Minh always had something to give to the beggars who gathered in the temple courtyard. In the Tu Dam Temple, I met the Most Venerable Thich Thien Sieu, a very famous scholar monk in Vietnam. He translated the Chinese Dirgha Agama and many other sutras into Vietnamese and wrote articles on Buddhism. Sometimes Thay would quote from these articles in the Dharma talks in Plum Village. He was very shortsighted, almost blind. When I was introduced to him I called him Thay. This was incorrect. "Thay" is only for ordinary bhikshus. Here was a high monk, and so he had to be addressed as "Hoa Thuong" or at the very least as "On." Having been corrected, I was more careful in addressing monks after that.

We visited Bac Sieu who was very ill in his home. In Hue he was known by many people as a bodhisattva. Along with a party of supporters Bac Sieu would go into remote regions to bring aid. When houses were damaged by flooding they would bring bamboo cane to make repairs. Like Sister Chan Khong he organized a programme where people would put a handful of rice into a special pot every time they cooked rice. At the end of every month he and his party would collect the rice that had accumulated and take it to distribute to the hungry. He had been a very important social worker in

Hue, connected with Sister Chan Khong and Plum Village. He had visited the poor on his bicycle. I hoped that he was happy to meet a representative of Plum Village and Sister Chan Khong.

We had to be very careful in the hotel we were staying in not to talk about anything to do with Plum Village or our plans whilst in Hue, because the security police were always there listening. Whenever the security police came to Dong Thuyen Temple I would hide, but because they knew about my transmitting the Five Mindfulness Trainings, I was brought to the security police headquarters. We had to wait a very long time there, and then I was interrogated by a policeman whose English was not up to the task. So in the end we had to talk Vietnamese. I was a little annoyed and impatient with what I considered a tedious and unnecessary process. You find yourself in a situation which is completely unreasonable and at the same time you are powerless to do anything about it. Apparently I had broken the law by transmitting the Five Mindfulness Trainings, because I was a foreigner and foreigners were not allowed to hold religious ceremonies. The net result was that I was fined and told to leave Vietnam in the next twenty-four hours. I had an upset stomach and asked for another two days to recover, which they granted.

I did not leave Vietnam but flew south to Saigon with the Venerable Dieu Dat where we stayed in a Catholic hotel, because it was a place that would arouse the least suspicion, and I remained undetected by the security police. During the day we would go to a bakery shop and spend our time behind the shop in the living quarters of the shop owners.

The owners of the shop were lay disciples of the venerable nun Vien Minh and gave us our meals. The Venerable Vien Minh was also a very important elder nun associated with the Hong An temple in Hue and was known to Thay and Sister Chan Khong. One of the lay friends who would come and visit us encouraged me to learn to read and write Chinese characters and there was a small Buddha Hall right at the top of the building where I transmitted the Five Mindfulness Trainings in the name of Thay to a small number of laywomen who knew about Thay and had read Thay's books that had been distributed underground. At that time all Thay's books (except *The History of Vietnamese Buddhism,* which was published under a pen name) were banned in Vietnam. Sister Chan Khong would meticulously photocopy Thay's books zoomed down to a tiny size so that many pages would fit on to an A4 sheet of paper, and in this way Thay's books were smuggled into Vietnam.

It was much easier to keep out of the sight of the security police in Saigon than it was in Hue. We even managed to lead a Day of Mindfulness for 200 people in the Giac Lam Temple and also to talk to a gathering of monk and nun students there. It was the first time a nun had taught in that place. The Giac Lam temple held a Day of Mindfulness regularly led by the abbot there so it did not need to be advertised. Advertising would have attracted the notice of the security police. The Buddhist congregation in Vietnam who knew about the teachings of Thay were eager for any opportunity to put them into practice and there were also those who were curious and would be in touch with these teachings for the first time.

After the Giac Lam Temple, which is the oldest temple in Saigon, we visited the Tu Nghiem Temple. There were many nuns living in the temple and some of them were making nuns' robes when I came. The abbess spoke to me and encouraged me in my practice. It was here in 1967 that Sister Nhat Chi Mai immolated herself to call for peace. The Tu Nghiem Temple had been connected to the School of Youth for Social Service, which Thay and Sister Chan Khong had founded and to which Nhat Chi Mai belonged. She was also, along with Sister Chan Khong, one of the first six students of Thay to receive the Order of Interbeing ordination in 1966. She was deeply moved by the Twelfth Mindfulness training of the Order of Interbeing, which encourages us to do all we can to prevent war. Burning herself to death was a way to show her deep aspiration for peace in her country. So many people at that time wanted peace, but to write articles calling for peace was a crime. It needed a drastic measure to make this deepest desire known. She left ten letters and poems which show that her action came from a pure heart where there was no hatred. We saw the place where she had set light to her body and renewed our deep aspiration to continue her desire to build peace and prevent war.

The temple where I felt most at home in Saigon was the Dieu Giac Temple for nuns. I spent several nights there. The temple had been founded by the most venerable Dieu Khong whom I had met when I was in Hue. The abbess of the Dieu Giac Temple was relatively young for an abbess. She was welcoming and very kind. The Sangha there felt like a family with the abbess as a mother. Since the monastery was founded from Hue, the nuns were from central

Vietnam and their accent was quite different from the southern Vietnamese most people in Saigon were speaking. The temple had a programme run by the vice abbess for poor children who could not go to school because they had to make a little money for the family by scavenging plastic bags and cans from rubbish heaps. In the early evening they would come to the temple, receive a meal, and then have lessons from the nuns in reading and writing.

One day a week the children of the Buddhist Youth Association came to the temple. I was asked to speak to the children who were between eight and twelve years old. They were impeccably well behaved and quiet although it must have been difficult for them to understand my broken Vietnamese.

During this trip in Vietnam I was surprised that I never felt nervous when asked to teach or give a Dharma talk. I felt very relaxed and giving a talk was fun more than an ordeal. The venerable Dieu Dat said that the best talk I gave was at the Phap Van (Dharma Cloud) Temple. Thay had stayed in this temple during the Vietnam War and there was a memorial stone to Thay Thanh Van and the five social workers, disciples of Thay who were murdered by the Viet Cong just because they belonged to the School of Youth for Social Service. It was the temple base for social work during the war and next door was the School of Youth for Social Service. The temple had a thatched roof. Thay very much liked thatch-roofed temples and was disappointed when the Dieu Nghiem Temple in Hue replaced its thatch with tiles. When I visited Phap Van Temple, we sat outside on benches and I talked about the practice with lay friends who had worked under Thay in the SYSS during the war and been ordained as core members of the Order of Interbeing.[8] The atmosphere was very inspiring, as Thay would say, "the air was filled with the Dharma," and it was easy for me to speak in Vietnamese about the basic mindfulness practices and how they can be applied in the daily life of a social worker.

I also visited the Truc Lam Temple where I saw Thay's hut because Thay had sometimes stayed and taught at this temple with three other like-minded monks in 1961–1962. It was the hut where he had written the poem entitled "Perception's Embrace."[9]

> This is because that is,
> This is not because that is not.
> The bell vibrates after a long sleepless night,
> I wait for the flowers and leaves in the garden
>   to manifest.
> It is not yet light,
> Yet in the heart of this deep night
> I know you are there . . . .

Thay told me that he wrote that poem because at three o'clock in the morning on hearing the bell he had risen from a sleepless night and walked on bare feet on the cool earthen floor to the window. Opening the shutter and looking out into the darkness he wondered when he would see the flowers and leaves, and then he realised that they were there in the embrace of his mind. The flowering tree was out there because Thay was there.

These two temples did not have a monastic Sangha. Each

had a sole resident monk and both of these monks were physically and mentally in poor health. As the Phap Van temple was politically sensitive because it was so closely linked to the life of Thay, the communist government had installed there a monk who was not compos mentis so there was no way the temple could prosper and grow.

When I left Vietnam for Australia a crowd gathered around us as we waited outside the Tan Son Nhat Airport building in Saigon. We sang Dharma songs. The crowd had gathered because they were curious to see a Western nun and we taught them to sing: "Breathing in. Breathing out. I am blooming as a flower . . ." in Vietnamese. The officials in the airport searched every centimetre of my luggage and confiscated all my books and cassette tapes, even blank ones. They even read my diary. For many months after I left Vietnam I dreamt about being followed by the security police.

I was in Vietnam for about six weeks. Although it was, and still is, a communist country I felt it more as a Buddhist country. After all, Vietnamese people have been Buddhists for more than two thousand years. Everywhere I went in the centre and the south there were many people eager to learn the Dharma. (Now that thirst for spiritual practice has reached the north of Vietnam also). Many people knew of Thay or had known Thay when Thay was in Vietnam. They were very kind to me as if I was Thay's ambassador.

In many ways I should have liked to stay longer in Vietnam. I appreciated deeply the opportunity to be in touch with Vietnamese Buddhism in Vietnam. The ancient temples in the North, some dating from the Ly era (eleventh and twelfth centuries), had been imbued with the practice for so long. The depth of the practice, of self-sacrifice, and simple living that I saw in so many places was a real inspiration for me. Another inspiration was meeting venerable elder nuns. In Plum Village I had Thay and sister Chan Khong as my much appreciated and respected elders, but I never expected to meet nun elders who had practised for so long, some of them for fifty or sixty years, and had remained devoted to the monastic life through very hard times during the war and afterward under communism.

It was Thay and Sister Chan Khong who had decided that I should go on to Australia after Vietnam since I was already more than half the way there. Thay had not been to Australia since 1986–1987 so the Australian Order of Inter-being who were organizing the retreats were happy to have a Dharma teacher from Plum Village. I stayed in the houses of the lay Order of Interbeing members who were Vietnamese and many of the events were for Vietnamese students of Thay so I could keep speaking Vietnamese.

I enjoyed Australia very much because it was new and at the same time familiar due to the British ancestry of so many Australians. In Sydney we went to two Vietnamese temples to lead a Day of Mindfulness. The monks in one of the temples had been to Japan to study Buddhism and there in the monastery they had been trained to eat quickly. In Plum Village our training had always been to eat slowly. We usually take anything from thirty to fourty minutes to eat a meal. We chew every mouthful about fifty times and this gives us a chance to be very aware of what we are eating and visualise the food as it grew in the field, being nourished by sunshine and by rain. We also have time to look around at the sisters and brothers who are eating with us and feel our appreciation for them. Eating a meal slowly like this is relaxing and can be healing for body and mind. After I had taken two spoonfuls, the monks in the temple had finished and the dessert, a sweet soup, was brought in. Because I was hungry I ate this more quickly. In Brisbane I gave a Dharma talk in a nuns' temple. In the front row was an audience of Vietnamese women. It usually happens when I give a Dharma talk in Vietnamese the audience listen very carefully. They need to listen carefully because Vietnamese is a tonal language and you understand the meaning of words according to its musical tone. My Vietnamese is not perfect and I make mistakes with the tones. These women were very kind and whenever I made a mistake with a tone they would correct it for me so that the rest of the audience could hear and understand. It made me smile but sometimes I lost the thread of what I was talking about.

The family of a Vietnamese practitioner who had lived for a time in Plum Village invited us to his home in Tasmania from where we could organize a retreat. We called him Bac Tu, Uncle Four, which meant he had two elder brothers (or sisters) who would be called Uncle (or Aunt) Two and Three. He had had a hard life as an orphan and when he married and had his own children he treated them rather harshly as he himself had been treated. He was also a talented musician. Somehow he came to Plum Village where he learnt how we can practise mindfulness in order to be able to transform the suffering that has been handed down to us by our ancestors. At first it was not so easy for him to live in a community but he learnt mindful breathing and mindful walking which transformed his life and as a result he wrote several songs which he would sing to the accompaniment of his mandolin expressing his enjoyment of tea meditation and other practices. Years later he became very sick with cancer. He was in hospital and the doctors thought he was about to die. He practised mindful breathing and recovered much to the astonishment of the doctors who pronounced that it was a miracle they could not explain. He wrote and told Thay that one breath was worth more than a million Australian dollars. He lived on for a few years more, experiencing the miracle of being alive and breathing. His house was not far from the sea and we could sit on the rocks looking out over to Mount Wellington. I was lucky to be able to go to Tasmania, because it was such a beautiful place, a pure land with its deep blue sea and green mountains.

Not only did I have a chance to go to Tasmania, I could also go to New Zealand. At that time there were no Vietnamese monks or nuns living in New Zealand. The laypeople had a small house which they used as a place to chant the sutra and hold Days of Mindfulness. So of course they were very happy to see me and the OI member sister, Chan Truyen, but we did not stay with them. We stayed in the countryside not far from Auckland with a Dutch practitioner and his wife, and from there we led a couple of retreats. One was in a forest where there were ferns and so many other trees. Many children came to that retreat and we practised hugging meditation with the trees as part of our walking meditation. It is rather like hugging meditation with another human being. You first ask the permission of the other person to give them a hug. Following your breathing you take that person into your arms. As you breathe in and out three times you can be aware of the warm body of the other person and the miracle of life. You are both alive and that is a miracle. You enjoy deeply the present moment of being together. When you hug a tree you feel the same respect as when you hug a person. That tree contains the whole universe. It withstands the winter's cold and the summer's heat. Its roots go deep and its branches reach high. In another retreat in a countryside camp we were unlucky when a bird fell into the drinking water tank. Many retreatants became ill. Those of us who were well took care of those who were sick and we went from room to room chanting the name of Avalokiteshvara Bodhisattva to help them feel safe and relaxed. Chanting the name of bodhisattvas is a practice of sending spiritual energy. Avalokiteshvara is the bodhisattva of compassion. As we chant the name we summon up in us the energy of compassion and feel we are sending that energy to the one who needs it. If we do this with concentration so that our mind is not dispersed, it is an effective practice and the person who is receiving the energy feels it immediately whether they are near or far away. On our return to Sydney, another temple there asked for a Day of Mindfulness so I delayed my return to France. After that the organizers of the practice had another event for me to go to. When I called Sister Chan Khong and asked if I could change my ticket a second time I received a firm "No." It was time to go home.

I returned to Plum Village in February 1993 after being

away for four months. I felt very comfortable in Australia and I think I was a little spoilt by the people who hosted me. When I received requests to lead retreats or Days of Mindfulness I thought it was only right to say "Yes" so I forgot about the benefits of being in Plum Village for my training and development.

More and more people were coming to Plum Village to practise and the Red Candle Hall in the Lower Hamlet was not big enough to hold them all. Thay wanted to build a new meditation hall, very simple, following the form of farm buildings consisting of iron girders and a corrugated iron roof. The girders and the roof were put in place just in time for the next annual Summer Opening and Thay gave Dharma talks in a building with no walls. This was the precursor of the Compassionate Nectar Dharma Hall. It was very pleasant sitting half-outside and half-inside and seeing the trees and hills around when the weather was not too hot but because the roof was of galvanized iron it became unbearably hot when the sun reached its zenith and Thay and others would take the hose and spray cold water on the roof to cool us down.

Thay very generously had someone build a hut for Sister Chan Khong and a hut for myself in the grounds of the Lower Hamlet. All I had to do was to varnish the floor. This was a place where we could meditate and work on translating the sutras and books of Thay in a quiet atmosphere. The Lower Hamlet is situated in a valley amidst rolling hills. Sitting on the wooden floor of the veranda of the hut you could look up the hill, over fields of sunflowers and forests, to a château as you watched the sunset. There was a water faucet on the

Daffodil festival in Upper Hamlet, 1993.

veranda so that I could boil water and make tea. I was surrounded by the natural world of flora and fauna. In the hut
there was a wooden stove which functioned well and kept
the hut very warm. Advances had been made in the design
of wooden stoves since I arrived in 1986 and this new stove
stayed alight much longer. The hut nestled amidst trees and
bushes and through the window above my desk I could look
out on an elder tree.

I had a computer on which I worked to translate the
teachings, which Thay gave me in 1993-1994. When I was

ordained we had no computer in Plum Village. It was only in 1990 that we acquired two in the Upper Hamlet. Two disciples of Thay, Arnie and Therese, brought them from the US and showed us how to use them. Before that we had used a word processor without a delete function. Many of Thay's books in Vietnamese were typed by Sister Chan Khong on this machine and then printed and bound by Thay in his hermitage.

In the monastery we have a daily schedule of classes, work, meditation, and rest and sisters work in teams to do the cooking and washing up in a rotation. In the early 1990s Thay came to me one day and said I did not need to work in the rotation team anymore. When I asked Thay why, Thay said that my pen should be my plough. This meant that I had plenty of time to translate. It also meant that I became a little isolated from the rest of the Sangha because, although I was present for the sitting and walking meditations and other sangha activities, I did not have the kind of connection the sisters have when they work together. So after a time Thay suggested that I sleep in the dormitory except for a few days before going away to lead a retreat and a few days for resting when I came back. One day I said that my head was tired of translating and on the next day Thay brought me a large radio and told me where to find France Musique so that I could listen to that for refreshment. I enjoyed very much listening to the classical music that I had not heard since becoming a nun.

The *préfet* of Lot et Garonne and the *Équipement*—a department of the Ministry of Public Works—began to pay their attention to the Lower Hamlet and its buildings. They were not happy about our compliance to safety regulations and threatened to close down Lower Hamlet. Thay was not worried about this and said, "They have their work to do and we have our work to do, and if they do not allow us to stay in Lower Hamlet, we shall find somewhere else to do our work." This was one of the reasons for Thay and Sister Chan Khong to start looking for another location to expand into. In 1995 they found a property about sixteen kilometres away, which Thay named the Loving Kindness Temple, now more commonly called the New Hamlet.

In September 1994, I went to Russia and Poland to share Thay's teachings on mindfulness in daily life. Russia had still not recovered from the dissolution of the Soviet Union in 1991. The people who had lived under Communism for so long were thirsty for spiritual practice. Many of them were searching for a spiritual path and their attendance at a retreat was part of their search. It seemed as if they were comparing the different spiritual paths of all the different teachers who came to offer their practices to find out which was the best for them.

From my observation, the Russians were endowed with a deep spirituality. The Russian Orthodox Church was needing to compete with new rivals like Buddhism and Hinduism from outside of Russia. I visited an Orthodox church and saw the faithful prostrating before icons with a great deal of devotion. We heard the choir sing and then sat down to hear the priest deliver a homily. I found myself under his gaze and from the translation which our lay friend and hostess was giving I realised that I had inspired an attack on non-Christian religions such as Buddhism.

During our retreat in Moscow, we held a tea meditation. Usually tea meditation in our tradition involves offering a cup of tea and a biscuit to each of the retreatants, which we then drink and eat in silence with joy, concentration, and mindfulness. The organizing team thought it would be easy enough to find some herbs that could be used for the tea but what were we going to do about biscuits? It was hard to buy bread let alone biscuits. In the end people who had relatives living in the countryside agreed to bring what they could, so we had a pot of jam and some bread to spread it on. Because of the food shortages in Moscow people were lucky if they had relatives who had some land in the countryside where they could grow vegetables and fruit and preserve them by pickling.

From Moscow I went on the night sleeper train to St. Petersburg. Although it was only the end of September, it was already snowing. The sleeper compartment was very warm and had four bunks, two of them occupied by men talking loudly in Russian. I felt rather lonely and longed to be back with the people who knew about the practice of mindfulness. Once in St. Petersburg I was very happy to be greeted by two kind friends who knew Plum Village and were organizing for us. I was not feeling well and they took good care of me. At first I could not eat anything and then when I felt better I began to eat what was to be our daily fare of buckwheat and pickled vegetables. We went to the venue where the retreat was to be held. It was a small house with a large wood-burning stove which kept us all warm. We were only twenty people or so on that retreat but almost everyone was new to the Plum Village practice. It was like being in a family. We sat crowded in the small living room of the house with the stove so hot that the people could be in shirt sleeves and I described to them the practice of mindful sitting, walking, and eating. Since it was so cold no one dared go outside until the afternoon, and that is when we practised walking meditation along snowy paths into a forest. I could not help but feel what a safe environment we were in, when I thought about the past.

In the first five years after I was ordained a nun, I travelled to many parts of the world and experienced teaching the Dharma to people belonging to different cultures. I was surprised how the practice of mindfulness was universally accepted and helped people to transform their suffering. I grew to appreciate the wisdom of the teachings Thay has offered to the world, sitting in small Dharma sharing groups and hearing about how people were applying the practice and how it was helping them. In those years my teachings were still immature at times but I also had some insight that I could use to help people transform. Sometimes when I meet people they remind me of what I had said more than twenty years ago. I am pleasantly surprised by what I said then and people are grateful for what helped them but they also see that I have made progress as a teacher and there is more depth to the teachings now.

At the end of 1994 I went again to Vietnam and then Australia. This time Thay also had the idea that we should hold retreats in the north, centre, and south of Vietnam. Sister Doan Nghiem was my second body. Sister Doan Nghiem is Vietnamese with British nationality. I had already met her when Thay came to England in 1986. She is one of the elders of the Plum Village nuns' Sangha and she travels every year in order to be able to share her time and her teachings in Thailand, Europe, and the United States.

Officially, I was not allowed to go to Vietnam because of what had happened two years earlier with the security police. However I managed to obtain a tourist visa through a tourist agent and flew to Hanoi. In the meantime the security police had discovered that I was on the flight to Hanoi and after we landed and I had walked down the steps on to the tarmac, I was met by two security policemen. They told me that I was not welcome in Vietnam and I should have to fly back to France on the aeroplane I had arrived in. The first thought that entered my head was "no way." I was looking forward to being in contact with Vietnamese Buddhists. Thay and Sister Chan Khong had gone to a great deal of trouble to organize the trip, and many people were looking forward to retreats and days of mindfulness, but trying to persuade the two policemen was beyond my capacity. All I could think of to save me having to reboard the aeroplane was the money Sister Chan Khong had given me, which I could use as a bribe.

At the sight of the hundred dollar bill they took me to their office and told me I could stay for a couple of days to rest before returning to France. They then told me to pick up my luggage and open it. They went through all the contents and confiscated video tapes of Thay's Dharma talks. Sister Chan Khong had told me that the security police often watched or read the material they confiscated and there is a good chance they benefit from Thay's teachings so that was some consolation at least.

Su Thay Dam Nguyen, (Su Thay is the title accorded to

bhikshunis in the North of Vietnam), the abbess of Dinh Quan Temple, was there to meet me. I had come to know Su Thay in Plum Village where she came to stay after she had been told by the doctors that she only had three months to live. Under Thay's direction she practised dwelling in the present moment very diligently and in fact lived for another nineteen years.

The Dinh Quan Temple is in a small village twelve kilometres from the centre of Hanoi. Su Thay talked to the police and somehow they reached an agreement with her that I could stay in her temple for a month. They would come and visit me every day, but I was strictly forbidden to go anywhere else. The security police from the Committee for Religious Affairs used to come and talk to me, asking questions about Vietnamese Buddhist congregations in Europe and the United States. They asked me about the activities of certain Vietnamese monks in North America, of whom I had never heard. They said they would like to have the publications of these organizations and if I could send them such materials, they would make it easy for me to come to Vietnam whenever I wanted.

On this trip I could not, as I had hoped, visit the centre and south of Vietnam. Still, somehow Su Thay Dam Nguyen managed to arrange for me to leave the temple to go to a couple of sacred sites in North Vietnam. We went to the Yen Tu Mountain and the Fragrant Mountain as on my last visit, and this time the road to the Yen Tu Mountain had been repaired. We also went to the Tiger Mountain, in the province of Nam Dinh, not far from Hanoi, unobserved by the security police. We hired a car and a driver for these trips.

Before we left Plum Village, Thay had done some research and discovered the address of the Young Mountain Temple where Princess Huyen Trang had come to practise after being ordained a nun and he instructed us to visit this place. Princess Huyen Trang was the daughter of King Tran Nhan Tong, the king who had become a monk in the fourteenth century. I had been helping to translate Thay's historical novel, *Hermitage among the Clouds*, about this nun who used to be a princess.[10] Su Thay Dam Nguyen hired a car and we were driven there from Hanoi. The stone-built hermitage with just three rooms has a shrine room that was still used by the local people. That place was not policed and some of the village people were far from friendly, but one old man accompanied us up to the hermitage and showed us around. He had in his possession some ancient documents about the temple but I could not understand them.

I was astonished at how small the hermitage was. The shrine room was the largest and the other two rooms, the kitchen and bedroom, were not more than a couple of metres square. It is always a joy to visit the place where the practice of understanding and compassion has been realised and especially for me because in this case it was the practice of a woman.

When we came down again a man was standing in the road threatening to throw a rock at the car and we had to wait some time before some local people managed to subdue him. He was hoping maybe that we would pay him some money in order for him to give us passage.

Another small hermitage we visited was the Huong Hai Hermitage. It had belonged to the realised nun Dieu Nhan who lived in the eleventh century. She was the chief lineage holder of the seventeenth generation of the Vinitaruci school, one of the Zen schools of Vietnam, which was founded by an Indian Zen master in the sixth century and continued until the thirteenth century. This was another place that inspired my confidence in the capacity of female practitioners.

In Dinh Quan temple I had time to do walking meditation in the large garden and eat the delicious grapefruit that grow there. Su Thay Dam Nguyen wanted the people who came to her temple to learn about the Plum Village teachings and practice of mindfulness, so she would organize a Day of Mindfulness from time to time.

During this second visit to Vietnam, we had a chance to teach about the Plum Village practice of Buddhism, although it was rather limited. Sometimes we would walk through the village on our way to the main road and talk to the children, and there were the little old women who came to do volunteer work in the temple. They were so small in size, but they still managed to carry building materials. I used to contemplate on what they had been through. They had been brought up in an atmosphere of Buddhist culture and practice, had been through the French occupation, the Famine of 1944–1945, and then suddenly found themselves under Communist rule where the practice they had known was strongly discouraged if not repressed. Now they had a chance to come back to their local temple and practise without being under threat. We had a tea meditation and they sang the lullabies they had sung to their children.

It is a privilege to be able to experience a culture that is not your own. The kind of Buddhism practised by the older women from the village was different from that which we practised in Plum Village. It was much more devotional, but still very sincere, and early in the morning I would see an old lady come to practice repentance, kneeling before an altar as she chanted and prostrated. During my second trip to Vietnam I had a chance to stay in a Buddhist temple for two months. This already made it quite a different experience from the one I'd had two years ago. The practice in the Dinh Quan temple under the direction Su Thay Dam Nguyen had many elements of the practice of Plum Village, since Su Thay considered herself a disciple of Thay and had brought his practice to North Vietnam. There was a chance to do sitting meditation together and to chant in the Plum Village way (in Vietnamese not Chinese, which in Vietnam was the traditional way of chanting).

I left Vietnam for Australia as I had done two years previously and would not return to Vietnam again until 2001. This time I just stayed in Australia one month. We held a retreat at the Wat Buddha Dhamma which had been founded by Ayya Khema. Ayya Khema (born 1923) was of German Jewish extraction and became a nun in Sri Lanka. She ordained women as Buddhist nuns and she organized the first International Conference on Buddhist Women from which the Sakyadhita (International Association of Buddhist Women) conferences arose. Wat Buddha Dhamma is in beautiful Dharug National Park, and is very simple with some huts and a meditation hall. I stayed in the hut which Ayya Khema had built for herself on top of a rock so the rock was the floor and you had to climb over the top of the rock when you came in the door. At that time there were no monks living in the Wat as there now are and our organizers had hired the location for our retreat. We could walk in a most beautiful environment of unspoiled nature. The practice during the retreat was based on the meditation on the six elements. These elements are earth (which symbolizes what is solid), water (which symbolizes what is fluid), fire (which symbolizes heat), air, space and consciousness. All these six elements have come together to make our body and our mind. They are not only in us but also in nature around us, the rocks, the brook, the eucalyptus trees. When we die our body and mind do not become nothing and when we are alive it is the same, our body and mind are constantly intermingling with the six elements around us.

While in Australia I had to apply for visas to visit China because I was to go from there to join Thay and other monks and nuns on the first Asian tour.

CHAPTER SIXTEEN

Asia with Thay

ONE OF THE great benefits and joys of being a monk or nun in the Plum Village tradition was to go on tour with Thay. Apart from the three-month Rains' Retreat Thay was almost always on tour either in Asia, Europe, or North America.[11] It was a joy and privilege to go on tour with Thay because you would learn so much and at the same time you had the chance to be in touch with mountains, ocean, and forests in faraway countries. You would see the world through the eyes of Thay and the Dharma, and Thay was so at home in all the different cultures. Wherever Thay went he was dignified, courteous, and very skilful in dealing with people in difficult moments. Thay's commitment to sharing the Dharma in the most relevant way possible in the countries he visited meant that even when Thay was not in good health he would appear fresh and joyful as he taught the Dharma.

The first Asian tour was organized in the spring of 1995. Thay's Taiwanese lay disciple, Dr. Yo, wanted Thay to visit his country of Taiwan and also mainland China. He was among many Taiwanese who were trying to help a revival of Buddhism in mainland China, and they financed the restoration of many old temples there. Besides China and Taiwan, Thay had disciples in Korea and Japan who wanted Thay to visit their countries. This tour with Thay would include four East Asian countries. In the beginning we were a delegation of five monks, five nuns (including Sister Chan Khong who always accompanied Thay when he travelled), and less than a dozen laypeople: Thay Doji, a French monk who had been ordained and practised in the Japanese tradition, Thay Shariputra, also French, who had been ordained in the Theravada tradition of Sri Lanka, and Brother Phap Tang from the US, as well Thay Thien Son who was Vietnamese and acted as tranaslator. The nuns included Sister Dieu Nghiem (Jina), Sister Tu Nghiem (Eleni) and Sister Vien Quang who was the disciple of an elder nun closely connected to Plum Village. She was of Chinese descent and spoke Chinese, but had been brought up in Vietnam. In each country to which we travelled different students of Thay would join the delegation.

TAIWAN

I flew from Australia to Taiwan to join the rest of a delegation that had arrrived a few days before I had. Taiwan is a Buddhist country and the temples and monasteries are well endowed and supported by the laypeople. We stayed in the house of a layperson in Yangmin Mountain where there are hot sulphurous springs and, at that time, azaleas in bloom. Thay led us on walking meditation among the azaleas and we bathed in the invigorating natural hot water of the springs. At first I thought that maybe there were no poor people in Taiwan. Everyone we saw looked so affluent. Dr Yo wanted Thay and Sister Chan Khong to meet the venerable nun Cheng Yen because she is one of the most influential and dynamic figures of Taiwanese Buddhism in

helping the poor. The venerable nun Cheng Yen told us how she had been inspired to make sure poor women have better hospital treatment, when she had witnessed how, in one maternity hospital for women who could not pay for treatment, the floor was covered in blood and there were not enough doctors and nurses to help. She started a charitable foundation and eventually was able to build a very large modern hospital for the poor.

In Taiwan I learnt about the relationship between the lay and monastic practitioners there. When we went by taxi, the driver did not take a fare. Once when we went into a shop to buy some pastries, we inadvertently chose one that was not vegetarian. The shop vendor refused to sell it to us because monks and nuns in Taiwan are expected to be vegetarian in accord with the precept of protecting life. I was impressed with how Buddhism is part of the society and culture in Taiwan and how the people want to help the monks and nuns practise purely.

We had a seven-day retreat in a monastery where the normal practice was Pure Land Buddhism. The abbot of the monastery noticed that each one of our monastic party had a different kind of jacket and he said that it would be better if each of us could be dressed the same. He bought for each one of us (including Thay) a brown cloak with a black lining and wherever we went in Asia after that we would wear this cloak. After we returned to France we continued to wear the cloaks for a while. The abbot also supplied everyone with a good thermos and thermos holder, and a stainless steel set of a bowl, chopsticks, and spoon. The intention was goodwill for the environment. He wanted us not to use the disposable bowls and chopsticks that were available everywhere in Taiwan.

In Taiwan it was the first time I had seen so many "baby" monks and nuns (children of five years and upward) laughing and playing in the cloister. Sometimes a mother and a father wanted to enter the monastic life and their children would be ordained along with them. Thay asked if the children would normally remain monks and nuns for the rest of their lives. A monk told us that many of the nuns stayed on, but at the age of eighteen the young monks had compulsory military service and would have to leave the monastery. They felt the freedom of being able to do as they liked, and once they had taken certain steps in that direction, it was difficult for many of them to return to the monastic life. A few would realise from their experience in the army how precious the monastic life was and return to the monastery when their military service was over.

I had heard much about the Chinese Buddhist master of the seventh century Xuanzang who had made the dangerous journey by land from China to India, along what is now known as the Silk Route, to bring back the Buddhist scriptures to China and translate them. In Plum Village we had studied some of his translations of texts on Buddhist Psychology, which the master himself had studied in Nalanda University. I was perplexed when I heard that we would visit a Xuanzang monastery in Taiwan and wondered how he could have come to be there. When we came to the temple I learned that the master had come there only thirty years ago in the form of a relic. We had a chance therefore to pay respect to a monk who had gone through much hardship in order to preserve the Dharma.

KOREA

The backdrop for our visit to Korea was the religious climate of the country which Thay explained to us when we arrived. Traditionally Korea has been a Buddhist country with some interruptions since the seventh century. Now, according to the census, only 25 percent of the population of South Korea claim to be Buddhist. For reasons of social status people are afraid of saying they are Buddhist. Many say they are Christian but secretly go to the Buddhist temples especially on festive days. Christianity is seen to go along with progress and Buddhism as something that is out of date and not in line with the recent economic growth.

There is also tension between certain Buddhist groups and Christian groups in South Korea. For many professed and non-professed Buddhists, Thay's books and presence were very healing. The books of Thay that had been translated into Korean were a part of the tour, for Thay had been invited to Korea by the publishers of these books.

As far as Thay is concerned there is nothing wrong with double belonging. This means that someone can belong to Buddhism and another religion at the same time. I am personally grateful for this because my Christian roots are still alive in me. Thay did not want to tell people to stop being Christian, he only wanted them to be aware of their Buddhist roots and what an important role they played in the Korean culture. People who are Christian can use practices that have their roots in Buddhism such as the practice of mindfulness. In a skilful way Thay often referred to the teachings of Jesus such as: "Leave your offering before the altar, and first go and be reconciled with your brother, and then come and offer your gift." (Matthew 5:24) A Korean professor of Theology at Union Seminary in New York, Dr. Chung, played an important role on this trip, interviewing Thay in such a way that helped people see how Buddhism could complement Christianity.

In Korea we stayed near Seoul in a Christian establishment with magnolia trees that were then in flower. Thay taught us to meditate on the tree in bloom: "I am here for you," and "I know you are there and I am very happy." Standing under the trees, looking up at the blossoms against the blue sky, we would be wholly present for them in the here and the now. We recognized that because we were there for the tree, the tree was there for us.

I had not known before that there were descendants of the Vietnamese Ly kings in Korea. In the thirteenth century in Vietnam, the Ly dynasty fell. The politician who wanted to instate a new dynasty of kings from his own family ordered the massacre of members of the Ly family or sent them into exile in remote mountainous regions. Prince Ly Long Tuong, along with his family and court officials, fled by boat and landed in Korea. His descendants still live in Korea and Thay wanted to meet them. It was a chance for Thay to talk about the Ly dynasty of Vietnam and how as practitioners of Buddhism the kings had made Vietnam strong through the exercise of compassion and understanding. They listened very carefully and were determined to keep the values of the Ly kings alive in their own family.

In Korea many old monasteries are in mountainous set-
tings. Among other temples we visited the Haeinsa Temple
where the Korean Tripitaka is housed. Korean Buddhists
have their own Tripitaka, their own Buddhist canon. It had
been written down by hand in the thirteenth century and
we saw one volume that a monk had written by hand using
his own blood. We visited the large Unmunsa nunnery
where Thay was invited to give a talk to the nuns. They
had been taught not to look at the monk who was teaching and so everyone was looking down at the ground or
closing their eyes. In Plum Village we look at Thay as he is
teaching us.

We learnt that in Korea cooking food is a practice. We met
a monk who was a chef and had written a recipe book. He
emphasized cooking for good health. I enjoyed his rice soup
made with ground pine nuts and tried cooking it myself
after we returned to Europe. In one temple the monks made
a drink out of pine needles, said to be good for the lungs. It
had accidentally become somewhat fermented, so we felt a
little light-headed after drinking some and politely declined
to have any more. Most temples in Korea plant pine trees in
order to enhance the quality of the air for the lungs of their
practitioners.

JAPAN

The place of monks and nuns in Japanese society is very
different from that in Taiwan. The code of discipline,
which monks and nuns receive in most Buddhist countries, does not exist in Japan. While we were in Japan, we

did some research on the monastic code (Pratimoksha) and
it appeared that it had ceased to be practised by Japanese
monks since the eighth century. Therefore, monks marry
and have property and do not appear to be any different
from laypeople. While people may feel respect for their Zen
master, they may feel a certain disrespect for other monks
and nuns. Thay was able to speak to monks and nuns and
give them advice and encouragement on their path of
practice.

We stayed for a few days at at Kojirin Monastery on
Mount Hiei outside of Kyoto where we had a Day of Mindfulness. The monastery was in the middle of a forest. There
was light rain or mist most of the time but this also enhanced
the beauty of the place. Walking in the forest you could hear
the water dripping from the branches of the trees as well
as the sound of a nearby stream. The tops of the trees were
enshrouded in a fine mist. Walking in the forest there was a
practice I shall always remember.

We visited a Pure Land temple and gave a Day of Mindfulness there. It was springtime and the camellias and cherry trees were blossoming beautifully. In the grounds of the temple there were more than one thousand tiny statues of Bodhisattva Kshitigarbha (Jizo) placed there in a ceremony by parents to help absolve the guilt and loss they felt for having gone through abortion. The Pure Land temple reminded me of a Christian church, so I felt quite at ease there explaining the basic practice.

We had a four-day retreat in a forest camp near Kiyosato. Thay introduced the Three Touchings of the Earth in the retreat in Japan. Up until then we had been practising the Five Touchings of the Earth, which is a meditation done as you place your body in the prostrate position on the earth. First you meditate in order to feel your mother, father, and all your blood ancestors continuing in you. The second time you touch the earth you see your teachers and all your spiritual ancestors continuing in you. The third time you touch the earth is to feel how you continue the energy of the people, animals (past and present), plants, and minerals of the land in which you are living. The fourth time you touch the earth is to send the strength of your ancestors to your loved ones and to feel at one with your loved ones. The final touching is to make the deep aspiration to understand and love those who make you suffer. The Three Touchings of the Earth take these teachings deeper. In the first touching we feel our connection not only with our blood and spiritual ancestors but also with our blood and spiritual descendants and we accept them all without reservation. In the second touching we feel our oneness with all beings alive on this planet now, whether they are suffering and afraid or liberated and free from fear. The last of the Three Touchings is to see that we are not really born and we do not really die. We are like waves on the surface of the ocean, arising and going back to the ocean water which has no beginning and no end.

It was a large retreat with more than a hundred retreatants, which was held in a conference centre. On the last day of the retreat we were due to take the train after lunch. Thay led the last walking meditation in the grounds of the retreat centre. The walking went on much longer than one hour and by the time we arrived back, we had to get on the bus to go to the railway station without being able to have lunch. The lunch that we missed caused all who ate it to go to the hospital. Someone had misidentified a herb on the mountains and put it in the cooking. Thay must have had a sixth sense that told him to lead a very long walking meditation that day.

It is unfortunate that I have only once been to Japan, that one time in 1995, but my monastic brothers and sisters have since regularly gone there to teach and lead retreats. Thay had been to Japan in the 1960s and even remembered the Chinese restaurant in Tokyo where he had gone then. He went there with a few of us for lunch one day. The tidiness of Japanese people impressed me, as well as their ability to live in a very small space. Many laypeople hosted us and served us food presented in an aesthetic way. The beauty of the flowering trees and shrubs in spring is unforgettable and no doubt has an effect on the consciousness of the people who present everything in a beautiful way.

CHINA

Dr. Yo was also instrumental in organizing Thay's trip to mainland China. For his part Thay had long wanted to be able to go to China to touch the roots of Chinese Buddhism and pay his respect to the great Chinese Buddhist masters, and this was to be the first visit of Thay to that country. Dr. Yo, though from Taiwan, was involved in encouraging the restoration of Buddhist temples in China and was eager that the young Chinese monks and nuns could hear the teachings of Thay. As a disciple of Thay, I also had that longing to visit the country from which we have received so much to help us in our practice of Buddhism.

This first visit of Thay to China, taking place in 1995, was ostensibly a tourist visit. Nevertheless, a programme of visiting Buddhist temples and institutes had been arranged by Dr. Yo and many previously unarranged teachings were also made possible spontaneously. Due to Buddhism's long history in China since the third century CE, we could still feel the presence of Buddhism despite the Communist regime, and we could be in touch with the beautiful scenery of the mountains which had supported the practice of Buddhist practitioners and Zen masters. Many of the ordinary people we met still had the seeds of Buddhism which had been handed down to them from their ancestors. In successive trips to China later on, Thay's visit would be organized by the Chinese government's State Administration for Religious Affairs. However, while Thay was in Italy in March 2008, he spoke out about Tibet, saying that, just as Thay had been allowed to return to Vietnam, China should

allow His Holiness the Dalai Lama to return to Tibet to teach the Dharma, and Thay expressed that he was willing to go with the Dalai Lama to Tibet to support him. After Thay made this statement, the Chinese government never organized for Thay to go to China again, and they wrote to Thay expressing their outrage at Thay's public announcement about Tibet.

We were assigned official tourist guides whose chief task was to watch over us and make sure we did not do anything the Communist government might disapprove of. They were young men and women who seemed to enjoy their task of being in touch with foreigners. Every day they had to make a report to their superiors on what we had done and said. While in Beijing we were taken by our guides to the official tourist sites. After a while Thay expressed his wish that we go to a Buddhist temple. This request is only too easy to understand. As a Buddhist monk, when visiting any place, you go first of all to the altar of the Buddha to pay your respect, and only after that do you pay your respect to the land ancestors. This request probably put our guides in a dilemma so they did not comply. It was a little frustrating, not only for us but also for the guides who had probably never had to deal with tourists like us and had not been instructed to take their clients to Buddhist temples. However, we took it with a sense of humour and Thay, as always, was calm. In the end, Thay said that we would refuse to get off the bus until we were taken to a Buddhist temple. It was fun doing a sit-in on the bus outside the Forbidden City. We practised breathing and smiling and sat in silence. This had its effect and the bus was directed to a Buddhist temple, Biyun Temple in the Fragrant Hills Park. The place was crowded with many local people enjoying their free time. Thay wanted to light incense in the temple and offer it on the altar, but for fire safety reasons the curators of the temple (which was now considered a museum) would not allow it. Finally Thay held up an unlit stick of incense he had brought with him, chanted the incense offering in Sino-Vietnamese, and then invited the bell. We touched the earth deeply on the dusty floor (in China people do not take off their shoes to go into the temple), feeling that we had fulfilled our desire to pay our first respects to our Chinese spiritual ancestors.

At the beginning of our visit to China, Thay had gathered us together and told us that we might not be able to share our practice by giving teachings on this trip so we should need to share our practice by the way we walked. As soon as we took a step, we should come back to our practice of mindful walking. After the incense offering and bowing in respect we went out into the park and some of the people who spoke English came up to ask us questions. We sang a song, written by Thay and put to music by Betsy Rose, first in English and then in Chinese which caused yet more people to gather around us. Thanks to Thay's deep practice, and maybe our walking meditation, Thay had a chance to share a teaching about the practice of mindfulness and relationships, and people were visibly moved.

Somehow after that we had the support of our ancestral teachers in China, and were allowed to share in words the teachings of the Buddha and be genuine Buddhists rather than tourists. Perhaps the guides helped by relaying messages to their superiors about how our interest in Buddhism was beneficial for the people. Thay was invited to give teachings to monks in a Buddhist Institute and in the headquarters of the Chinese Buddhist Association to monks, nuns, and laypeople. Thay's deep desire to repay his gratitude to the Buddhist masters of old by giving teachings that were relevant and helpful to this modern time, made the teachings very practical and inspiring. This first visit was the foundation for the other visits in years to come that would be organized by the Chinese government. Once a government official, after hearing Thay praise the wonderful heritage of Buddhism in China, said, "Thay, we have a wonderful jewel which we have put into the rubbish bin."

After Beijing we moved south, going first to Shijiazhuang in Hebei Province. There, while we were walking, there was a child who looked at Thay and met Thay's eyes. Thay said that sometimes you feel a deep connection with a child.

In Hebei Province, our party had the chance to visit the Bailin Temple and the Linji Temple. The situation in 1995, after forty-six years of Communist rule, was that many famous ancient temples were inhabited by just a very few elderly monks and were not in a good state of repair. More recently, many famous temples have been restored but unfortunately they have also become tourist sites, which means that the monks have to take care of tourists and the presence of tourists detracts from the atmosphere of Buddhist practice that has been there over the centuries.

What was new for me about visiting ancient Chinese temples was their size. At one time they must have housed so many monks. In Vietnam the ancient temples are so much smaller. The Bailin Temple is famous for its master, Zhaozhou (778–897). Thay gave a teaching to the monks there, telling a famous story connected to this temple. One day a young monk came to the master and asked him: "What is the real significance of Bodhidharma coming from India?" The master replied: "The cypress tree in the courtyard." This story was an excellent inspiration for a Dharma talk. Thay taught how that monk had lived several years in the temple and had never noticed the cypress tree. We need to live our lives awake to the miracles around us and not be caught in intellectual ideas. If you walk mindfully across the courtyard, you will be sure to see the cypress tree as a miracle of life.

We were also able to spend the night in the temple and join the monks for sitting meditation and chanting. Sometimes I could make out what we were chanting because the pronunciation of Sino-Vietnamese is sometimes close enough to that of Chinese.

Not far from the Bailin temple is the Linji temple. Linji is the name of a ford not far from the temple and the master was called by the name of the temple and the ford. He came here to live and teach in the first half of the ninth century. The Zen lineage to which Thay and Thay's disciples belong was established by Master Linji.[12] While in the temple, we were shown a plaque in bronze on which were inscribed the chief lineage holders of each generation of the Linji line. Thay belongs to the forty-second generation and Thay's disciples to the forty-third. Thay touched the plaque with great reverence as if being in touch with all the spiritual ancestors.

In the grounds of the Linji Temple, Thay prostrated with great reverence before the stupa of Master Linji. Of course we followed Thay's example, but I confess I felt uncomfortable about laying my forehead on the dust. Thay's reverence was so great that you could feel it in the atmosphere all around him and it took away my hesitation about touching the earth.

From Hebei we went to Shanxi Province to visit Wutai Shan, the mountain which is sacred to Manjushri, the Bodhisattva of Great Understanding. Traditionally Manjushri is depicted with a sword to cut through the bonds of ignorance. During this trip to China we might stop anywhere on our journey to eat in a local restaurant. It was not always clean and most of us at one time or another underwent some kind of stomach upset. When we arrived at our lodgings at the foot of the Wutai Mountain, Thay's stomach was not at all well. We were worried Thay might not be able to make the climb planned for the following day. The next morning we were due to walk up the 1,080 steps to the top of the mountain with our guides. Thay had not been able to sleep all night and we wondered if he would be strong enough to make the climb. To our great happiness Thay appeared and gave instruction on how we were to walk up the mountain; this was meant for us all, including our two Communist Party guides, who listened respectfully. Thay told us that we were to take one step for a whole in- and out-breath. We could say to ourselves the name of a loved one and imagine we were walking for him or her. Later Thay told us that he had practised for each of his monastic disciples one by one. Usually in Plum Village we practise walking meditation taking two or three steps to an in-breath and three or four steps to an out-breath. The much slower way of walking proposed by Thay that morning was very healing and by the time we reached the summit Thay was healed.

People believe that Manjushri frequently appears on the mountain in the form of a pilgrim or a monk. Thay said that walking in this way we would meet Manjushri at every step. Every time we came to a turning point in the steps we would stop and enjoy the magnificent view. We watched people rushing past us huffing and puffing and we just continued our slow walk, which must have been very strange at first for our guides. We would stop often and enjoy the wonderful views from the side of the mountain and we could feel we were looking with Manjushri's eyes. When we arrived at the top, none of us felt tired. We were welcomed into the monastery at the top of the mountain by the resident monks wearing their sanghati robes. Thay asked the abbot, "Are you Manjushri?" Maybe this was not the first time he had been asked this question, because tradition has it that Manjushri is still on the mountain and appears to the faithful in different forms. He replied, "No. I am Manjushri's dog." We took photographs and walked slowly back down the steps. This time we went separately in small groups of two or three and we continued the mindful walking that Thay had taught us on the way up so that once again we could enjoy the splendid views of the mountains that surrounded us.

Sister Vien Quang was a Vietnamese nun with Chinese parents and she understood Chinese. The guides did not know anyone in our party spoke Chinese so they would speak freely about us to each other within our hearing. She told us afterward that one of the guides had said, "'that old monk' (a respectful way of address for a senior monk in China) was something extraordinary." It was the first time she had walked up that mountain and not felt tired. She was writing her report of all that Thay had said to hand in to her superiors, but she said she was going to keep a copy for herself because the teachings were so important for her. In subsequent trips to China, Thay's teachings also impressed our guides and they began to put them into practice. One guide even came to Plum Village.

The last province we visited was Fujian Province in the southeast of China. There in the Guanghua Temple we sat with Thay as he spoke to the young thirty-year-old abbot. In the Upper Hamlet of Plum Village we have an abbot who is not yet thirty years old, but being an abbot in Plum Village is rather different from being abbot of a Chinese monastery. In Plum Village the abbot is more like a father caring for his brothers. He is not a decision-maker or the one who is in charge. However, maybe at that time Thay first thought about having a young abbot in Plum Village.

In Xiamen, our last port of call, we stayed in the university hall of residence, which was very close to the Nanputuo Temple where our retreat was held. This temple includes a famous Buddhist college. We had the support of the Venerable Miao Zhan who was the abbot of Nanputuo Temple. When he heard that Thay was in Xiamen he spontaneously invited Thay to give a retreat for the monks and nuns in the temple. He said nothing would stop him from going ahead with this retreat whether the government officials gave permission or not. The Venerable Miao Zhan and Thay held each other in mutual respect and it was with sorrow that later that year in Plum Village we learned of his death. On the last day of the retreat the monks and nuns sang the song: "I Have Arrived, I Am Home," which someone had translated into Chinese, as Thay stepped down from the teaching podium and we walked out of the lecture hall. This song was written by Thay and put to the music of the Christmas carol "Infant Holy, Infant Lowly." It describes the practice of feeling at home wherever you are. Everyone was very moved. We also visited a nunnery there, higher up in the mountains, and Thay talked to the abbess. We spent time talking to the nuns. Whenever we went to China, Thay always had time to go to nunneries and enquire about the practice there and give advice.

We learnt a great deal from Thay during this trip. What

we learnt above all is that the practice of meditation is not hard work. It is for our enjoyment. We had so many opportunities to practise meditation in beautiful places. Every moment of a retreat could be nourishing for us as well as for the retreatants. Travelling with Thay on a teaching tour is like going on a spiritual holiday. You see new people and new places and learn how people in different cultures live. We watched Thay and how he interacted with our hosts in different countries. His politeness, gentleness, and firmness when needed, were wonderful lessons. It looked as if Thay was at home in any culture. Not only did Thay have to give all the Dharma talks, he also had to take care of his delegation of disciples. Even when Thay was not in good health, he was there for the retreatants and no one knew that Thay was not well. Sometimes we were not in harmony. In Japan, Thay told us, Thay had had enough merit to be able to avoid us having to go to hospital, but our party did not have enough merit to prevent the incident of food poisoning from happening. We needed to practise more diligently to be in harmony.

Later on that year Thay and Sister Chan Khong discovered a property for sale in the *département* of Gironde. It is just over half an hour's drive from the Upper Hamlet. It was designated as the New Hamlet, a sisters' hamlet that welcomes women and families. The main house was originally built as a large private house for a well-to-do family and had been transformed into a number of *gîtes* (apartments) for holiday makers as part of a summer camp. These gîtes became dormitories for the nuns. More and more nuns were being ordained, most of them of Vietnamese descent and in their twenties, and the sisters needed more space. A few sisters came as a vanguard to begin the work of transforming a holiday camp into a nunnery. In 1996 all of us came to live there from the Lower Hamlet and lay friends stayed in the Lower Hamlet. Now there are nuns and laywomen in both New Hamlet and Lower Hamlet.

When I first came to visit New Hamlet, Thay was standing in the garden in front of what is now the Buddha Hall. He asked me if New Hamlet was beautiful. I looked around and saw that it already had some beautiful trees and also had the potential to be more beautiful. Although it has two minor roads on two sides of the garden, it is in a rural setting and there is not too much traffic. All around are forests and arable land. The nearest village is called Dieulivol which you can interpret as "God wants us to be here." The village church is a particularly attractive place. It has wonderful acoustics and we would go there, request the key from the woman who lived in the former rectory, and go in to recite the sutra. Now it is not so easy to gain entry. You have to have permission from the mayor before the postmistress will give you the key. The church, which is of twelfth-century Gothic style, is on top of a steep hill with wonderful views all around. On Lazy Day we can walk there and sit on the low wall of the porch outside the church door, contemplating the scenery, the deer, the sheep, and the birds below us.[13] The New Hamlet, just as the Upper and Lower Hamlets fourteen years earlier, had a disused building which was very quickly made into accommodation for nuns. What is now the Buddha Hall had once been a large barn which was then converted into a ballroom and then into a Buddhacum-meditation hall. With New Hamlet's founding in 1996, Thay appointed Sister Trung Chinh as abbess. Sister Trung Chinh had ordained as a nun and received full ordination in Vietnam. When she came to stay in New Hamlet, Thay was struck by the quality of her bearing that came from her training in Vietnam and her loving kindness. She was the first nun Thay appointed as abbess, and after that came Sister Jina in Lower Hamlet, myself in Green Mountain Dharma Center and, when Sister Trung Chinh was sent to be abbess in the Deer Park Monastery in California, Sister Dinh Nghiem was appointed abbess of New Hamlet. Many sisters have moved to New Hamlet from the different Plum Village centres throughout the world and it now has about seventy nuns in residence and has expanded even further with the recent purchase of several properties in the vicinity.

As nuns we practise what is called "changing hamlets." This means that we do not stay in one monastery for our whole life. Plum Village has three monasteries in the US, two in France, one in Germany, two nunneries and a small monastery in Vietnam, one monastery in Thailand, and one monastery in Hong Kong. We are asked, or we request, to go to a different monastery in order to broaden our experience of the practice and to give other sisters from the smaller monasteries a chance to live in the larger centres of Plum Village France and Plum Village Thailand. Some laywomen who enjoy the practice have built huts for themselves on the hill behind the New Hamlet so that they can join the daily meditation of the nuns.

By 1996 I had already been in Plum Village for ten years. During that time I had concentrated my energy on learning and practising Buddhist meditation as transmitted by

Thay. I had also had the opportunity to teach and translate. Because I was able to translate Thay's Dharma talks from Vietnamese to English, it gave me a chance to become acquainted with a wide range of Thay's teachings. Thay gave me the freedom to be myself and to cross the bridges that I needed to cross. Thay remained a strong pillar of support outside, but also allowed me to find my own teacher inside. A good teacher is not someone who makes you dependent on him or her, but someone who helps you find your own teacher within.

After one year in the New Hamlet I was sent to the United States. We had a goodbye tea meditation in the Floating Cloud Meditation Hall of New Hamlet. I made a formal request to leave the New Hamlet and go to the United States. Although I had had a persistent feeling that I would not be in the New Hamlet for the approaching three-month Winter Retreat, the only time in the year when monks and nuns do not go anywhere outside the monastery, I had no idea I would be going as far away as the US.

It was already late October when I received a telephone call from Sister Chan Khong telling me that Thay wanted me to go and live with a new group of monks and nuns in Vermont. I knew that this was an opportunity for me to make a new start and it was with determination to do the best I could that I knelt down and asked permission of the Sangha to leave.

CHAPTER SEVENTEEN

Establishing Monasteries Outside France

MAPLE FOREST MONASTERY, VERMONT

EVERY OTHER YEAR Thay, along with a substantial delegation of his monks and nuns, would spend three months in North America, giving public talks and leading short retreats in different locations. It is called a tour because we would move from one location to the next. In 1997 Thay and the delegation found themselves in Florida where Thay led a retreat on Buddhist Psychology. It had been arranged by Pritam Singh, a student of Thay who had been a disciple of a Sikh master but who also appreciated the teachings of mindfulness.

While Thay was in Florida, two Vietnamese young women and one young man asked to be ordained as a novice monk and nuns. They had come to the US as refugees and did not have passports, so they could not join us in Plum Village in France. Where were they to study and practise after their ordination? Pritam said he had a farm in Vermont where the monks could live and he could rent a house nearby for the nuns. Vermont is one of the most beautiful of the states of the US, though all of them have their own beauty. It was established 200 years before we arrived, in 1791. It has few built-up areas and no large towns. It has a beautifully green range of mountains called the Green Mountains and that is

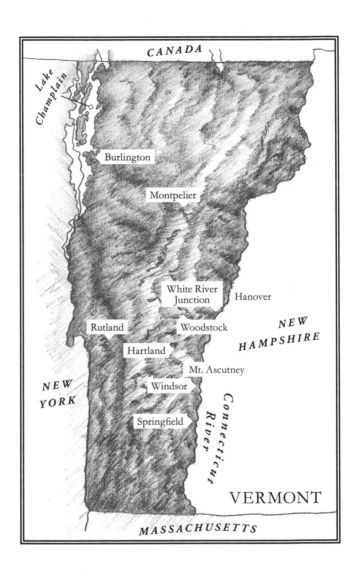

the origin of the name of the state. Many French-speaking people came there from Canada to escape the hardships of discrimination. They farmed the land and now the forest has taken over again. It is a perfect place for meditation: remote, with good air (when the wind is not blowing from the industrial complexes of Toronto) and no noise of traffic. Thay asked me to go and be with the nuns as an elder sister. At first there were only two monks at the farm, Brother Phap Lac and Brother Phap Chau, a South African monk, so they used to join the nuns for sitting meditation. We were seven nuns altogether, the two newly ordained ones, three other sisters who had been ordained in France but could not remain for a long time because they were applying for US citizenship, and one elder sister who was there, like me, to help. All were Vietnamese except for myself.

When I arrived, there was snow everywhere; it was knee-deep on the ground in early November and it did not melt until late March. The first thing I was offered by Ann, Pritam's wife, when I came to Vermont was a pair of boots for walking in the snow and a thick lined jacket. Each monk and nun had a pair of boots that came almost to the knees so that we could walk in deep snow. There was a dirt road between the monks' and nuns' hamlets and a beautiful path over the hills. I had never known so much snow. In Plum Village when it snowed it never lasted for more than a week. After a month my eyes became used to the ground being white with no green to be seen. In March, I had to fly back to France to renew my visa. When we were coming in to land in Charles de Gaulle airport, I caught sight of green grass. It came as a complete surprise and filled me with wonder.

Thay called our monastic community in Vermont Maple Forest Monastery, and our nuns' house was called Pine Gate. I had thought that Canada was the only place for maple syrup but now I came to know that Vermont has many sugar maples and produces maple syrup according to a tradition of hundreds of years. We used to see the sun rising red in the morning and it turned the whole snow scene pink. It was very warm in the house and we had a wood-burning fire as well as central heating. Every day we would practise walking meditation in the snow. The leader of the walking meditation would leave tracks in the snow that everyone following could place their steps into. If you are the first one, walking in the deep snow takes more effort because you have to pull your feet out of the snow every time you make a step.

When I first arrived in Vermont, Thay had already returned to France but he had stayed in the house of the sisters for a week or so before leaving. During that time the two young brothers and the sisters had established a custom of reciting the liturgy and meditating every morning and evening of the week. The morning meditation was at 5:30 a.m. I was impressed by this because in Plum Village we had what was known as a Lazy Day every week, when we did not recite the liturgy or practise sitting meditation as a community. Here they also had a Lazy Day, but it included gathering as a community twice a day to recite the sutra and meditate, rising at 5:30.

The three-month Winter Retreat began on the fifteenth of November, two weeks after I arrived. The Winter Retreat is a time when we have a chance to study in depth and practise solidly without having to travel anywhere. During that retreat, Thay would teach a specific topic in depth on Thursdays and Sundays in Vietnamese. In 1997 it was not possible yet to upload talks to the Internet, and then download and listen to them. In Plum Village the monks would make a videotape of the talk and Sister Chan Khong would take it to the post office and send it by express mail to us in Vermont. We could not have dreamt of streaming at that time. The tape normally took about a week to arrive. We were usually two weeks behind Plum Village as far as listening to Thay's Dharma talks was concerned. I translated the talks simultaneously because there were usually some non-Vietnamese friends who came to listen.

At Pritam's suggestion we organized a Day of Mindfulness for local people on Saturday instead of Sunday, because many of them were Christian and would want to go to church on Sunday. There was always a children's programme on the Day of Mindfulness, which was held in the sugar house in Maple Forest Monastery. The sugar house was the meditation hall in the Maple Forest Monastery. In that part of Vermont there are many sugar maple trees used for making maple syrup and the sugar house is the building where in early spring the sap which has been drawn off from the maple trees is boiled down to make the syrup. The house has a roof which is open at its apex so that the smoke and steam from the boiling process can escape. This sugar house had been converted so that the open roof was closed with glass and there was a wooden floor and central heating. Before I arrived Thay had given a talk there for sixty people.

We celebrated Christmas in Maple Forest Monastery and

there was a Christmas day when so much snow fell during the day that the sisters could not go home and slept in the meditation hall of MFM. Yes, Buddhist monks and nuns in Plum Village tradition do celebrate Christmas. When I first came to Plum Village, before being ordained as a nun, about a week before Christmas Thay told me that we were going to celebrate Christmas Eve in the Upper Hamlet. At that time of year no one was living in the Upper Hamlet. He asked me to cook some Western food. Five young Vietnamese men and Sister Chan Khong also came to the celebration. The young men did not appreciate the food I had cooked and when they had sat with the three of us for a polite period of time they went away to make their own noodle soup. That first Christmas was a modest affair but it showed how Thay and Sister Chan Khong are people of two cultures, able to be as at ease in the European as in the Asian culture, and I felt how kind of them it was to allow me to celebrate Christmas. Thay has emphasized the importance for Buddhism to adapt to the spiritual background of the country it comes to, just as it did in the past in Japan and Tibet for example. Now Christmas has become a very important event in Plum Village attended by more than a thousand people who are looking for the spiritual Christmas that has largely been lost in our time of consumerism. Plum Village Christmas is a wonderful blend of Zen Buddhism and Christian culture with a little bit of Vietnamese culture added in.

The roads that lead to Maple Forest Monastery, like most other minor roads in Vermont, are dirt roads—just earth with no tarmac. The people who live there have agreed to keep them like that to discourage road traffic. The climate is very cold in winter and the earth freezes to a depth of 1.3 metres. In April or March when the thaw comes, the dirt roads become deep, slippery mud. One has to be a very good driver to navigate such roads and many vehicles become stuck.

We could not receive lay practitioners in Maple Forest Monastery; it was just a couple of houses with room only for the monks and nuns (though later Pritam renovated the sheep house in the grounds of the Maple Forest Monastery farm to be a place in which laymen could stay). Pritam generously helped us buy another nearby property, a horse ranch, which Thay called the Green Mountain Dharma Center. The monks continued to live in Maple Forest and the nuns went to live in Green Mountain in April 1998. The Sunday Day of Mindfulness was held in GMDC and the Thursday Day of Mindfulness in MFM. Some monks and nuns would walk or bicycle the distance between the two hamlets; others went by car. The GMDC was a large property with 120 acres of land including some beautiful forests, a stream, and pastures. The main house was up on a hill and there was a large riding arena which could be turned into a Dharma Hall for seating one thousand people. Thay called it Buddha's Horse Hall, named after the horse who carried the prince Siddhartha away from the palace to become a monk.

As the crow flies, Green Mountain was very near Maple Forest, just over Mount Ascutney. Green Mountain Dharma Center was at the foot of Mount Ascutney. This mountain stands all on its own and is not part of a range. Another side of the Ascutney mountain was visible from MFM. If we had been birds, we could have flown only a distance of five miles to arrive at GMDC.

The route on the tarmac roads was about seventeen miles and went through the local town of Woodstock, but there was a shorter way on the dirt roads that was only ten miles. Since it was April when we moved to Green Mountain, the ice and snow were beginning to melt and the unpaved roads were sticky ribbons of mud. We went in two cars to take up residence in Green Mountain Dharma Center and because we became stuck in the mud we did not arrive until it was already growing dark. Pritam tried to use the larger van to nudge the smaller car out of the mud but it did not work. I had already been shown the property by Pritam, but this was the first time we all went there as a Sangha. We looked for a room that could serve as a meditation hall and, upon finding it, immediately chanted the verse asking for protection from the Dharma protectors. Then sister Hy (Joy) Nghiem swept the floors and we began to settle in to our new home.

Thay wanted to give us words of encouragement so he gave a Dharma talk on the telephone from France on the morning after we had arrived in Green Mountain Dharma Center. The only telephone was in the harness room by the riding arena. It was still very cold. Our friend Tim managed to put on the heating and about a dozen of us huddled in the small room to hear Thay on the speakerphone. We sang: "I Have Arrived, I Am Home." for Thay. Thay told us that Green Mountain Dharma Center did not belong to us; we belonged to Green Mountain Dharma Center. Since it was a telephone conversation, we could also talk to Thay and

Sister Chan Khong in France about our settling in. Thay wanted us to live in harmony so that we should have something to offer to the people of New England.

Green Mountain had its own water supply from a couple of deep wells. We had a vegetable garden with asparagus and raspberry bushes. One of the things all our monastic centres have is a vegetable garden. Gardening is one of the activities that occupy us during the hours that are devoted to work every day, and we can grow vegetables organically. In Vermont the growing season is quite short but once the snow has melted it is surprising how quickly things will grow. Sister Thuan Nghiem (Harmony) and sister Thang Nghiem (Victorious) were two of our gardeners growing arugula, mangetout (snow peas), French beans, and asparagus (before someone mistakenly dug it up).

In GMDC we also had a meditation hall. It was called the Avalokiteshvara Hall. It had been a hay barn, painted dark red outside, as is the custom in Vermont. It was converted for us into a warm meditation hall by a kind Vermonter friend called William. He did not charge us anything. The monks and nuns helped to make the new ceiling and floor. When Thay came to GMDC in May and saw it, he appreciated the exposed curved wooden beams that held up the roof, which reminded him of the ribs of the emaciated Siddhartha when he was practising asceticism. The Buddha Hall in Maple Forest Monastery and the meditation hall in Deer Park Monastery in California. would be built according to the same design with a rounded roof and ceiling. Thay led a ceremony to consecrate the building. The hall was very cosy with a carpet and you could look out through the large windows to the east at the White Mountains of New Hampshire in the background and a pond in the foreground. When I had free time I would come and sit there and admire the view. We could roam freely on Green Mountain Dharma Center's 120 acres of land. One time I came up behind a deer standing in the long grass. Turning its head and seeing me, it ran away into the distance. In winter we would lie down on the crisp snow and look up at the deep blue sky; then before standing up we moved our outstretched arms up and down so that the form of an angel was imprinted on the snow. In Green Mountain Dharma Center we had everything, including a swimming pool which we made into a waterlily pond. The compensation was that on our neighbour's land there was a pond in which you could swim.

When Thay came to Green Mountain Dharma Center, he saw the view of Mount Ascutney and he said once again: "We belong to the mountain; the mountain does not belong to us." This sentence always moved me. You could say it of the planet Earth: "The Earth does not belong to us; we belong to the Earth." Looking in this way, we have a great deal of freedom and we take good care of our environment.

The Ascutney Mountain Resort became the place where Thay twice led large retreats for many people. During the retreats we had a Day of Mindfulness in Green Mountain Dharma Center. In the early morning we climbed on to school buses that brought us to GMDC. The activities were held in the Buddha's Horse Hall, which had been carpeted. Thay had a stage where the monks and nuns came to chant, and then Thay gave the Dharma talk. We had a wonderful

Sister Annabel in Vermont, 2000.

walking meditation, a packed lunch, total relaxation and Touching the Earth led by Sister Chan Khong (in short, the recipe for all our mindfulness days), and then we went back to the resort. We had only one large retreat at GMDC and that was in 1998. It was a retreat for Vietnamese young people. They slept, (men on one side of the arena and women on the other), meditated, and listened to the Dharma in the Buddha's Horse Hall. Legally we were not supposed to have public events in the Buddha's Horse Hall and the living conditions were extremely basic, but the event was greatly enjoyed by the young Vietnamese friends.

Thay was keen that we renovate all the buildings in

GMDC as we had done in Plum Village, turning stables, sheep houses, etc., into living accommodations for guests and the horse arena into a large Dharma Hall. Thay said that two or three hundred people could come there to hear True Virtue give a Dharma talk. Unfortunately many obstacles arose in our designs to convert this farm into a Dharma centre. We enjoyed the Avalokiteshvara Hall for eight years but we were not able to convert any other buildings and later we were told that even that building was illegal. Plans were drawn up, architects' designs were submitted for approval, but the authorities never granted permission for us to begin to build. We came up against other legal difficulties. There was a great deal of opposition to our building a larger septic tank, which the law required us to have in order to be able to receive guests. The opposition was led by a group of environmentalists who took us to court, but was funded by one of our neighbours who was very rich and perhaps feared having a Buddhist centre next door. Since we could not build the septic tank, we could not build any guest accommodation. In the midst of these difficulties, Thay encouraged me to contemplate the moon whose light was always free.

On the one hand we had a beautiful place to live. On the other hand we could not pursue our ideal of building a centre that would be a place of refuge for many people.

While these struggles to develop Green Mountain Dharma Center were taking place, in Maple Forest at Thay's request Pritam was building an enclosed monastery where the nuns could take it in turns to go and practise to develop concentration and insight. It was not far from Maple Forest

Monastery and was built in the Shaker style of architecture as two beautiful buildings just below the Buddha Hall, which had been built some years before. The Shakers were a Christian movement in the United States and they lived in celibate communities. Thay always said that it would be funny to live in the US and build a monastery in an Asian style, that we should use the style of the people who live there. Just like when Chinese and Indian Buddhism came to Vietnam, the architecture and music used was Vietnamese. Pritam explained to me that the Shakers had made a very positive contribution to North American culture, and by building in the simple style they had used, we were paying respect to their ethical way of life. One of the houses, Crane House, had a kitchen and dining room downstairs and bedrooms upstairs. The other, Pine House, had a library and common room downstairs and two or three bedrooms upstairs. The houses were very fine and built of wood. We made a rotation so that sisters could take it in turns to stay at Pine and Crane. The length of time each sister could spend there was three months in one year. The sisters used these houses to live in seclusion and have more time to study and meditate. This was a great luxury and a wonderful idea.

Those who stayed in Pine and Crane practised sitting meditation in the Buddha Hall which was a five or ten-minute walk away. At five in the morning we would walk across the hill to come to sitting meditation. Sometimes there was a blizzard and it was difficult to see where you were going. Yesterday's path in the snow would have already been obliterated by new snow. If someone else had arrived earlier and lit the candles, then you could see your destination; if not you had to guess. It was very pleasant to arrive, shake the snow off your boots, and close the meditation hall door against the wind and thick falling snow. Even though we had only been walking for ten minutes or so, the contrast between inside and outside was very great.

Inside the meditation hall is always a little different from outside. You place both hands on the door handle and gently push for the door to open. You feel immediately the atmosphere of peace created by those who are already sitting there. Pritam built this Buddha Hall on the summit of a high hill above Maple Forest Monastery; it is made of wood and painted white. It has a platform all around the edge of the walls for sitting meditation, and sitting on the platform you have windows to look out of and from which you can see the surrounding mountains that stretch far into the distance. It is surrounded on the outside by rose bushes, and leading up to it from the south are granite steps. It is lovely to sit on those steps and contemplate the mountain ranges in the distance. In the winter, the sun rises directly in front of the French windows of the hall and fills it with its red light.

The construction of Pine and Crane was completed in October 2005, and Thay was able to visit as part of the US tour that year. I was sleeping in the upper hallway of the Pine House where Thay had his quarters. At 4:00 a.m. the snow started to fall thick and fast. I sat up and watched it out of the window. Thay came out of his room and suggested we walk to the Buddha Hall in the snow. We went downstairs and put on our snow boots. I was moved to see how mindfully Thay held the boots and tied the laces. If I had been a good attendant, I would have tied the laces for Thay. I was not yet familiar with the path to the Buddha Hall and led Thay around in circles. The snow was already thick and the going not easy. We did not have a torch.

When we arrived, we took off our snow boots and walked into the Buddha Hall. There we found sister Dao Nghiem meditating; she brought us cushions to sit on and placed them in front of the French windows where we could watch the snow fall. After sitting for some time, it was still dark and we saw two lights. Thay said it was Thay's two attendants carrying torches and coming to look for us. But the lights did not come any closer and we realised that what we had seen were two lamps outside two doors of Pine House. I knew Thay was giving me a teaching and I thought of the phrase in the Diamond Sutra: "Where there is a sign, there is a deception." Much of the time we live in a virtual world and our perceptions are not the reality. When dawn came, the snow stopped falling and we walked back, enjoying the sunrise. After breakfast we all went for a walk in the Maple Forest. It was like a fairyland, the snow on the branches sparkling in the sunlight.

"If this place is not the Pure Land, the Kingdom of God," Thay would ask, "then where will you find the Kingdom of God?"

For nine years we enjoyed the humid summers and the dry winters in Vermont, with brilliant blue skies and thick snow on the ground.

The potential of Green Mountain was great, with many old farm buildings that could have been converted as had happened in Plum Village. Thay told me that Green Mountain was a wholesome healing place and we should not give it up, but in the end after nine years we realised that we could not do our work of offering retreats there and we should have to move somewhere else. Another reason we felt the centre would not work was that Vermont was very remote and far from large airports. It was not very encouraging for the ordinary person to have to travel all that way. Leaving Green Mountain Dharma Center also meant leaving Maple Forest Monastery because we needed the monks to take care of the new centre along with the nuns. When we saw that we could not continue in Vermont, we thought about looking in New York State for a suitable place that was not too far from New York City.

When some of our neighbours heard we had gone, they wrote a letter expressing their regret that we had left the area. We used to go at Christmas to offer spring rolls to our neighbours. There is a special tradition in Plum Village that at Christmas the Sangha makes spring rolls. This is a vegetarian dish of Vietnam. There is a filling of carrots, cabbage and tofu wrapped in pastry and then fried. You can almost guarantee that anyone, whether Vietnamese or not, will like this dish. Having made the spring rolls, if possible while they are still hot, a group of monks or nuns will take these rolls and distribute them to our neighbours.

In GMDC some of our neighbours lived at quite a distance, at least a couple of kilometres away, so we would go by car to do the distribution. For those who lived near, we would go on foot. For the nine years we were in Vermont there was only one year when at Christmas there was no snow on the ground. Taking spring rolls to neighbours is a modern version of going on the almsround. During this almsround we have a chance to be in touch with our neighbours and offer them a taste of the practice—not only in the love that we have put into the spring rolls but also by the way we comport ourselves in mindfulness, with every smile, every word, and every step.

Our not-so-friendly neighbour was afraid of many things and had built a great wall and fence around his property. It was not possible to come inside without someone taking a look at us first. On the traditional almsround it was not possible to miss a house, rich or poor, friend or foe, Buddhist or non-Buddhist; the monks and nuns went from house to house, stopping at every house. So we went to our neighbour's house in that spirit and the janitor let us in the first gate, but the second gate we could not enter. He took the spring rolls and gave them to the lady of the house and a few days later she brought to us a box of biscuits she herself had made. We had another neighbour who had horses who let us go there and ride sometimes. The horse just walked gently around the field as we sat on its back. If you read the traditional precepts you will see that a nun should not ride horses. That is because in the time of the Buddha riding a horse was something very luxurious. We did not spend very much time riding horses, just very occasionally for fun.

We had another neighbour, Lillian, who was over ninety years old. She lived alone in a cottage and her son lived in a house on the opposite side of the road. The cottage was high up and had splendid views of the White Mountains of New Hampshire. It was small, just a few rooms and of course the mudroom. Every house in Vermont has a mudroom. That is the place where you leave your muddy or snowy boots and coat before you enter the main part of the house. With her family she made and sold maple syrup. Whenever we were going to visit one of our hamlets in France we would buy it from her to take as a gift. She would tell stories of when she was a child in Vermont and she wrote books, her latest of which was on the ecology of Vermont.

Some of our neighbours were such good friends, some were indifferent, and some were hostile. Some did not know whether to support us or to listen to those who wanted us to leave. After we left, in the collective letter we received from our neighbours, they said how much they missed us and that they regretted they had not stood up more strongly to support us so that we could have stayed.

We also felt regret at having to leave because Green Mountain Dharma Center and Maple Forest Monastery were such ideal places for the practice of meditation. We felt a little sad that we had not been successful in winning the support of our neighbours. However, the monastic practice of Plum Village has its component of leading retreats and having guest accommodation so that the laypeople can come and practise meditation alongside the monks and nuns; so we were happy at the prospect of finding a new centre where we would have the facilities to welcome guests and begin anew in our aspiration to practise for the sake of all beings.

Maple Forest Monastery and Green Mountain Dharma Center were an opportunity for Plum Village to have a hamlet in the US for the first time. Even though that place no longer functions as a meditation centre, it still leaves beautiful memories in the hearts of people. They are part of our path of coming from nowhere and going nowhere. All kinds of causes and conditions led to the founding of MFM and GMDC and to their subsequent dissolution.

Thay never said that he wanted us to leave GMDC. He said this place is *dat lanh*, that we should not leave, and in my heart I have never left. Dat lanh means "wholesome earth," a wholesome place where people can benefit from the practice. Sometimes the pressure is too much; there are forces that want us to stay and forces that want us to leave. People feel threatened by a different religion and a different culture; they know nothing about us but they imagine that we are a threat. If we can demonstrate to them that we are not a threat, then we can stay. If we fail to demonstrate that, then we have no choice but to leave. Thay has always said, "I am not attached to any hamlet." If the government forces us to leave, then we can find another place to go to. We are like the deer; we can get up and go to another part of the forest at any time. We do not have to suffer because of the loss of a hamlet. We do our best to make things work and cooperate with others, but when it's clear that the causes and conditions aren't right, then we can leave without a lot of regret. People can put pressure on us and tell us that we have to do this and that, but we also have our way of practice and we are guided by that rather than feeling we need to comply with everything others tell us we have to do.

BLUE CLIFF MONASTERY, UPSTATE NEW YORK

There were many properties in New York State that could be made into a retreat centre. The area of the Catskills, an hour or so away from New York City, was dotted with old hotels and summer resorts that had been built for New Yorkers to escape the oppressive heat of the summer months in the city. We went as a Sangha to look at them. Some of the resorts were very large and we felt that we would not be enough people to manage them. Some needed so many repairs that we could not afford them. In the end we chose the place that is now called Blue Cliff Monastery, and in April 2007 all the monks and nuns from MFM and GMDC, about twenty of us, moved there from Vermont.

Blue Cliff was an old hotel resort but it had a very pleasant atmosphere, which we could feel as soon as we arrived, and we felt at home there immediately. The thing I felt drawn to when we saw the property for the first time was the lawns with two very large old fir trees. The buildings were perhaps less attractive, chalet-like cabins of different hues. The sisters lived in the old hotel buildings and the brothers, who were fewer, lived in the house across the road where the former hotel owners had lived. There was a separate building on the sisters' side large enough for the community to use as a meditation hall, but not large enough to use in this way for the big retreats led by Thay. Blue Cliff also needed many repairs and much had to be done before Thay came in the autumn of 2007 from France for the US tour. We were fortunate to have Brother Phap Vu (Dharma Rain) to help us settle in and make the necessary repairs.

The US tour that year was set to begin and end in Blue Cliff in September and October.

Thay chose the name Blue Cliff from the Blue Cliff Records, a famous Zen manual for koan practice. I do not know why Thay chose that name but one day, looking at the mountains from where the present meditation hall is, I saw some cliffs that were in fact bluish in colour. Thay, however, had never been to the place when he gave it its name so perhaps it is just a happy coincidence that the name suits the place so well.

As the original resort had been built mainly for use in the summer, the buildings were not suitable for year-round habitation and it has been expensive to winterize them. The water is very good there; it comes from two wells and does not have to be brought in from outside.

Not far from Blue Cliff there is a state park in the Sha-wangunk Mountains. We went there to practise sunrise or sunset meditation from what is called Sam's Point, the highest point of the range. Thay once said we can just enjoy the mountain without having to buy the mountain. During the first summer family retreat held at Blue Cliff, we would sometimes leave the monastery before sunrise and arrive in time to see the sun come up and then eat our breakfast on the mountain. The air was fresh and cool.

On Thay's 2007 US tour we went on an outing to the nearest part of the range where the mountain is covered with wild blueberry bushes and a very rare species of pygmy pine trees, and where there are also caves. When Thay went there with us we visited one of the caves and then sat outside it to eat a snack. Thay recited the lines: "Having come to the deep cave of the immortals, we only leave when the elixir of immortality has changed our bones," letting us know that when we come to a practice centre we should not think of leaving it until we've experienced that deep transformation of our mind.

When Thay arrived I was not in good health. Some people suggested that I should not go with the Sangha on tour to Colorado and our monastery in California, Deer Park. Someone even said that I might not survive the rigours of being on tour. Thay said the opposite. He laid his hand on my head for a long time and said that the Sangha energy on the tour would be the best thing to revive my health. I also was determined to go.

First we went to Stonehill College in Massachusetts where Thay led a retreat for 800 retreatants. Thay suggested I give one of the Dharma talks, if I felt well enough. I was already feeling better at that time and then I continued with the tour to Colorado and Deer Park Monastery, not far from San Diego. In Deer Park Monastery the parents of one of our monks had invited a Chinese doctor from Beijing to come and he treated many of us.

We came back to Blue Cliff for the final retreat of the tour. I was feeling much better. It was mid-October and the weather was cold. We had hired a large marquee for the Dharma Hall and the freezing wind blew through the cracks. There was a gas-fired heater in the centre of the marquee that roared during the Dharma talks. Many people had to stay in local hotels because we did not have enough accommodation on site.

In all I only spent six months in Blue Cliff. I was still the abbess during that time. It was an interesting time of settling in to another part of New England. Although we kept our daily schedule of sitting and walking meditation in the early morning and in the afternoon, there was much work to be done. Thay wanted us to build a large meditation hall at Blue Cliff, and we had to do the work of seeking planning permission. Thay insisted that the design of the meditation hall should be in the traditional style of New England.

At the end of October 2007 I went back to Plum Village.

European Institute of Applied Buddhism (EIAB)

While in Blue Cliff in the autumn of 2007, Thay shared with me his vision of an Institute of Applied Buddhism in Germany. At that time Thay had looked at different properties in central-west Germany, not too far from Holland and Belgium where Thay had many students. Thay had some aerial black and white photographs of the building that he thought most suitable to house an Institute of Buddhist Studies. The photos were of the building that now houses the institute in the town of Waldbröl.

Thay asked me to help write the catalogue for the courses that were to be held there and suggested I go back to Plum Village to do this. This catalogue was based on the various retreats that Thay had led in different parts of the world: retreats for congresspeople in Washington, D.C., for police and prison officers in Wisconsin, for businesspeople in Plum Village, and so on. So after the US tour that year, I went back to the New Hamlet of Plum Village. The introductory paragraph of the the catalogue reads as follows:

> Distinguished programs of Buddhist Studies may be found at any number of universities around the world. There is, however, a crucial element missing from most, if not all, of these programs: training in concrete methods for using the wealth of the Buddha's teachings to relieve suffering and promote happiness and peace in ourselves, our families, our communities, and across the world. The European Institute of Applied Buddhism (EIAB) offers a complete program that fully integrates the study of Buddhist texts with concrete applications at all levels of the students' daily life.

During the Winter Retreat 2007–2008, I put together the catalogue and revised Thay's book of guided meditations *The Blooming of a Lotus*.[14] Those of us who have been sent from Plum Village to build practice centres elsewhere always feel happy to come back to our root, our mother house in France. For thirty-two years Thay shaped Plum Village by his presence, practice, and teachings and that energy is still very palpable.

The Institute was to be first and foremost a monastic centre where monks and nuns could study and practise and learn how to lead laypeople in the practice. Thay described it as a peach. The kernel of the peach was the monastic Sangha who would practise permanently on the campus of the Institute, thus lending the place an ambience of mind-

fulness, concentration, and insight. The flesh of the peach symbolized the lay friends who would come and practise. So that the monks and nuns would not be overloaded by leading retreats, Thay also invited lay Dharma teachers to come and help with the teaching.

Thay appointed me Dean of Practice at the Institute but said I could come and go between Plum Village and Germany as I liked, and that especially when Germany was too cold I could come back to Plum Village whenever I wanted.

I arrived in the town of Waldbröl, Germany, in early November 2008, two months after the other brothers and sisters had begun to live there. Sister Bi Nghiem, our only German nun at that time, was with me. She was a Dharma teacher and in the beginning the only one of us who could give teachings in German. All the other monks and nuns were Vietnamese, except for one monk who was North American. Sister Bi Nghiem had just led a retreat with me in the Woodbrooke Quaker Centre in Birmingham, England. It had become a custom to have a retreat there every year with the Quakers. I learned some important things from them about how to facilitate a meeting and I was always impressed by their capacity to listen deeply in Dharma sharing.

Waldbröl means "The Bröl in the woods." The Bröl is a river that runs into the river Sieg. It begins as a source in the woods that lie a five- or ten-minute walk from the Institute. Whenever I am there, I walk to the spring to bring water home to drink.

I had seen aerial photographs of the Institute but until I was there I had not realised just how big it was: a stark five-storey building from the Nazi era with a flight of concrete steps to the entrance, wide, high corridors, and flights of marble stairs inside.

The abbess, Sister Huong Chau, came to greet me and introduced me to the daily programme we should be following. Thay Phap An, the eldest monk, also greeted me and I was shown around. At that time the Brandschutzamt, the authority for fire protection, had not yet prevented us from using the building and we had the run of the whole of it.

I had many emotions as I stood on the second floor and looked out of the windows of the rooms we used as a meditation hall. I wondered how long I would stay here, whether it would be the last centre I was to live in, and whether I would die here. I was aware of all the people who had lived and died here before, most recently the military doing research into chemical warfare. The name on the wall outside my room was the name of an officer in the military.

I was shown to my room, which I was to share with an attendant. I had a bed, a desk and a chair, a cushion and a mat for sitting meditation, and an electric kettle to boil water. The room was carpeted. Outside the window of the room was a beautiful straight tall birch tree in which blue tits spent their days looking for food. The room had its own bathroom en suite, the first time I had known such a luxury in monastic life. There were other things that were not so luxurious, like the absence of drinkable tap water. Our closest neighbour was a home for people with disabilities, and they were kind enough to supply us with all the water we needed for cooking purposes. Two monks would go and fetch it every day. The heating system was antiquated and unreliable, and it would often fail. The only telephone (we did not have cell phones in those days) was in a remote area of the basement. It was quite an ordeal to get there through different parts of the basement in the semi-darkness and many of us, especially our Vietnamese brothers and sisters, were afraid of ghosts.

For lighting in the many corridors we put small desk lights at intervals. The days had already been drawing in. I was heartened by how well my Vietnamese sisters and brothers adapted to this strange environment. The one who felt the most depressed there was our North American brother. It was the daily routine of sitting, eating, and walking meditation together as a community that made us feel more at home. Thay came that month to be with us monks and nuns in the Institute and to lead a Day of Mindfulness. Since we did not have a Dharma Hall, we had to rent the auditorium in the nearby hospital, only a few minutes' walk away from the Institute.

Before Thay left, he invited us to sit and contemplate the moon early in the morning. We all sat before the windows in the hallway that leads off from the main entrance hall. In those early days we still had the run of the whole building but it was not long before the fire protection officials came and stopped this. We had to migrate next door to the building of the former Civil Service School and wait until one fifth of the Institute building had been brought up to standard before we could go back and live there again.

Even now, the other four-fifths of the building, apart from the ground floor, remains out of bounds and has been walled off by the fire protection authority. Because it is a listed building, the authorities are particularly strict about all the fire protection regulations, which in Germany are already more stringent than in other European countries. The reason we could not continue to renovate was that we did not have the funds. Recently, in 2018, we have received some donations and begun to renovate another fifth of the building.

The building has a complex, dark history. When Thay and the group of monks and nuns who were to live and practise in the Institute arrived in September 2008, Thay had gone into each one of the four hundred rooms and sprinkled consecrated water to purify the karma of the place. Many of us have had dreams of children being cruelly treated and some have even seen ghosts, but as the years have passed the atmosphere has become less and less heavy. The original building had been a hospital for people with disabilities and paupers. The intentions of the Evangelical priest and the doctor who founded the hospital appear to have been wholesome, but it seems that patients were maltreated from early on. Once the Nazi regime came in, the situation became much worse. In 1938, 700 patients were forcibly removed from there and never seen again.

Then the hospital was made into a kind of hotel for Nazi youth where young Aryan men and women could stay and become acquainted with each other and thus continue the Aryan race. When World War II ended, the building was commandeered by NATO and made into a hospital again, this time for Allied soldiers who had been wounded while fighting in Germany. It then became a civilian hospital for Waldbröl until a much larger new hospital was built nearby in the 1960s. After that, the building was taken over again by the German Army for research into chemical warfare. Some of our local lay practitioners remembered coming to the place to stage demonstrations against chemical warfare.

The army had abandoned the building only three years before Plum Village bought it in 2008.

The history of the building did not endear many of Thay's German disciples to it. They could not understand why Thay should have chosen a building where such terrible things had happened. Of course the German people are horrified by this period of their history and I can understand that they do not want to be reminded about it. Thay said we did not choose Waldbröl but Waldbröl chose us. Thay felt that the Dharma was needed there and our practice of tolerance and compassion could be like lotuses growing out of the mud of fanaticism and cruelty.

In fact there had been acts of compassion in the building in the past and it is possible that these tiny acts of kindness and courage served to tilt the balance and make it possible for the Sangha to be there and practise. For example, it is documented that when the Nazis came to take the patients away, there were doctors who tried their best to save their patients' lives by refusing to sign their release papers, concealing the number of patients and their names, and so on. The building had borne witness to unspeakable cruelty but also to compassion and bravery to counter the Nazi regime.

In the beginning Thay advised us to organize a short ceremony every day to help transform the heavy energy in the building. During this ceremony we use the power of mindfulness and concentration to give rise to compassion for those who died and suffered there and for those who perpetrated the acts of cruelty. To prepare for the ceremony, a small altar is situated before an open window or door. On it are placed a censer, candles, and some food, including a thin rice soup. At their time of death victims of cruelty and injustice may produce feelings of fear, anger, and hatred— who cares about them? who will bury them and pray for them? We care for them by making this offering and helping transform the fear and hatred with our compassion. Thay wrote a text for us to use in this ceremony.

Dear friends, dear children,
Seventy years ago you were badly treated. Your life was ended by euthanasia or you were sterilized so that you could not have a continuation. Your suffering was enormous and not many people were aware of it. From then on you have suffered.

Now the Sangha has come. The Sangha has heard and understood the pain and the injustice you underwent. The Sangha has practised mindful walking, sitting, breathing, and chanting. The Sangha has asked the Buddha, the bodhisattvas, the spiritual ancestors, and other great beings to transmit to you their merit and all their attainments so that you have a better chance to be liberated from your suffering and the injustice done to you, so that you can be reborn and be able to manifest again in new and wonderful forms of life.

The people who caused you suffering and injustice had themselves suffered greatly. They did not know what they were doing. Therefore allow compassion and forgiveness to be born in your hearts so that these people too may have a chance to transform and be healed.

Please support the Sangha and the succeeding generations of Dharma practitioners so that they can turn this place into a place of transformation and healing, not only for Waldbröl but for the whole of Germany and the world.

Our walking meditation on the stairs and in the hallways replaces the sound of military boots and we are aware as we walk of the punishing hard work of labourers putting those heavy marble slabs into place. We send compassion and gratitude to them as we walk.

In the beginning, the ground floor hallway was an empty place. Now at the weekends and at other retreat times it is filled with retreatants who are looking for a way to bring peace and joy into their lives, their families, and society by the practice of mindfulness, and the Institute has become a place of spiritual refuge for many people, many of whom attend retreats not once but several times every year.

We feel happy when we are able to contribute something to the lessening of suffering. What has encouraged me most at EIAB is the diligence and devotion of my younger monastic sisters and brothers. They have continued to offer their services to the guest practitioners who stay with us. They have learned German in order to be able to do this, although German is a very difficult language for Vietnamese people; it could not be more different from Vietnamese. Living in the Institute has also been an opportunity for me to learn German and to appreciate many positive aspects of the German culture. I am sometimes a little daunted when I walk on to the campus and see the huge main building, the Ashoka building, but I know that one day it will be filled with people who meditate in order to offer compassion to the world and that makes me happy. It just needs time to find funds to renovate the building and we need to be patient. Thay has taught us that we never need to be afraid of not having material resources and that as long as we practise diligently the resources will manifest.

THAILAND

In March and April of 2013, Thay and Sister True Emptiness allowed me to join the Asian tour in Thailand. As well as a biennial US Tour, Thay conducted a biennial Asian tour to Thailand, Hong Kong, and Korea. Hong Kong and Thailand have their own Plum Village monasteries, and Thay's students there were so happy that Thay could come and visit them every two years. The Plum Village Thailand monastery is also called The Nursery Garden, meaning the part of the garden where seeds are planted and the seedlings are taken care of. The reason for this name is that the monastery is chiefly a place for young monks and nuns who have recently been ordained as novices. They come mostly from Vietnam where Plum Village has two small nunneries and an associated small monastery, but there are also more and more young Thai nationals who want to ordain. Of course there have to be elder monks and nuns to take care of the younger ones, but the number of monks and nuns who are

Chiang
Mai

BURMA
(Myanmar)

VIETNAM

Hanoi

LAOS

Vientiane

Gulf of
Tonkin

THAILAND

Hue

Tu Hieu

Thai
Plum Village

Bangkok

Siem Reap

CAMBODIA

Pattaya

Phnom
Penh

Gulf of
Thailand

Ho Chi Minh City
(Saigon)

THAILAND

over forty years old is very small. After being taught for seven or eight years, the monks and nuns become teachers themselves and take care of the new recruits coming in.

During the month I was in Thailand, we held a retreat for one thousand people in a resort some hours' drive away from the monastery, which was newly built and only had accommodation for monks and nuns and a very small guest-house. The retreat included a traditional almsround and I began to understand the nature of Thai culture more. It is a joy to offer to monks and nuns and it is a joy to receive. The almsround is a deep practice. You stand before the donor and he or she puts something in your bowl. You follow your breathing and the donor follows her breathing. You look deeply and you see the interbeing nature of the one who gives, the one who receives, and the object given. If there were not these three elements there could not be giving.

Every two weeks or so a group of about seven or eight monks and nuns from Thai Plum Village go into the villages on an almsround. We walk as a group from house to house and when there is a donor who wants to give, we stop and receive the offering. After that the donor kneels or squats and we chant in Thai to offer up the merit of their giving for their health, well-being, and liberation from suffering.

When we came back to the monastery after the retreat, I was following Thay around the nuns' residence. As we finished walking down one flight of steps, Thay stopped and turned to me. Thay asked: "Why do you not come and practise here in Thai Plum Village for a couple of years?"

I was a little surprised. It had not occurred to me to live for a longer time in Thailand but I trusted Thay's insight and that his suggestion was to help me progress on the path of practice. When I went back to Germany, I asked permission to go to Thailand for the three months of the Rains' Retreat. The Rains' Retreat in Thailand is from the end of July until the end of October. The community in Germany asked me not to go until after the large retreats there that would be led by Thay in August 2014. Thay was not in good health and was confined to his room on the third floor of the Ashoka Institute. I went to ask permission of Thay to go to Thailand. Thay reminded me to be sure to find an elder sister to replace me while I was gone. Sister Doan Nghiem from Plum Village Thailand was happy to replace me, and now spends six months a year as the eldest bhikshuni in the EIAB, so that I can be away in Thailand.

Thay had suggested that when I go to Thailand I teach Buddhist Psychology in the Mahachulalongkorn Buddhist Monastic University. Thay had a very good connection with that university, had led retreats for monks and for laypeople there, and was respected by the rector and the vice rector of the university. In 1995 I had visited Thailand for the first time to lead retreats. While in Bangkok I had given a teaching to a small gathering of monks on the university campus in Bangkok, the first time a bhikshuni had ever taught there. We discussed, with the head of the Buddhist Psychology Department, the possibility of my teaching for a term, but because I did not have a doctorate they were reluctant to allow me to teach the monks at the university level and, in the end, we just led a Day of Mindfulness for the monks and some laypeople.

Whenever we lead retreats and Days of Mindfulness in Thailand there are always monks from the Thai Theravada tradition present. They sit and listen respectfully to a bhikshuni teaching, something I find heartwarming because it contrasts with what I have experienced when teaching in a Thai Buddhist temple in England; as soon as I ascended the teaching podium the monks would stand up and leave.

I went to the Plum Village monastery in Thailand in October, 2014 and stayed until March 2015. I enjoyed my time there much more than I had expected I would. The energy of the young monks and nuns made me feel younger and I had very few responsibilities. My teaching responsibilities were light: a precepts class for newly ordained bhikshunis, occasional classes on how the West had influenced Buddhism and on Right Mindfulness, and the occasional Dharma talk in the practice centre and in Bangkok. I had the chance to go to the north of Thailand, where we led a retreat for young adults. The retreat was held in a camp surrounded by very high mountains. I enjoyed being with the young laypeople we were teaching and the young monks and nuns who were leading the retreat.

The second time I went to Thailand was for three months in 2015. Because my mother was ailing, I did not dare stay away too long from my parents in case I was needed. This time I was able to teach young Thai men and women on a special programme which is held only in our monastery in Thailand, a three-month ordination programme. In Thailand there is a tradition that every young man ordains as a monk once in his life. This time spent as a monk is seen as a special training that can benefit the person as well as society. In Thai Plum Village this programme is not only open to young men but also to young women and now there are young people from other Asian countries who come to Thai Plum Village for three months and ordain as a novice nun or monk during that time. If they like the monastic life they can stay on for another five years or for their whole life. I enjoyed this kind of teaching and as I walked along the cloister to the class I would feel I was the happiest person in the world.

I felt very at home in Thailand. I remembered the time when I first asked to be ordained and Thay had said that if I wanted to ordain as a nun I should do so in Asia—in some ways, it is easier to practise Buddhism in Asia. As Thailand is a Buddhist country and the Buddhist tradition of mindfulness has seeped into the country and culture, it has an atmosphere that is especially conducive to practice. Our community of monks and nuns in Thailand were predominantly Vietnamese, and for Vietnamese people, on the whole, the Thai climate and culture is much closer to their own than what they would find in Europe or North America. Nevertheless, most of our Vietnamese monks and nuns adapt well to their new environment in Europe or North America and are able to serve and offer help to many Western practitioners.

The numbers of Westerners who are being ordained as monks or nuns in Plum Village centres for five years or for their whole life is also growing steadily. In the Vietnamese monastic tradition when you ordain to be a monk or a nun it is for the whole of your life, and it was like that in the time of the Buddha. Since the time of the Buddha, in the Theravada tradition temporary ordination has been a skilful means to help young men taste the discipline of the monastic life as a training to help them in their future career and position of paterfamilias. Thay recently introduced the Five-Year Monastic Programme for young Western men and women under thirty-five who want to see if monasticism is truly for them. They can ordain for five years and, if it suits them, can then continue for the rest of their life. This step was made to help monastic Buddhism become rooted in the West.

As I write this in 2018, in the Upper Hamlet of Plum Village the number of non-Vietnamese brothers is slightly higher than the number of Vietnamese brothers, although the numbers of non-Vietnamese sisters are comparatively few.

CHAPTER EIGHTEEN

Fragrant Stream

I N 2012 Thay told me that since my parents were advanced in age, it was important that I visit them frequently. Those of us who are in a monastery in Europe and have parents in Europe are given time to visit them for two weeks every two years. Thay felt I should be visiting my parents more often than that. Since I was in Germany at the time, I began to visit my mother and father frequently. It was not always easy. Their way of life had been very different from mine. That does not mean that I did not have much to learn from them. They did not have any kind of computer or other electronic gadget and lived very simply. Their meals were much more simple than those we have in the monastery.

My mother was diagnosed with vascular dementia at about that time. Fifteen years earlier she had asked me what I thought about assisted suicide in the case she was diagnosed with dementia. As Buddhist nuns we are not allowed to condone acts of killing but we are also practising to develop compassion. Of course I did not want to lose my mother but at the time she was showing no signs of dementia. I told her: "Mummy, we'll take care of you. You have nothing to fear." After she was diagnosed with dementia she kept expressing her wish to die. She asked me to take her to Switzerland, where there is a clinic that provides legal assisted suicide, but I could never agree. Whenever I was staying with her and someone would come to pick me up to take me to the local Sangha meeting for meditation, she would ask to come along. I gently persuaded her to stay at home because I was afraid she would disturb the gathering but I was touched by the fact that she remembered her experience of being in the Sangha as a positive one. She also repeatedly asked to go back to Germany with me to the Institute but my father would not allow it.

My mother kept her compassion and understanding up until the end. In one Dharma talk Thay had suggested that we ask our aging parents: "Mother/Father, is there anything that you have wanted to do but have not been able to? Please tell me and maybe I can do it for you." My mother, who had then already been diagnosed with dementia, said: "Yes, I wish I had spoken less and listened more."

"Mummy," I said, "I shall do my best to practise that for you."

The night before she died, I was sitting on her hospital bed. I had just come back from leading a Day of Mindfulness in Devon. I had a very bad earache. I told her that she would always continue in me and her children and that her children were her. I sang her the poem of Rumi:

> Silence is the ocean, language is a river.
> When you need the ocean, don't go to the river.
> Listen to the ocean saying:
> "That's enough for now."

I did not know it was the last time I would see her and I said: "Mummy, I have quite bad earache. Is it OK if I go now?" She did not complain as she usually did, saying I had to let her go home with me. She said: "Yes, yes." The next day, 11 December 2015, the hospital rang me to say my mother had died peacefully.

My greatest regret was that I had not complied with my mother's wish to bring her home to die. We had tried to take care of her at home but it was too much for me. She refused to eat and drink and, because of this, was not able to walk—but she would always try to walk. It meant we had to sit with her all the time to stop her getting out of bed. She was hospitalized after a bad fall, which severed her ear. I felt very bad for not being able to stop her from falling and cried. The home nurse saw this and said it was too much for me to take care of my mother at home.

It had been difficult for my father to retire, although my parents were very happy in their new home once they became used to it. At the time of my youngest brother's marriage, my father had not yet retired, and my brother bought a house in the nearby village of Mylor. When my father retired, he and my mother went to live in my brother's house, and my brother, his wife, and by now their two children, went to live at the farm. The house in Mylor was a small cottage at the end of a row of cottages. It was quiet there and you could hear the sound of the brook in the valley below when you sat in the garden.

By the time my father retired, farming had become a way of life for him and even though in the end he agreed to move out of the farmhouse, where he had lived since he was in his twenties, he used to drive up to the farm every day to give advice and lend a hand to my brother who was just beginning to farm. It was not always easy for my brother since he had his own ideas and did not necessarily want to continue to farm in exactly the same way as his father had done. My father, until he was ninety, would come and help my brother in harvest time, to sit by the grain dryer watching the grain dry, a monotonous and dusty job.

In his nineties he became crippled with arthritis and also had to take care of my mother who was developing dementia. Still he was cutting the grass on his lawn, repairing things for his own house and sometimes for the farm of my brother. He devoted the rest of his time to caring for my mother, cooking, washing up, and so on. So it was a devastating blow to him when my mother died in 2015—and he never recovered from it.

At first he was numb. He had to go to the funeral and appear brave, then go to the wake; but the wound he received by losing my mother could not be healed, and fifteen months later, he died. When my mother died, I asked him if I could stay and take care of him, since I was sure my community would allow this. He said he was only one person and I had so many people to take care of. If needed, he would go into a home. He wanted me to continue doing the work of service I was doing. So I had to be satisfied with coming to visit him every three months or so.

During my visits we would sometimes fall out with each other. I wanted him to have better care when I was not there, to have a carer come in for more than fifteen minutes a day and do certain things around the house that he could not do. He became very angry about this. As he was shouting at me I followed my breathing and reminded myself that I and my father were one and, in being angry at me, my father was being angry at himself. I felt compassion for him and suddenly he stopped shouting. He said, "I am sorry for being so beastly." This was the first time I had heard my father apologize to me. I realised how much he had changed in these last years.

He had a very bad fall about the time of my mother's birthday in October 2016, while I was visiting our monastery in California. He told my brother not to let me know what had happened, but of course my brother told me. The monastery bought a ticket for me to fly to England as soon as possible.

When I arrived in the hospital he had gone through a six-hour operation in his ninety-ninth year and was in a state of delirium. He refused to let anyone come near him and thought everyone wanted to destroy him. I was wearing my jacket over my usual brown habit, so he didn't recognize me at first. I came to his side and embraced him. He asked who I was and I said, "Your daughter, Annabel." He said: "I know you are a Buddhist nun and you do not lie." After that he came out of the delirium and began to accept my two brothers and sister.

That winter I would go from Germany to England every couple of months to spend time with him in the hospital. Six months later I was in the annual monastic retreat in Plum Village when I heard from my sister that he was not doing well. I was due to give the Dharma talk on the first day of the retreat and I thought that after that I would go to England. But then I heard from my sister that he was doing better so I decided to wait until the retreat was over before going. The day before the retreat was going to end, I felt it was urgent that I go to my father. The brothers in Upper Hamlet bought me a ticket straightaway and I had twenty-four hours to be with my father before he died.

My father had signed a document to the effect that in the case of death he did not want to be resuscitated. The day before he died the doctor had asked him if he wanted resuscitation and he had said he did. I asked the doctor what resuscitation would involve. She told me that he would have to be moved to the county hospital as soon as possible. Then when he died they would apply an electric shock to the heart. Sometimes it worked and sometimes not. I talked to my brother. Did he think it would be good to renege on the advance directive and make a new one? Both he and I felt that my father was too ill to make possible any significant recovery after resuscitation. So I told my father about the need of going to the county hospital, the defibrillation, and he was silent. He did not ask again to be resuscitated.

The immediate cause of his death was pneumonia. It was very difficult for him to breathe and as I sat alongside him, I recited under my breath the name of the bodhisattva of compassion. A few minutes before his death his breathing became completely normal. His last breaths were very peaceful.

He died in the nursing home and I could sit with him for six hours after his death, which in the county hospital would not have been possible. I recited the Discourse on Love from time to time because I felt the emotion of love would be the most transcendent and helpful energy at that time.[15]

I felt a great deal of grief at my father's death for more

than a year. I thought I had been well-prepared by all the teachings and meditations I had heard and practised on no-birth and no-death. These teachings helped me to remain peaceful and unafraid while my father was dying but after the funeral was over I began to experience grief. My father had come close to death as a young man and always had the determination to survive and not to die. He had not heard teachings on no-birth and no-death, and any death to him, whether he knew the person or not, was a cause for sadness. I felt I received from him some of that inability to accept death. I wanted to be able to practise better to be able to accept death.

One part of Plum Village in France is the Fragrant Stream Cloister. It is adjacent to Thay's Hermitage. The Cloister is a secluded place for personal practice. It is here that monks and nuns can ask permission to come in order to practise alone. In 2017 and 2018 I stayed in this cloister for a couple of months at a time to do this kind of practice.

From time to time monks and nuns feel they need a period of solitary retreat to be able to develop concentration and look deeply into the matter of birth and death. We all have an inborn fear of dying, which may take time to heal and transform. During sitting or walking meditation it is possible to feel a deep peace that surpasses understanding. That kind of peace is very healing for body and mind and is easiest to maintain when we do not have to be in touch with many people or take care of many events. When our mind is very still, concepts of birth, death, and separation dissolve and we no longer feel afraid.

Fragrant Stream Cloister has a stream at the edge of the grounds, which are spacious with many trees. There are walnut, fig, and plum trees, which all do very well in that part of France. The largest trees are three deodara cedars. Thay would hug these trees. He usually hugged all three of them. It was Thay's way of practising equanimity. Thay also taught me how to hug trees. You receive the energy of the tree and offer the tree your respect and appreciation. You can hang your hammock between the trees and listen to the music of the stream and the birds.

Thay spent his time at the hermitage when he was not leading retreats in Plum Village and other parts of the world. It was the place he came back to in order to regain strength. In earlier days, when Thay was not so busy leading retreats, he planted many of the trees and spent time gardening in a small vegetable garden. Thay also did much research and writing in the hermitage as well as lying in his hammock. So the atmosphere there is filled with the presence of Thay. Whenever I visited Thay in the hermitage, he would encourage me to go out into the garden and lie in a hammock. It was an antidote for being too busy.

After Thay had a stroke, he was very eager that we rebuild some of the ruined buildings in the grounds of the hermitage. Some of the building work is in progress now and we hope that some day Thay will return and stay there.

Forty years earlier I had received the symbolic staff in Athens when I heard: "You are on your own now" and the cane by the door fell into my hands. A cane is a support helping us up to the terrace where we can look out at the moon and the stars, the wonders of life that are available to us when we practise mindfulness. You are on your own in the sense that only you can do the practice to transform your body and mind, but that does not mean you are without support. The cane, which in early Vietnamese Buddhism is a hallmark of a monk, stays with you although you have left your family and the comforts of worldly life. The abbot's cane which I received from Thay in Green Mountain in 1999 was also an encouragement to practise the spiritual life for myself and for others. What we need to transform is our actions of body, speech, and mind, which in Buddhism we call karma. From the time I was a child I had a strong awareness of karma, the fact that whatever we do has its consequences and if we cause others to be happy or to suffer we too shall be happy or suffer sooner or later. Karma is not just individual but there is also the karma of our ancestors which we receive through our parents. This has to be resolved and put to rest by means of the practice of mindfulness in our daily life. We have that staff which is the practice of mindfulness, concentration, and insight to support us. The staff is our Sangha which provides the collective energy to do this work of transformation.

Sometimes I am afraid of being alone, or rather the little child in me is afraid of being alone. I remember how afraid I was of being separated from my mother and father when I was a child. If I had to go away somewhere the idea would come into my head: "What if the house is bombed and mother and father are no longer there when I come home?" I do not know why I had this idea of the house being bombed. I was born after World War II. It was the fear of some little child who did live through the war and that fear continued in me. My little child is also the little inner child of my father and my mother. It is my part as a nun to take care of this little child as Thay has taught us: "Every day you need to talk to the child in you." Leaning on the cane, you practise to come back to the island within yourself and when you do come back you find that yourself is made up of millions and millions of feelings, thoughts, perceptions, and events stretching out into eternity.

Afterword: Reflections on Living in Spiritual Community

I N WISCONSIN in 2003, when Thay was leading a retreat for policemen, prison wardens and guards, and judges who worked in the US criminal justice system, we stayed in a conference centre that once had been a Catholic nunnery. It was a large building with cells for at least a hundred nuns. Since the room I slept in had once been the room of nuns, I used to ask myself what would have happened if I had become a Catholic nun, something I had contemplated as a young adult. I could imagine her looking out of the window, especially at moments when she may have gone through difficulties or disharmony with her sisters or her superiors. During that retreat I would spend time on my own walking in the garden and I sometimes saw Thay and his attendant walking there too. I wondered if there was something wrong with walking alone like that, and the look of acceptance in Thay's eyes assured me that there was nothing wrong, but I could join Thay if I liked.

For several years when I was living at the Green Mountain Dharma Center in Vermont we would go to Pennsylvania and lead a retreat at a Franciscan nunnery. There were about five elderly nuns still practising there. The building was also large and must have housed nearly one hundred nuns in the past. I would walk in the convent's graveyard and see the ages of the nuns when they had entered the nunnery and when they had died. Many of them had become nuns when they were still under twenty. I have also had the chance to be in contact with Christian nuns in interfaith gatherings. I always felt that the practice of the Christian nuns I met was deep and sincere and I admired their humility. On one occasion I led a Day of Mindfulness for Catholic nuns in New York City. In the Dharma talk I spoke about creation as something that is happening in every moment—the living God and the living creation—and how the creator and the creation are not two separate realities. The nuns were very interested and accepting of these ideas.

The reasons for the decline in Christian monasticism must be many and varied but in the Christian church we see not only the decline of monasticism but also that of the larger lay congregation and no doubt to some extent these two things go together. In Buddhism we talk about the fourfold Sangha: monks, nuns, laymen, and laywomen. These four elements protect and support each other. The strength of any community also has something to do with the teachings. Thay has often said that Christianity needs renewal just as Buddhism does. The teachings and practices of a spiritual path are something living. They change in the way they develop according to the society in which they are manifesting. Thay's deepest wish, from the time he was a young novice until today, has been to renew the teachings of Buddhism so that they are relevant to the present time. Renew means to rediscover the spirit of Buddhism which has become lost in certain outer forms that may bring a temporary relief but do not help us transform the suffering that we face. The purpose of the monastic community is to preserve the Dharma in its deep form and create Dharma doors that can help people.

My own monastic community is still very young. It began in 1988 and continues to grow. Most of the novices are young: teenagers, or in their twenties and early thirties, and most of them are Vietnamese although the number of young Western male novices is growing fast.

When I became a nun, I did not know what I was embarking upon. It is like when you are a child, you feel safe in the environment of your family and you do not think about what it will be like when you grow into adulthood. As a monastic, you are in the safe environment of your teacher and the Sangha. When I became a nun, our monastic Sangha was very small so it was in my teacher that I took refuge most of all. I saw my task as that of teaching the Dharma in the way that Thay did.

As our monastic Sangha grew I saw that all of us were continuing our teacher in our own way and that my way was to teach, translate, and study the Dharma. When I say teach the Dharma I do not just mean in words but in my way of walking, speaking, listening, and interacting. My way of walking and breathing helps me to relax, to be in touch with my body and help my body deal with discomfort or pain. Although my health has not been strong in recent years, largely because I suffered from anorexia nervosa for many years, the spiritual practice has made it possible for me to continue teaching and enjoying life.

When I was asked to go to the US in 1997, I had to leave the side of my teacher, but frequently I continued to feel his presence very strongly. What I did miss was his verbal guidance on specific matters and his physical presence in difficult moments, such as when we were not sure in which direction to go. Since 1982 Thay and Sister Chan Khong had lived in Plum Village, France, and the Upper Hamlet especially had become imbued with a spiritual energy that is difficult to describe in words. When I was sent to Maple Forest and Green Mountain in the United States and then to the EIAB in Germany, I realised that I and the Sangha had to create the Plum Village energy from scratch. In Green Mountain we had the beauties and silence of nature to help us. In EIAB Germany, if we look, we can also find beauties of nature to help us. Now whenever I need advice from Thay I sit up straight, establish concentration by means of mindful breathing, and talk to Thay as if he were there before me. I listen, and I hear his counsel and write it down so that I do not forget. I see clearly that Thay is always there within me and around me.

From very early on in my monastic life I was leading retreats and giving teachings. My younger sisters now have to train for eight or nine years before they receive the authority to teach the Dharma in the form of the Dharma Lamp Transmission. Before that they can only begin to describe basic practices like walking and sitting meditation to guests who come to join us.

Teaching the Dharma is also to learn the Dharma. When I give a teaching, I speak about what I am currently practising or have practised in the past in order to encourage myself to keep practising and go further. In order to be able to teach, one has to continue the practice. It is not in the spirit of Buddhism to teach theory without practising it.

Leading a retreat in Stourbridge, England, 2017.

In Buddhism, we have the equivalent of the Christian monastic principles of chastity, poverty, and obedience; the only modification being that our obedience is not to the abbot but to the Sangha of fully ordained monks and nuns. Following these principles of living has helped me in my monastic life—along with the practice of mindfulness of body, feelings, and mental formations—not to go down paths that cause me to suffer and make others suffer, as well as to recognize when I have gone down them and then begin anew.

The reality of living in community, obedient to the consensus of the community, with no personal belongings and no special emotional attachments, is not easy for someone like myself who has been brought up in the individualistic and materialistic environment of the Western world. That is why I have needed to train myself by studying the monastic precepts often. Fortunately, I have always enjoyed living a simple life from the material point of view.

As a Western nun, I do not have aunts or uncles, brothers or sisters who are monks or nuns, unlike many of my Vietnamese brothers and sisters, who more often than not have a relation or relations who have been ordained as monks or nuns. It is not in my blood to devote my life to monasticism. I have had to train to go through the difficulty of feeling that I am different from the majority of my sisters who are Vietnamese. They, for their part, accept me as I am, embrace me as I am, and that is what has made it possible to go through the difficulties that largely come from my own perceptions of inferiority.

Some people ask if the world needs monasticism. Monks and nuns who are living in accord with the principles of monastic life can create a collective spiritual energy that people can feel. So when someone sees monks and nuns living and practising together in a spirit of harmony, they can remember that the spiritual life is available and they can come back to the present moment. We have our habit and our shaved head or headscarf as the outer form to remind ourselves and others of the practice. In Christian communities, after Vatican II, the habit was largely abandoned. Listening to elderly Catholic nuns I realised that this

Teaching in Upper Hamlet in the 21-Day Retreat, 2018.

was a shock for the nuns who had lived in it for decades. One elderly Catholic nun who came to practise with us for a while in Plum Village said that seeing the monks and nuns wearing a monastic habit reminded her of the time when she had to give up wearing her habit and how difficult that had been. The habit is important if the person who wears it is practising spiritually because it draws attention to the spiritual life, which all of us humans need. Even though I have only been ordained for thirty years it is hard to imagine what it would be like no longer to be able to wear the habit that I have grown into. It would certainly be a strange feeling of not being properly dressed.

I have had to learn to grow into monasticism. Like marriage, the ceremony of ordination is just an outer sign of official recognition. The real practice begins when I accept my weaknesses and put my heart into transforming them. In order to do this, I have relied on the Sangha that has surrounded and supported me. I have a community before which I can confess my shortcomings, and this helps me to be more diligent in transforming them. The monastic Sangha is not perfect. Sometimes I acknowledge that a lay practitioner is practising better than I am. This does not give me an inferiority complex or make me feel I should be a layperson. It shows me that although the monastic way and the lay way are different, both ways can lead to liberation. If I were a good practitioner, I think I should not need to be a nun, but I know that I need the monastic way to keep me on the path.

The value of monastic life is freedom and brotherhood and sisterhood: to have the time and the space to meditate and realise the truth that nothing is born and nothing dies and to take care of our fellow nuns or monks. When we enter the monastery, we learn to offer service by cooking and gardening. Some monks and nuns will continue to work in the kitchen or the garden until the end of their lives because they feel happiest in this kind of work. In my own case, I can teach or translate or write, but I am under no pressure to do these things. So, when I want to practise walking or sitting meditation, I can sit under a tree or walk in the garden. We think that in order to write a book we have to sit at our desk and write, but most of the writing happens before we do the physical act of writing. We can only write when our mind has something to write.

As I approach my seventieth birthday, I feel a deep gratitude that I have been able to practise the monastic life according to the teachings of the Buddha. It is an enormous privilege to be able to sit still and do nothing, to walk in the present moment, and to touch something that is ineffable, beyond our concepts of right and wrong, birth and death, here and there. It is also a privilege to be able to serve, to sit and listen to someone who is suffering, to help them breathe peacefully and smile.

Notes

1. Thich Nhat Hanh, *Call Me By My True Names: The Collected Poetry of Thich Nhat Hanh*, Berkeley, CA: Parallax Press, 1999.

2. Thich Nhat Hanh, *Be Still and Know: Meditation for Peacemakers*, London: Pax Christi and the Fellowship of Reconciliation, 1987.

3. To know more about this, the reader can see Sr. Chan Khong's book: Sister Chan Khong, *Learning True Love: Practising Buddhism in a Time of War*, Parallax Press, 2007.

4. Thich Nhat Hanh, *The Sun My Heart*, Parallax Press, 1988.

5. Venuvana, or Bamboo Grove, near Rajagriha was offered to the Buddha and his monks by King Bimbisara.

6. Vulture Peak was a favourite retreat of the Buddha, where he is said to have given many teachings.

7. Jivaka had been the doctor for the Buddha and monastic Sangha, and had allowed the Buddha to use his mango grove.

8. The School of Youth for Social Service was officially inaugurated in 1965 as part of the Van Hanh University. The students went to offer their services in "pilot villages." It was financed wholly by donations from local people. The students would bring education, health care, and sanitation to the villages, and would help to rebuild villages that had been bombed.

9. Also see the poem "Non-Duality" in Thich Nhat Hanh, *Call Me By My True Names*, pp. 160–161.

10. Thich Nhat Hanh, *Hermitage Among the Clouds: An Historical Novel of Fourteenth Century Vietnam*, Parallax Press, 1993.

11. The Rains' Retreat in Plum Village has traditionally been held from mid-November to mid-February. It is the time when the monks or nuns do not leave the monastery and spend three months studying and practising in depth together.

12. In 2003–2004 Thay gave teachings on *The Record of Master Linji* for three months. See Thich Nhat Hanh, *Zen Battles*, Parallax Press, 2007.

13. Lazy Day is a wonderful invention of Thay. It is always on Monday because on Sunday we organize a Day of Mindfulness for whoever wants to come, and we may need to take care of many guests. On Lazy Day we have no timetable and practise sitting, walking, writing, or drinking tea just when we feel like it. We can even stay in bed a little bit longer if we feel like it.

14. Thich Nhat Hanh, *The Blooming of a Lotus: Guided Meditation Exercises for Healing and Transformation*, Beacon Press, 1993.

15. Metta Sutta, Sutta Nipata 1.8.

Monastics and visitors practice the art of mindful living in the tradition of Thich Nhat Hanh at our mindfulness practice centers around the world. To reach any of these communities, or for more information about how individuals, couples, and families can join in a retreat, please contact:

Plum Village
13 Martineau
33580 Dieulivol, France
plumvillage.org

Magnolia Grove Monastery
Batesville, MS 38606, USA
magnoliagrovemonastery.org

Blue Cliff Monastery
Pine Bush, NY 12566, USA
bluecliffmonastery.org

Deer Park Monastery
Escondido, CA 92026, USA
deerparkmonastery.org

European Institute of
Applied Buddhism
D-51545 Waldbröl, Germany
eiab.eu

Thailand Plum Village
Nakhon Ratchasima
30130 Thailand
thaiplumvillage.org

Asian Institute of Applied
Buddhism
Lantau Island, Hong Kong
pvfhk.org

La Maison de l'Inspir
93160 Noisy le Grand, France
maisondelinspir.org

Healing Spring Monastery
77510 Verdelot, France
healingspringmonastery.org

Stream Entering Monastery
Beaufort, Victoria 3373, Australia
nhapluu.org

The Mindfulness Bell, , a journal of the art of mindful living in the tradition of Thich Nhat Hanh, is published three times a year by our community. To subscribe or to see the worldwide directory of Sanghas/local mindfulness groups, visit mindfulnessbell.org.

A portion of the proceeds from your book purchase supports Thich Nhat Hanh's peace work and mindfulness teachings around the world. For more information on how you can help, visit the Thich Nhat Hanh Foundation at tnhf.org.

**PARALLAX
PRESS**

Parallax Press, a nonprofit publisher founded by Zen Master Thich Nhat Hanh, publishes books and media on the art of mindful living and Engaged Buddhism. We are committed to offering teachings that help transform suffering and injustice. Our aspiration is to contribute to collective insight and awakening, bringing about a more joyful, healthy, and compassionate society.

For a copy of the catalog, please contact:

Parallax Press
P.O. Box 7355
Berkeley, CA 94707
parallax.org

31901065019210